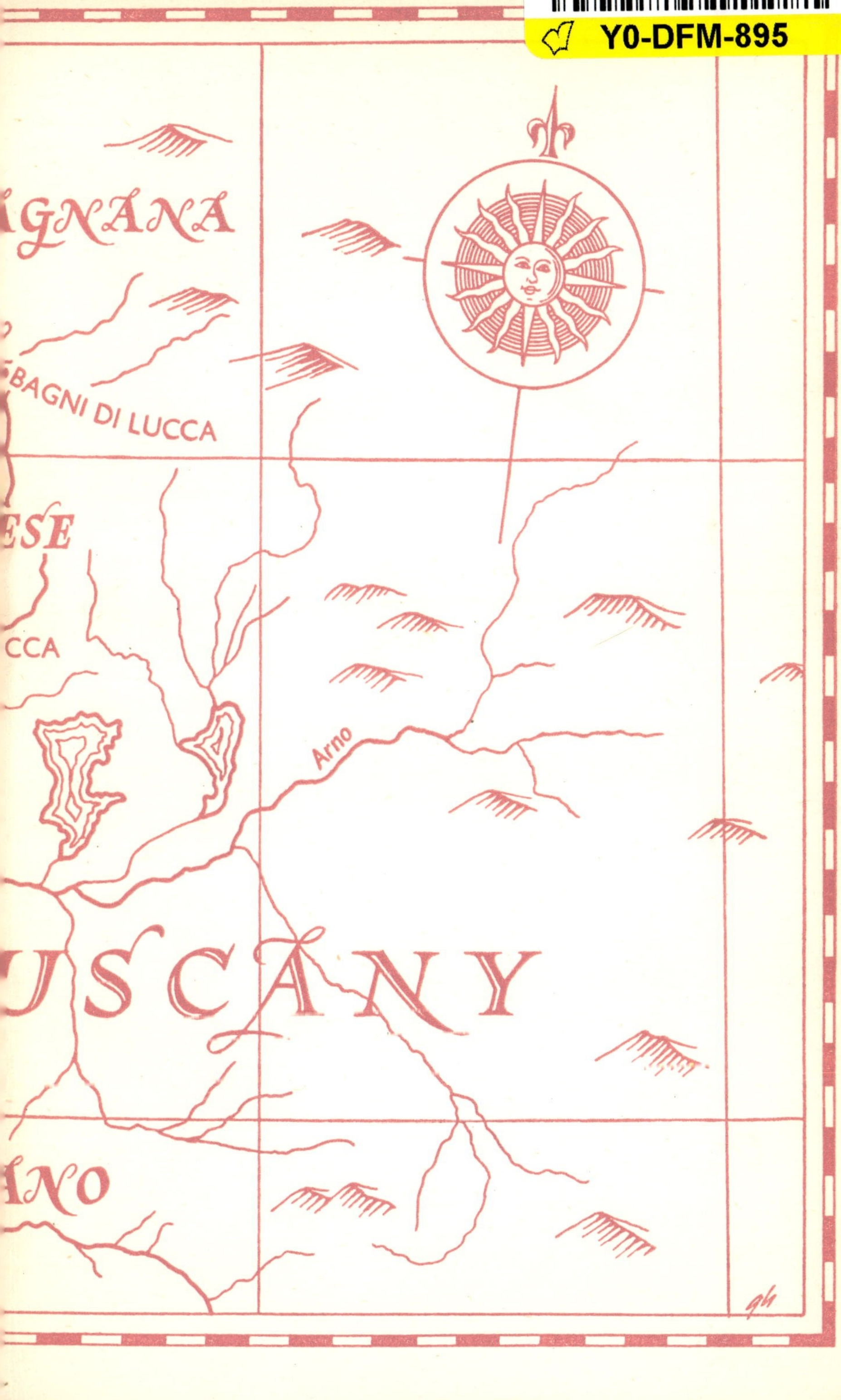
GNANA
BAGNI DI LUCCA
ESE
CCA
Arno
USCANY
NO

SHELLEY: THE LAST PHASE

IVAN ROE
has also written:

The Breath of Corruption
An Interpretation of Dostoievsky

Novels
The Green Tree and The Dry
The Salamander Touch

"One frail form": how nineteenth-century admirers imagined Shelley

SHELLEY

The Last Phase

By

IVAN ROE

HUTCHINSON
Stratford Place
London

Hutchinson & Co. (Publishers) Ltd.
London   New York   Toronto
Melbourne   Sydney   Cape Town

First published 1953

Set in eleven point Monotype Old Style No. 2
one point leaded
Printed in Great Britain
by The Anchor Press, Ltd.,
Tiptree, Essex

CONTENTS

	Introduction	*Page* 9
Chapter I	Chaos in Commotion	15
II	The Silent Centre	36
III	Weird Archimage	58
IV	The Towers of the Future	70
V	Of Kings, and Priests, and Slaves	87
VI	The Lamp in the Dust	114
VII	The Changeful Year	159
VIII	The Quenchless Lamp	187
IX	The Silent Isle	213
X	The Goal of Time	227
	A Shelley Chronology	243
	Bibliography and Sources	247
	Index	249

LIST OF ILLUSTRATIONS

P. B. Shelley: Posthumous Painting
   by Joseph Severn   *Frontispiece*

	FACING PAGE
Casa Magni: in the Nineteenth Century and Today	64
Val di Magra	65
Lerici	80
La Spezia	81
Page from a Shelley Notebook	144
Lerici from Casa Magni	144
Carrara	145

INTRODUCTION

> If you can't swim
> Beware of Providence.
> *Julian and Maddalo*

IF I could say that this book was simply an account of the last sixty-nine days in the life of Percy Bysshe Shelley I should be happily excused the task of writing an introduction to a subject of such perennial interest that it scarcely seems to require a preface. But I must detain the reader for a few moments in order to explain the scope and method of the narrative.

Like many people who enjoy what Shelley wrote, and who are inexhaustibly interested in what others write about him, I have long been impressed by the many dimensions presented by his life and work. His life of barely thirty years is so remarkably well documented that he springs to life more readily than the average writer and it is easy to feel that in spite of the passage of a hundred and thirty-one years he has not long been dead. This may be because the materials of biography—journals, letters, notebooks, Press cuttings—are so plentiful. But I think it is also because his ideas and interests are so similar to our own: we feel that his debates on English and European politics, religion, morals and the nature of love are our own still unfinished debates.

The picture of Shelley's personality that emerges from his works and letters and from the many biographies and memoirs is deceptive because dazzling. We have to view the man through the distorting glass of his friends' love, dislike, vanity, envy and several other disturbing emotions. Nineteenth-century idealizing and emasculating, twentieth-century debunking—these add distortions to our own view. Let us face the fact that everyone who writes or thinks about this man is in some way disabled by admiration or resentment. Shelley is like the chameleon in his poem on poets:

> Poets are on this cold earth,
> As chameleons might be,
> Hidden from their early birth
> In a cave beneath the sea;
> Where light is, chameleons change:
> Where love is not, poets do.
> Fame is love disguised: if few
> Find either, never think it strange
> That poets range.

The heat and pother that he caused among biographers and critics reminds us that Shelley was like a pigeon among cats. Some writers like to think that they have gobbled him up; others that they have dissected him and left only a few dry bones and feathers; others that they have buried the remains. All this scratching and snarling among Shelleyans and others is in vain, for the general reader, who is the final arbiter in these matters, goes on reading Shelley and extracting something valuable from his words. All the opinionizing of critics, all the modern apparatus of criticism, cannot diminish his work if it contains something that will continue to illuminate the mind and touch the emotions of readers, as distinct from writers. Shelley arouses anger and enthusiasm but never boredom; for the ideas that gave all the nobility (and the burlesque) to his life and poetry are ever-present, still-unresolved realities: why and how men and women love, and what they seek in love, why they hate, how they govern and misgovern themselves, how their gods and devils colour their vision of life. These if anything are the materials of literature, the blood and bone and marrow of a poet's expression.

In posterity as in his contemporaries Shelley encouraged an addiction to extremes. One extreme has labelled him an ineffectual angel; the other has dismissed him as a humourless blackguard. Perhaps it is the result of my own distortion, but I cannot visualize him except as a virile person, subtly humorous as only a master of language can be. In attempting to fuse his personality and his works I have tried wherever possible to give his view of life rather than his friends' view of him or their assumptions about what he saw and felt. In other words, I have tried to let Shelley speak for himself.

This is not always possible. There are mysteries in Shelley's life, and there are some parts of the periphery of that life which we, posterity, know better than he knew himself, because we can read letters and overhear conversations of which he knew nothing. Probably no group has been more fully documented than the Shelley circle, but we must not forget that letters in general give less than half the truth about personalities. If you want to see the world from within a poet's skull, you read his creative work rather than the letters in which he presents his chameleon-self to friends, half-friends and enemies. Our deepest crimes, our self-betrayals (and our best actions and impulses) are not as a rule the things we record in letters, or speak into the telephone, or discuss within hearing distance of the recording machine. Hardly anyone quite fails to lie in some degree in every letter that he writes. Letters are fascinating and indispensable tools for scholars, but they are not all of scholarship. For one man with the genius for self-revelation of Van Gogh we have a thousand with the talent for self-concealment that literary men in general possess.

Because Shelley's life seems to me a palimpsest of ideas and emotion I have risked presenting the record of his last sixty-nine days as a kind of palimpsest. That is, I have tried to create from his life and poetry the extra dimension, the special depth of focus, sometimes sharp, sometimes blurred, that his whole life dimly presents through a mass of books and papers. To do so, I have had to move backwards and forwards in time: not only within the span of Shelley's life, but in the eighteenth century to indicate what kind of world he lived in, and in the nineteenth century to indicate the kind of world his works helped to make.[1]

[1] A chronological summary of the chief events in Shelley's life will be found on pages 243–5.

The story of the last two months in his life is dramatic and moving enough in itself, and all the more so if one goes back to the part of Italy where that life played itself out. The story is all the more absorbing if one attempts to link up with his last days what were probably his final preoccupations and thoughts, arising out of the loves, hates, problems and mysteries of his life.

One reason for my distrusting the exclusively chronological method of writing about a man's life arises, I confess, out of my prejudice as a novelist, which makes me hold to the belief that a man does in truth live his life more as if it were a manuscript greatly over-scored and corrected than as if it were a clock or a calendar. The happenings in the life of a man of Shelley's imaginative intensity are overlaid in the memory: that in my view is the meaning of his twice-used phrase "dead memory". To observe chronology alone is to produce a false perspective: a man's life is not like a railway journey photographed by a ciné-camera mounted on the engine—a camera has no memory, none of the distortion and secondary elaboration of the human memory, none of the power of emotion which real life tells us paints the true picture of our lives even if the perspective of that picture is not the camera's perspective. We remember, forget, confuse and lie to ourselves *about* ourselves: but the result is our life, the dome of many-coloured glass in place of the thin thread of nylon fabric which, too often, is the result of using the chronological method to the exclusion of all others.

The last days of Shelley were spent at San Terenzo, on the most hauntingly beautiful part of the Tyrrhenian shore. The house he lived in still stands there; the pines have the same scent and the cicadas in the olive groves utter tirelessly the same excited and rasping song that Shelley heard. If you go there knowing even a little about the happiness, misery, anxiety, hope and pain endured by the group of English people who lived there for a little while in 1822, you will find it hard to resist the conflicting atmosphere of timelessness and mortality that pervades the Bay of Lerici. The melancholy that the indolent air produces in you may be mere imagination; perhaps after all nothing is left save an old house with arches, a few inaccurate legends passed down by the villagers through the intervening decades, and the dry memory of a poet who embarked too hardily on the treacherous sea.

Perhaps, however, a great deal more is left when, as in the following chapters, certain aspects of Shelley's life are surveyed as he himself might have surveyed them during that summer by the sea, as he stood on the terrace of Casa Magni and looked across the bay towards Corsica. I should like to think that among my readers there are several who, knowing little of his life now, and having read little of his work, will turn from this book to the poetry of Shelley himself, thereby embarking on as eventful a mental and spiritual voyage as I believe his own life to have been.

IVAN ROE

One

CHAOS IN COMMOTION

> It is a sweet thing, friendship, a dear balm,
> A happy and auspicious bird of calm,
> Which rides o'er life's ever tumultuous ocean;
> A god that broods o'er chaos in commotion.
> *Epipsychidion (Rejected Fragments)*

ON 30 APRIL, 1822, Shelley took possession for six months of Casa Magni, at San Terenzo, a fishing village lying in a bay on the eastern side of the Gulf of La Spezia, which forms one of the most picturesque parts of Italy's western coast. He was to live in this house for only a little over two months: it was the last of a formidably long list of houses and lodgings that he occupied during the ten years of his adult, and married, life. He was not yet thirty years old, but, as he had told a friend not long before, "You can put me down among the nonagenarians."

It is probable that he did not expect to live long, in spite of his springing from a long-lived family. He looked healthy but regularly had seizures caused by violent pains in the side; once, a doctor had written him off as hopelessly tubercular. He was living in Italy during the first quarter of the nineteenth century—a place where disease, violence or accident could soon put an end to a man who, like this poet, neglected even the elementary precautions that most men adopt in order to remain alive. Most important of all, his writings and many of his actions had demonstrated for four years that he did not look on death as an unwelcome companion; he had not been assiduous in stepping aside when some possibly fatal peril brushed near him.

He was a deeply unhappy man but not by any means a cheerless one. Contrary to the generality of melancholy poets, he kept his sorrows closely within the bounds of his verse and of his thoughts. The picture of Shelley during the last two months of his life, drawn for us by friends who wrote independently of one another, reveals such a lively companion that, glancing at his brief past, we may feel tempted to sum up his life and character by saying that he lived to make himself unhappy and his friends happy. Whether they liked or disliked him (none was ever indifferent to him), no one who knew this exceedingly unsuccessful poet at the end of his life leaves the world in any doubt about his good spirits.

He was not the half-mad sprite, the fantastic youth drawn with liberal distortion by Hogg, but a tall, stooping man, the youthfulness of whose face was belied by streaks of grey in his hair. He was not the shiftless dreamer of the popular romances that were later to be written about him, but a man who felt himself to be emotionally and materially a failure, a man keeping his family in an uncomfortable house, shouldering a great burden of troubles—his own, his friends' and his relatives'; snatching what time he could to satisfy his appetite for reading, his liking for boating, and his long-thwarted desire for solitude. His own words, in a reported conversation, dispel the legend of Ariel, the romantic sprite:

"Mine is a life of failures. Peacock says my poetry is composed of day-dreams and nightmares; and Leigh Hunt does not think it good enough for *The Examiner*. Jefferson Hogg says all poetry is inverted sense, and consequently nonsense. Every man should attempt to do something. Poetry was the rage of the day, and I racked my imagination to be a poet. I wrote, and the critics denounced me as a mischievous visionary, and my friends said that I had mistaken my vocation, that my poetry was mere rhapsody of words; that I was soaring in the blue regions of the air, disconnected from all human sympathy."

The summer colony at San Terenzo consisted of five adults and three very young children. Had a playwright invented these characters and placed them in their actual setting, he would probably have been condemned by the critics for labouring on a far-fetched situation. Casa Magni, the rugged house with its lower walls whitened by sea-spray, was a dramatic enough setting; and the situation of its tenants was extraordinary.

Shelley, the poet and exile, was in the eyes of most of his English contemporaries an unredeemed scoundrel. Firstly he was a scoundrel because, though the son of a Sussex gentleman of fairly old family and fairly large possessions, he had been expelled from the University of Oxford for refusing to lie about his authorship of a pamphlet on atheism. Secondly he was a scoundrel because he had written against the institution of marriage—though he had married two women and had actually observed the marriage ceremony three times. Thirdly he was a scoundrel because, following the failure of his first marriage, he had lived with the woman who ultimately became his second wife. Fourthly he was a scoundrel because his first wife, two years after their separation and when being adequately supported by him, had been found drowned. Fifthly he was a scoundrel because the Lord Chancellor of England implied as much, in depriving him of the custody of the two children of his first marriage following their mother's death. There were several other reasons for the general conviction that he was a blackguard; most of them were connected with his private life, several were the invention of tourists on the Continent, and the fact that the vanguard of his enemies included several professing Christians indicated the blackest of his offences, and incidentally the only one to which he himself pleaded guilty; in other words, he did not approve of the Church of England of his time.

To exile, money worries and the fact that he had to print his own works and never made a penny out of them, was added the recent memory of the death of two of his children, and of two others very close to him; it can readily be understood that a certain melancholy and an occasional bitterness were natural marks of his poetry.

So much for the man as he appeared to his friends and to his enemies. The deeper mysteries of his life, to uncover which would have delighted his enemies, were even more extraordinary than his public reputation. No one knew, for example, the cause of his separation from his first wife; why he had secretly adopted a child at Naples and registered her as the issue of his wife and himself; why he was so kind to his wife's half-sister; the why and wherefore of his association with one of the most notorious men of the time, Lord Byron.

His wife, Mary Shelley, was also something of an enigma to the world—which included the villagers of San Terenzo as well as the panjandrum critics of London and those who scrambled to perform the heavy task of guarding the sexual morals of Edinburgh. Mary was the daughter of Mary Wollstonecraft, the first Englishwoman to act and write in the belief that a woman had the right to be treated as a little more than a concubine, and of William Godwin, who as a young scoundrel had written an inflammatory book called *Political Justice*, and whose blackguardism had since been considerably toned down by excessive dullness and self-esteem. Mary had run away with Shelley, a married man. Now aged twenty-five, she was a writer: indeed, her successful novel, *Frankenstein*, had earned precisely ten times the amount of money made by her husband throughout his writing life, his sole earnings apparently being the £40 he made when a schoolboy out of a shocker called *Zastrozzi*.

Mary had had tragic experiences as a mother: her first child had died a few days after birth, her second at the age of twelve months, her third at the age of three and a half. She now had a boy of two and a half, and feared that the Italian fever would carry him off; she was expecting to become within a few months a mother for the fifth time. When it was suggested that one of his own illegitimate children should be adopted by the Shelleys, Lord Byron laconically demanded, "Have they *reared* one?" Percy Florence Shelley, the little boy who at two and a half played in the garden at the back of Casa Magni, lived into old age to confute the taunt.

Yet Mary's fears were justified. Had she ever climbed the hill behind Casa Magni and visited the graveyard of San

Terenzo she would have observed that many of the graves were those of infants. It would appear that the rate of infant mortality on that Italian coast has scarcely diminished since those days, for if you visit the graveyard amid the olive trees today, you will find that most of the graves made before 1930 have been removed to make room for San Terenzesi who have died since, that many of the tombs are those of children, and that a system of charnel-houses raised above the ground has had to be adopted to accommodate the dead on the hillside where the value of the earth has risen so steeply. For the people of the village, as for many others in Italy, death has long been a familiar. Death-worship is part of life in the pest-ridden sunshine. Whereas photographs of the recently dead are displayed in shop windows by the poorer people throughout Italy, in San Terenzo the images are displayed on the tombstones and on charnels that have the appearance of filing cabinets built in concrete. Death is celebrated magnificently in Italian poetry, the Italians usually make the sign of the Cross before entering the sea to bathe, and people make the same sign if in conversation you mention a dead friend: yet their idea of death is bound up with their idea of nature, and for them the grave has the beauty and friendliness, as well as the fury and savageness, of the drought-ridden earth, the treacherous sea and the shadowy mountains.

The third and fourth members of the party at Casa Magni, two lively and happy young people, were untroubled by thoughts of death. They went by the name of Mr. and Mrs. Williams, but were not in fact married. Edward Ellerker Williams, aged twenty-eight, had without regret ended his association with the British Navy and the Indian Army. The Shelleys probably knew that Jane was not his wife, but wisely, no one flaunted the "free union". Williams explained himself thus: "I was in the Navy at eleven years old. I liked the sea, but detested the tyranny practised on board men-of-war. I left the Navy, went into the Dragoons, and was sent to India. My mother was a widow; a man married her for her money. Her money he would have, and he defrauded me of a large portion of my inheritance. I sold my commission, marred my prospects of rising by marrying, and drifted here." Williams shared

Shelley's passion for sailing, and longed to write a tragedy in verse; the poet warmly encouraged him, but Williams too often found that he "could not collect his thoughts", and his writing frequently took second place to sailing or strolling. He was a sensitive man with a keen eye for the good and bad in the people he met but, apparently, with no malice in his nature.

Jane had been deserted by her husband, and had borne to Edward two children—Edward Medwin Williams, aged two, and Rosalind Williams, aged fourteen months. Williams was deeply in love with Jane, so deeply that two days before his death he lamented bitterly over their unaccustomed separation of four days. Some of her friends considered Jane to be shallow, and Shelley sometimes thought her selfish. The scoundrel Shelley wrote poems for her and—his enemies pointed out after his death—was cad enough to show them to Edward before he allowed her to read them.

The fifth member of the party, Claire Clairmont, sister two degrees removed to Mary Shelley (Claire's widowed mother had married Mary's father), had as remarkable a personal history as any of the others, except perhaps Shelley himself. She had aided Mary to elope and had accompanied the guilty couple, as interpreter, on their first strenuous Continental tour. A few months later—she was then only eighteen—she had secretly resolved to capture a tame poet for herself, and had misguidedly and ambitiously hit upon Lord Byron, who could be tamed by no one save perhaps the vicious, who would understand how to manipulate the bonds that his sensuality flung about him. The eighteen-year-old Claire, who then went under the less romantic name of Jane, offered herself to Byron shortly before he exiled himself from England. He granted her request for an interview, stipulating only that he should not be asked to go outside London to keep the appointment; it was more convenient to slip round to Dover Street, off Piccadilly.

The issue of this fleeting amour was Allegra, at first named Alba. Once he knew that she was to bear his child, Byron would have nothing more to do with Claire, and she had spent the intervening six years largely dependent on Shelley's support, forbidden to approach Byron, deprived of her child save for the occasional charity of being allowed to pay the girl a visit, and living most of the time with Shelley and Mary. Many years later she wrote of her fatal affair with England's most fashionable poet:

> "A happy passion like death has *finis* written in such large characters in its face there is no hoping for any possibility of a change. . . . I had one; like all things perfect in its kind, it was fleeting, and mine only lasted ten minutes, but these ten minutes have discomposed the rest of my life."

Though she did not know it on the bleak day when, with Mary, she joined Shelley at the house by the sea, her child had been dead for eleven days.

The village of San Terenzo, from which Casa Magni was separated by two hundred yards of rocky shore, was in 1822 a primitive cluster of houses run up on the shore near an ancient castle, and clinging to the steep hillside behind and around the grey fortress. In recent years San Terenzo has crept along the shore and taken the white house with arches to itself, though it cannot even now shelter it on wild days from the spray cast by the moody sea over the coast road.

Early in September the previous year Shelley and Mary went north from Pisa to look for a house on the coast in which to spend the summer of 1822. Shelley's friend Trelawny innocently thought that the poet wished Byron to go north, too, though this was the opposite of the truth. In the middle of April came news that two houses in which the Shelleys were interested were not to let. Byron's theory was that the Piedmontese Government objected to Shelley's living in their territory.

Trelawny recorded his impressions of the house-hunting in these words:

> "On the shores of this superb bay, only surpassed in its natural beauty and capability by that of Naples, so effectually had tyranny paralysed the energies and enterprise of man, that the only indication of human habitation was

a few most miserable fishing villages scattered along the margin of the bay. Near its centre, between the villages of San Terenzo and Lerici, we came upon a lonely and abandoned building called the Villa Magni, though it looked more like a boat- or bathing-house than a place to live in. It consisted of a terrace or ground-floor unpaved, and used for storing boat gear and fishing-tackle, and a single storey over it divided into a hall or saloon and four small rooms which had once been white-washed; there was one chimney for cooking. This place we thought the Shelleys might put up with for the summer. The only good thing about it was a verandah facing the sea, and almost over it. So we sought the owner and made arrangements, dependent on Shelley's approval, for taking it for six months."

On 23 April the Williamses and Claire went to reconnoitre and on 26 April Claire accompanied Mary and Trelawny to La Spezia to make arrangements. Because of the news Shelley had received a few days before, his aim was to remove Claire from Pisa as quickly as possible. He and the Williamses set off towards San Terenzo the next day, after seeing the two households of furniture loaded for the voyage up the coast.

On arriving at Lerici on 28 April the travellers learned from the harbour-master, Signor Maglian, that there was not a house to be had. Furthermore the Customs duty on the furniture would amount to at least £300. Thinking that it would be necessary to send back the furniture unloaded, Shelley went with the harbour-master next day to La Spezia, where the Customs officer authorized the goods to be brought ashore and stored in the Casa Magni till he received orders from his government at Genoa. In the meantime Mary had gone farther inland to Sarzana to conclude for the white house. The Williamses, disappointed in their hope of obtaining a house, stayed at La Spezia for the night, and next day found Mary waiting for the boats to be unloaded. The details of this confused house-moving typified Shelley's habit of moving precipitately from place to place; though there was a good reason for haste, not unrelated to Lord Byron. On the cloudy May Day the Williamses arrived with the children after breakfast; during the previous day's moving the Shelleys had decided that they could accommodate their friends in one of the back rooms of the house.

It has been said that Casa Magni was once a Jesuit convent —which is probably a legend suggested by the cloister-like appearance of the arches at the front. In 1822 it appeared to be more of a boat-house than a dwelling-house. The ground level, entered by five broad arches of white stone standing within a few feet of the rocks and the shallow sea, was used as a store-house. On the first (and only) floor there were five rooms, with rough-cast walls that had simply been whitewashed. The servants lived in an outbuilding. There was only one hearth for cooking, and in place of a stairway a ladder gave access to the upper storey. Over the arches ran a wide unrailed terrace, and nearby, a holm-oak cast its shade.

A writer who lived there later in the nineteenth century— Dr. Paolo Mantegazza, whose family still live on the hill overlooking the castle of San Terenzo—described the Casa or Villa Magni thus:

> "It is a rugged old house, with its feet in the sea, and a mountain behind it evergreen with pine trees and ilex. Solitary, and strong as the base of a fortress, with a terrace and porch opening on the sea. More like a ship than a house. The sea enters the porch as by right, bathes the walls and often sends a salt greeting even to the inhabitants of the terrace and the first floor. These savage caresses have given to the house still called 'Shelley's Villa' the wrinkled, rough aspect of some old sailor's features. The iron railings are eaten away like old cheese with rust, and on the weather-beaten walls the nitre creeps and marine salt sparkles."

The house still dominates the western side of the Bay of Lerici in melancholy dignity. In an annexe a photographer carries on his business. Another storey has been added, yet the house is still dwarfed by the towering building, housing an ice-cream bar, that marks San Terenzo's final approach to Casa Magni. In 1822 the place was isolated from the village. Local rumour had it that the owner was mad; the only remaining evidence for this is that instead of allowing profitable olives to grow on the steep hillside behind the house, he had the trees torn down and planted ilex there for his pleasure.

On the eastern side of the bay Lerici sheltered under the backcloth of the mountains, stretching a line of houses up the steep way to its ancient castle. With its five-sided grey tower soaring skyward, surrounded by a tireless cloud of swallows, the castle cast a romantic air over the whole bay. Shelley's instinct had led him to the place in which Petrarch, his own ideal among poets, had composed one of his characteristic sonnets. Five centuries before, he had written, at the foot of the castle:

Del mar tirreno a la sinistra riva,
Dove rotte dal vento piangon l'onde . . .[1]

Petrarch describes in this sonnet to Laura his stumbling into a stream concealed by grass, and his being pleased at least by having "changed style, from eyes to feet", that is, having bathed his feet for once instead of his eyes, which had so frequently wept for Donna Laura. Petrarch had the unusual ability of combining ironical humour with the most fervid expression of idealistic love in one and the same sonnet. Shelley, who admired the Italian's poetry so much and was at this period greatly influenced by it, could not do this in a poem, for his expression of love in poetry was more in the nature of a rhapsody or prayer than of a conceit. Yet like Petrarch he could do much the same thing in prose: he had a sad vein of humour.

The coast road (built later in the nineteenth century) did not then exist; to reach Lerici the occupants of the house had either to scramble along a rocky path for a mile or row across the bay. Seventy or eighty years ago, the old Lericini still remember, the sea came near to their doors too. Shelley was frequently in Lerici and no doubt knew the history of the once strategic harbour dominated by the melancholy fortress. There is a tradition that Dante as well as Petrarch knew the place;

---

[1] "Of the left-hand shore of the Tyrrhenian Sea, where the waves cry' broken by the wind . , ,"

he went to the castle against his will, however, as a prisoner, and after passing an uncomfortable sojourn in a dungeon shook the dust of the village from his shoes and swore never to enter it again. An older tradition relates that after the Battle of Pavia, Francis I, a prisoner on his way to captivity in Spain, was housed there for a few days because his captors learnt that the French galleons were lurking beyond Portovenere, the other horn of the bay.

Founded by the Pisans, Lerici was contested throughout the Middle Ages between the Pisans and the Genoese. It became the principal stronghold on the coast dominated by the Ghibellines, even when the Guelphs held Sarzana, where the Shelleys had to send their servants to do the shopping. Lerici was twice burnt down and in its gloomy fortress executions and murders by poniard and poison were no uncommon occurrence. Corsican rebels had known the smell of its dungeons. As for the origin of the name Lerici, the inhabitants have a romantic legend which tells how in some remote time a beautiful local girl was forced by her father to marry a brutal Turkish invader. On her wedding day she climbed to the western battlements of the castle and flung herself on to the rocks below. Her name was La Lericina and after her, say the townspeople, their home was named.

If Shelley, who looked forward with such eagerness to the liberation and unification of Italy, ever climbed the steep ascent to the castle, he might on reaching its foot have wandered along the narrow Vico dei Pisani and seen, in the Piazza del Pozo, a sailor of twenty-three, named Domenico Ginocchio, who was born there, worked there as a sailor, and died there still illiterate, yet who was named by Mazzini as his most trustworthy messenger and spy during the struggle for the unification of Italy later in the century.

Shelley, who had lived in Italy for four years, mixed little with the Italians, and had a low opinion of those he knew. During his first year (1818) in their country, he had written:

> "There are *two* Italies—one composed of the green earth and transparent sea, and the mighty ruins of ancient time, and aërial mountains, and the warm and radiant atmosphere

which is interfused through all things. The other consists of the Italians of the present day, their works and ways. The one is the most sublime and lovely contemplation that can be conceived by the imagination of man; the other is the most degraded, disgusting, and odious."

Mary's impression of the Lericini and San Terenzesi could scarcely have been lower:

". . . I hated that house and the landscape around it. Shelley used to scold me about it. His health was good, and the place suited him exactly. What could I reply to him? That the people were savage and antipathetic, that, notwithstanding the beauty of the position, I should have preferred a place more completely in the country, that housekeeping was difficult, that our Tuscan servants all wanted to leave us, that the dialogue of those Genoese was rough and unpleasant. . . . I had no words to describe what I felt. The beauty of those woods made me shiver, and feel as if I wanted to cry. So strong was the sense of repulsion which I felt, that I was content only when the wind and the waves permitted me to sail out to sea, so that I might not be forced to take my usual walk among the trees over which climbed the luxuriant vines. Things which I once loved now oppressed me."

The men of Lerici were not to be dismissed as such savages, however, if Mazzini is to be believed: he praised them above all others for their valour, and singled out a shipwright named Giacopello, whose grand-nephew, mathematician by calling and poet by choice, still lives in Lerici. He has written of the little riviera between the two ancient castles, of San Terenzo, "the flower of the gulf", and of Shelley's house itself under its local name—*Marigola la bruna.*

Whether noble or savage, the Shelleys' neighbours were noisy. Their habit was to go down to the sea, men and women in separate companies, and plunge in, singing wild songs, throughout the night. Shelley may have borne this image in mind when he wrote in the last of his poems, the unfinished *Triumph of Life*:

> The wild dance maddens in the van, and those
> Who lead it—fleet as shadows on the green,
>
> Outspeed the chariot, and without repose
> Mix with each other in tempestuous measure
> To savage music; wilder as it grows,
>
> They, tortured by their agonising pleasure,
> Convulsed and on the rapid whirlwinds spun
> Of that fierce spirit, whose unholy leisure
>
> Was soothed by mischief since the world begun,
> Throw back their heads and loose their streaming hair;
> And in their dance round her who dims the sun,
>
> Maidens and youths fling their wild arms in air
> As their feet twinkle; they recede, and now
> Bending within each other's atmosphere
>
> Kindle invisibly—and as they glow,
> Like moths by light attracted and repelled,
> Oft to their bright destruction come and go;
>
> .   .   .   .
>
> Yet ere I can say *where*—the chariot hath
> Past over them—nor other trace I find
> But as of foam after the ocean's wrath
>
> Is spent upon the desert shore;—behind,
> Old men and women foully disarrayed,
> Shake their grey hairs in the insulting wind.

The inhabitants soon took note of the English people who were to spend so short a time among them. Sometimes, as the village priest recalled, the sailors tried to dissuade Shelley from putting out into the bay in a cockleshell of a boat. They observed the poor spirits of his wife, and noted the comings and goings of Claire Clairmont. They did not know that she had been a mother. A long time afterwards, when the story of Claire's folly was common knowledge, and the cockleshell had fallen apart, and the sea had long taken Shelley, they adopted as fact the sensational allegation that the English poet lived in their village "keeping his wife and his mistress in the same house". They believe the story to this day—even the Mantegazza family who live in a villa on the hillside. In adopting this belief the San Terenzesi have shown an interesting resemblance to the villagers of Marlow, England; five years before, when for the sake of appearances Claire joined the Shelley household there with her infant daughter, the villagers, noting the fondness of that young woman for the little girl who passed as one of the Shelley children, correctly deduced that her love was genuinely maternal, and once they had discovered this fact, the convenient deduction occurred to them that Shelley himself must be Allegra's father.

For casual onlookers, this impression was hardly dispelled at any time by Claire's attitude of affection and admiration towards Shelley; though affection was surely a natural return for the help he had given to her. Mary and she quarrelled repeatedly. Throughout the years of her punishment, the five years of bitterness to which her infatuation with Byron condemned her, Shelley was the only person who consistently befriended her, treated her with courtesy, supported her, tried to dispel her indolence by encouraging her to study, and exerted himself on her behalf in the dreary quarrel with Byron. During the days of the Shelleys' elopement Claire's mother, reporting the scandal to a friend and utterly at a loss to explain Claire's running away with the delinquents, wrote: "I asked C. if she liked Mr. Shelley and she answered with her usual enthusiasm that she thought him absolutely perfect." She thought him "absolutely perfect" not only till the end of his life, but to the end of her own, and she was buried wrapped in a little shawl that he had given to her.

A number of well-known people in England looked on Shelley as a blackguard; the impulsive Claire thought him perfect; a number of his friends considered him the finest man they had ever known, and made no reservations about saying so; his wife, in her highly complex attitude towards him, knew the strength of his obstinacy, the unflattering truth of his desire for solitude, his nightmare-ridden nature. If he was such a contradictory personality, is it possible to form a clear picture of him today?

Leaving aside biographical facts, gossip and conjectures, it is interesting to see how even his physical appearance eluded precise description. Benjamin Haydon called him a "hectic, spare, weakly yet intellectual-looking creature". Horace Smith, who loved him, saw "a fair, freckled, blue-eyed, light-haired, delicate-looking person, whose countenance was serious and thoughtful, whose stature would have been rather tall had he carried himself upright; whose earnest voice, though never loud, was somewhat unmusical". Hazlitt saw him as a man with a "maggot in his brain, a hectic flutter in his speech, which mark out the philosophic fanatic. He is sanguine-complexioned, and shrill-voiced." Long afterwards, when Shelley was dead and had ceased to trouble critics, Hazlitt changed the portrait: "Mr. Shelley was a remarkable man. His person was a type and shadow of his genius. His complexion, fair, golden, freckled, seemed transparent, with an inward light. . . ." Peacock found Shelley's voice low and soft. Hogg, who was fond of caricature, described the violent, clumsy and awkward movements of the eighteen-year-old Shelley, but Trelawny, who had no thwarted aspirations as a novelist of the Theodore Hook school, was impressed by the poet's silent movements, which helped to make the nickname "serpent" stick to him. Hogg described his features as symmetrical, "the mouth, perhaps, excepted"; another writer, believed by Professor Newman Ivey White to be Leigh Hunt, described the mouth as "narrow, the lip protruding, the upper one being, a sculptor might think, too long". Medwin, who met Shelley in 1820 for the first time in seven years, found him emaciated, short-sighted, his light hair interspersed with grey, yet of youthful appearance. Trelawny, who came on to the scene only a few months before Shelley died, wrote, "There never has been nor can be any true likeness of him"—and he was referring to more than the accident that there exists no professionally-drawn portrait of the poet.

·   ·   ·   ·   ·   ·

Rain and cloudy weather greeted them all in what Shelley was to call "this divine bay". The five of them spent the first day, till four o'clock, putting the house in order, settling in the servants, who were soon to begin quarrelling, and sharing out the four bedrooms that flanked the single dining-room in the centre, overlooking the terrace. In the evening they sat there listening to the moaning of the sea and, as Williams noted in his diary, "talking over our folly and our troubles".

The bay is shallow, and on sunny days the water lies calm and clear, taking its shades of green from the plants on the rocky sea-bed. But it is a moody sea. The threat of bad weather from the south or from the west, in the direction of Corsica, which may be indicated at first merely by the presence of a few clouds high in the hot sky, or a light haze that obscures the line between sea and sky, will ominously announce itself in the mysteriously sudden formation of breakers. Where the shallows have been calm a moment before, they will now become turbid and dark green as the surf forms and rolls in to break on the rocks or dispel itself on the few score yards of ochre sand.

The two couples knew that Claire's child, Allegra, had died on 19 April, but no one cared to break the news to her yet. Shelley's reaction took the form of depression; for him, his four years in Italy had been haunted by children's ghosts. He had come to the country as a father bereaved by the Lord Chancellor of the children of his first marriage. Within six months the infant Clara was dead. At the end of that year, 1818, the mysterious Elena Adelaide Shelley, the poet's "Neapolitan charge", was born, to die eighteen months later. The mystery of her brief life is discussed in Chapter Seven. In 1819 William Shelley died, aged three and a half. Allegra Byron, consigned by her father to the pest-ridden convent of Bagnacavallo, might have lived beyond that April had Shelley's offer to adopt her been accepted by Byron. Only a month before Allegra's death, in March, 1822, Claire had conceived a desperate plan to kidnap her child from the care of the nuns, with the aid of Shelley and a forged letter. Shelley had dissuaded her from this insane plan, and Mary had pointed out that Byron was powerful and they were weak. Though unaware of the full extent of Byron's treachery, Shelley was prepared for a final break with Allegra's father. Now he had the duty of telling Claire that her only link with Byron had died.

The attitude of Mary, who might have been expected to convey the news, was cold. She had never lived in harmony with Claire. The authority for this statement is her journals and letters. But it is a statement true for scholars only: it is probably untrue in the deeper sense that has to do with human beings, who are never quite so literal in their interpretation of emotions as scholars are. A human relationship often eludes the grasp of the man who is content to be no more than a librarian. For the plain fact is that Claire and Mary lived together for many years, and corresponded for years afterwards, and there was never a clear break between them. At San Terenzo Mary was oppressed by premonitions of approaching disaster: of danger not to her husband but to her child. She hated the house, the village, the inhabitants, the need to share pots and pans with Jane Williams, who was housewifely whereas Mary had other interests and longed for a palazzo. Most important of all, Mary Shelley was ill; her pregnancy was not progressing normally.

It may be that Mary had never liked Allegra, and that the child's lonely death had not moved her in the least. Allegra's temporary guardians in Venice, at a time when Byron had turned his home, Palazzo Moncenigo, into something resembling a private brothel, had certainly disliked the child: but these people, the Hoppners, were not notable for tenderness of heart. During a bitter moment in her old age, Claire wrote of Mary:

> "What should one say of a Woman who should go . . . and gaze upon the spectacle of a Child led to the scaffold . . . yet she did so, she looked coolly on, rejoiced in the comfortable place she got in the show, chatted with her neighbours, and after all never winced once during the exhibition and after all was over, went up and claimed acquaintance with the executioner and shook hands with him.
> I never saw her afterwards without feeling as if the sickening crawling motion of a Deathworm had replaced the usual flow of my Blood in my veins. . . ."

In this figurative passage expressing Claire's hatred—very deep hatred, for she was old when she wrote the words—the executioner is no doubt Byron, who sent Allegra to the unhealthy convent when fully aware of the discomfort and threat of fever that awaited his daughter there. Byron did not like Mary, but some layer of her rather cold nature probably awoke in Mary an admiration of Byron. She was much more of a "literary person" than Shelley, who had none of the conceits of authorship, and she was flattered to know titled people. Before long she was to suffer bitter humiliation at Byron's hands, when as a poor widow she had to turn elsewhere for the wherewithal to travel to England.

As for the Williamses, this was not their affair, and they could do little but prepare to extend their sympathy to Claire. They were good friends of the Shelleys and of Claire. They knew Byron. Probably they did not know the full story of Claire's folly; they must have had to stand aside as somewhat embarrassed onlookers.

The Shelleys' attitude towards their guests calls for a note here, because it had an important bearing on what happened later. Edward and Jane had been introduced by Shelley's cousin Medwin in January, 1821. Williams had an unstinted admiration for Shelley's genius and Shelley liked Williams; there was nothing of the master-and-disciple relationship between them. Shelley criticized Williams's drama, but he also asked his friend to suggest a title for one of his own poems, and the suggestion, *Hellas*, was accepted, much to Williams's pleasure. The poet was not so sure of Jane. He wrote to Claire, "(Williams) I like, and I have got reconciled to Jane." Mary thought Jane lacking in imagination, and the more outspoken Trelawny considered her commonplace. At Casa Magni Mary and Jane did not get on well together, but to expect any two women, with young children, to live in harmony in that primitive dwelling would have been absurd.

Much later, Jane's vanity and the growing "legend of Shelley" were to make her boast that he had fallen in love with her at Casa Magni. Still later, in the days when anyone who could forge a Shelley letter was sure to be able to sell it for a considerable sum, a yet more remarkable legend was born.

One biographer, W. E. Peck, cited a letter of which the original was never forthcoming, in which Shelley is seen telling Byron, of all improbable confidants, that he had made love to his friend's wife while they were on their way home from a *festa*. Picking our way as carefully as possible among documented facts, autobiography, gossip arising out of vanity and downright forgeries, we can deduce that the atmosphere was heavily charged enough to produce an electric storm.

The second day dawned greyly. Rain fell from time to time. Shelley and Williams had a skiff that they had used on the Rivers Arno and Serchio; in this they went out to fish among the rocks. The sport was poor. The boat, which had been fitted up for river excursions, was flat-bottomed, ten feet long, and built of lath and canvas. It was really a marsh punt, but had been fitted, unsafely, with a rudder and sails. A year before, on a canal near Pisa, it had capsized and Shelley, who could not swim a stroke, had had to be rescued from drowning by one of his friends. Soon they hoped to have a worthier vessel, a schooner that Shelley was having built at Genoa. In the evening they went out in search of wild duck, saw no game, but were rewarded by the sight of the splendid scenery. That evening the wind rose, the unremitting sirocco wind that is called the *ponente*, and which gives its name to the riviera farther north, between Menton and Genoa, more attractively termed for the benefit of summer tourists the Riviera of Flowers.

A storm broke, and the four conspirators went to Jane's room at the back of the house to discuss how best to break the news that was becoming all the more terrible for having been kept from Claire for so long. She had given up her child at the age of fifteen months because she was penniless and Byron was rich, and could give Allegra the education and position that Claire considered to be the due of the poet's daughter. Instead Allegra had had her spirit broken and had died, aged five and a half, in a chilly nunnery.

Claire put an end to the difficulty by walking into the room: the silence told her the truth. It remained only for Shelley to tell her the details. The immediate effect was so alarming that Shelley thought Claire would lose her reason. Probably the next day, Claire wrote a letter to Byron, who blandly returned it to Shelley without answering it, as if he had been responsible for its having been sent. Shelley destroyed it. During the following fortnight Claire became calmer. She spoke of her wish to see the coffin, and to possess a likeness of her daughter and a lock of her hair. Now, if at any time, loss of a child might have brought her closer to Mary; instead, it seems to have brought her closer to Shelley.

The men spent as much time as possible away from the house: and 3 May brought fine weather. Shelley went shopping in Lerici, the servants having returned empty-handed from Sarzana, a few miles over the mountain. He reported to Byron that Claire now knew about the death of her daughter, and conveyed to him her requests—to see the coffin before it was sent to England, to receive a portrait of Allegra, and to have a lock of her hair, "however small". If Byron had only one portrait and wished to retain it, Shelley added that he would have it copied himself. Then, to put a note of cheer in a gloomy letter, he added, "Nature is here as vivid and joyous as we are dismal, and we have built, as Faust says, 'our little world in the great world of all' as a contrast rather than a copy of that divine example." He mentioned that Tita, a servant of Byron's, had arrived, "and has re-assumed his marine life. He seems as happy as a bird just let loose from a cage." He asked Byron to pay on his behalf ten crowns, which in the hurry of the departure from Pisa he had forgotten to leave for Mary's Greek master. He invited Pietro Gamba, brother of Byron's mistress, to "come quickly and stay long with us here". He gave the news about the Williamses, returned to the subject of Claire to point out that she was very ill, "although what I chiefly dreaded is spared, as she retains her senses", and concluded with a request for news, good or bad.

On Saturday, 4 May, the men went fishing, idled away the day, and tried fishing among the rocks again, only to lose their bait. A heavy swell drove them indoors late. It was the day when Mary gave up her journal, to resume it again at the beginning of June. That night the swell, sounding on the beach, as Williams noted, "like the discharge of heavy artillery", kept them awake all night. Next morning they tried to launch the boat through the surf, and were drenched on attempting to land. Once again they walked to Lerici.

In the house tension was increasing. Jane probably had the task of trying to console Claire; Mary made hysterical scenes with Shelley about the house and the housekeeping, for which she later apologized to him in private.

On Monday, 6 May, Williams went sketching and noticed something queer about the weather: heavy drops of rain were falling, though not a cloud was to be seen in the fathomless sky. After restlessly reading and taking Jane for a walk in the mountains, he came back to tea, then stood and talked with Shelley on the broad terrace, where San Terenzo produced the first of a number of nightmares.

Two

THE SILENT CENTRE

> Within the silent centre of the earth
> My mansion is; where I lived ensphered
> From the beginning, and around my sleep
> Have woven all the wondrous imagery
> Of this dim spot, which mortals call the world;
> Infinite depths of unknown elements
> Massed into one impenetrable mask;
> Sheets of immeasurable fire, and veins
> Of gold and stone, and adamantine iron.
> *Song of a Spirit*

"AFTER TEA," wrote Williams, "walking with Shelley on the terrace, and observing the effect of moonshine on the waters, he complained of being unusually nervous, and stopping short he grasped me violently by the arm, and stared steadfastly on the white surf that broke upon the beach under our feet. Observing him sensibly affected, I demanded of him if he was in pain, but he only answered by saying, 'There it is again—there!' He recovered after some time, and declared that he saw, as plainly as then he saw me, a naked child rise from the sea, clap its hands as if in joy, and smiling at him. This was a trance that it required some reasoning and philosophy entirely to awake him from, so forcibly had the vision operated on his mind. Our conversation, which had been at first rather melancholy, led to this; and my confirming his sensations, by confessing that I had felt the same, gave a greater activity to his ever wandering and lively imagination."

Shelley had been fond of Allegra, but the little girl in his vision, beckoning him towards the sea, may have had a more complex identity, as the compound of his own children dead, lost and unborn. He had lost Ianthe, daughter of Harriet; he had lost Clara, daughter of Mary; he had lost Elena Adelaide, his "Neapolitan". Mary was even now carrying another child, and her health was precarious. For Shelley, death was birth, and both were related to the ceremonies of love. He had written in 1820 some lines with a bitter twist at the end:

> Death has set his mark and seal
> On all we are and all we feel,
> On all we know and all we fear.
>
> . . . .
>
> All things that we love and cherish
> Like ourselves must fade and perish;
> Such is our rude mortal lot—
> Love itself would, did they not.

Shelley's vision of the child in the sea was the first of a number of hallucinations that afflicted the dwellers at Casa Magni as if portending the disaster that was to fall upon them before the summer had reached its height. To see a waking vision was nothing new for Shelley, for he was of a nature that causes dreams to merge with reality. A doctor might have explained this as a result of the excessive energy he threw into living. As his poetry reveals, he lived at a dangerously high emotional pitch; but he lived also under great physical tension. His whole life is a fevered record of travelling, reading, writing, grappling with the most distressing problems of practical life: he poured out such a stream of mental and physical energy that one wonders why the legend of an effeminate frame or personality ever became established.

The visions and premonitions that threw a mystery over the house that summer were not all Shelley's. Even Jane Williams, generally thought to be unimaginative, thought she saw ghosts by daylight. Since Jane was the last woman whose name has been linked (I believe wrongly) with Shelley's emotional life, she provides a natural starting-point for a discussion of what Shelley demanded of love.

The question of Jane Williams and the last two months of Shelley's life has long aroused curiosity. Because one of Shelley's last poems (*Lines Written in the Bay of Lerici*) has been associated with her, purely on the imaginary evidence supplied by another (*We Meet Not As We Parted*), it has been supposed that a mysterious relationship developed between them at San Terenzo. It is mysterious chiefly because biographers and others have made it so. Some favour the view that Shelley wished to make Jane his mistress, others that he was inspired by an idealized admiration. Everyone knows that when writers refer to Shelley's "Platonic mistress" they mean Jane. Yet the supposition, like so many relating to Shelley that are mere hypotheses unsupported by facts, has its being in a bubble. All the poems known to have been written for Jane express a light romanticism that does not occur in any other love poems having as object an identifiable woman. The scholars have fallen into a double trap. They assume that the poem *Lines Written in the Bay of Lerici* was an afterthought to *We Meet Not As We Parted*, overlooking the fact that there is no good reason to suppose that the latter poem was written about Jane at all, and furthermore that there is no conclusive evidence of its having been written at San Terenzo. Many of Shelley's poems are highly compressed autobiography. We must give them, as documents, value at least equal to that of biographers' suppositions, and some critics would rate them higher in the scale of truth.

Before turning to what Shelley himself wrote about his emotional state while he lived at San Terenzo, it is worth considering what opportunity or inclination he had to indulge in emotional platonics with Jane during that period. Between the middle of May and the end of June—after which he went away—he spent most of his waking hours either sailing with Williams in their new schooner or paddling about alone and writing in his cockleshell. Before that time he was beset by the difficulties of moving, Claire's tragedy, Mary's illness (which almost resulted in her death in the middle of June) and several dismal money problems that should have been the concern of William Godwin, Mary's father. These were hardly living conditions conducive to the development of a high romantic passion even if the discomforts of the house and the presence of Williams are to be overlooked. Jane soon began to quarrel with Mary. The gaze of posterity, fixed in fascination on Shelley, oddly overlooks the salient fact that during this time Williams, Jane's ardent lover, spent with her what time she could spare from looking after two infants and consoling the almost demented Claire.

Thus on 7 May, when in spite of fine weather the surf prevented the friends from boating, Williams stayed in and wrote a letter in the morning, and in the afternoon attempted to take Jane out in the flat-bottomed boat—an attempt that ended with his having to fish her, half-drowned, out of the sea. In the evening a heavy thunderstorm again confined everyone to the house. Next day Williams was again writing; he rowed over to Lerici; after lunch he bathed. News had arrived from Trelawny promising the delivery of the schooner next day and "every eye strained in hope of seeing the boat come in". On 9 May he tried to settle down to his drama, but everyone was unsettled and anxious to see the boat round Portovenere from Genoa; finally Williams went walking with Jane and then did some gardening for her. On Friday, 10 May, he was again attempting to write. The weather was threatening and news came from Genoa that the boat had not sailed because of the heavy seas. It was on Sunday, 12 May, that the boat arrived, and thereafter Shelley and Williams were absorbed for weeks, sailing and carpentering and absurdly planning Atlantic voyages.

The two families had been friends for nearly eighteen months, and turning to Shelley's writing for a picture of the relationship—a refreshing change from the confusion of letters and journals written by others—we find that Jane's first function was to take over the mesmeric treatment introduced by Medwin, fresh from the East. Shelley had for years been afflicted by a pain in the side which defied diagnosis, and which caused spasms of agony. Medwin's hypnotism eased the pain. Jane tried her hand at it, and the poem *The Magnetic Lady to*

Her Patient, no love lyric but a friendly jest, indicates that though the patient flattered the lady by commending her mesmeric powers, the hypnotic trance was far from deep:

> "The spell is done. How feel you now?"
> "Better—Quite well," replied
> The sleeper.—"What would do
>   You good when suffering and awake?
>   What cure your head and side?—"
> "What would cure, that would kill me, Jane:
>   And as I must on earth abide
> Awhile, yet tempt me not to break
>   My chain."

To this period belongs one of the more frequently quoted (and more solemn) references to Shelley's emotional life: his description of Jane on 19 June, 1822, as a *pure anticipated cognition* of the antitype of the lady in his poem *The Sensitive Plant*. Far from being a metaphysical solemnity, this was a joke, made at the expense of Kant and Coleridge and a forgotten philosopher named Drummond. Shelley's friend Peacock, in *Nightmare Abbey*, brought up the jest, a private one, in his friendly caricature of Shelley as Scythrop: "Scythrop's romantic dreams had indeed given him many *pure anticipated cognitions* of combinations of beauty and intelligence." In a mocking footnote Shelley had already used the phrase as a dig at philosophers who deduced truth from "anticipated cognitions *a priori*", and even at the age of eighteen, in the notes to *Queen Mab*, he was having fun at the expense of William Drummond when writing: "The consistent Newtonian is necessarily an atheist. . . . Sir W. seems to consider the atheism to which it leads as a sufficient presumption of the falsehood of the system of gravitation."

The friendship was still a lighthearted one when Shelley wrote *The Invitation*, in the spring of 1822. It was a poem posted on Jane's door, inviting her to go walking with him. In *The Recollection*, the verses that report the outing, the extravagant *cavaliere servente* note gives way to a sad autobiographical reference:

> Like one beloved the scene had lent
> > To the dark water's breast
> Its every leaf and lineament
> > With more than truth expressed;
> Until an envious wind crept by,
> > Like an unwelcome thought,
> Which from the mind's too faithful eye
> > Blots one dear image out.
> Though thou art ever fair and kind,
> > The forests ever green,
> Less oft is peace in Shelley's mind,
> > Than calm in waters, seen.

About this time Trelawny reports Shelley as having spoken of jealousy in the following terms:

> "Love is not akin to jealousy; love does not seek its own pleasure, but the happiness of another. Jealousy is gross selfishness; it looks upon everyone who approaches as an enemy; it's the idolatry of self, and, like canine madness, incurable."

Trelawny thought later that he was referring to his wife. In the winter Shelley had decided that Jane was "a sort of spirit of embodied peace in our circle of tempests". He was charmed by her music and, unable to obtain a harp for her, had bought the guitar that she received with the lines *With a Guitar, To Jane*, written

> > by permission and command
> > Of thine own Prince Ferdinand.

The emotional situation between Mary and Shelley, in the winter of 1821-22, is set down in the poem on a little pumpkin plant, *The Zucca*:

> > Summer was dead and Autumn was expiring,
> > > And infant Winter laughed upon the land
> > All cloudlessly and cold;—when I, desiring
> > > More in this world than any understand,

> Wept o'er the beauty, which, like sea retiring,
>   Had left the earth bare as the wave-worn sand
> Of my lorn heart, and o'er the grass and flowers
> Pale for the falsehood of the flattering hours.
>
> Summer was dead, but I yet lived to weep
>   The instability of all but weeping;
>
> . . . . .
>
> I loved—oh, no, I mean not one of ye,
>   Or any earthly one, though ye are dear
> As human heart to human heart may be;—
>   I loved, I know not what—but this low sphere
> And all that it contains, contains not thee,
>   Thou, whom, seen nowhere, I feel everywhere . . .

During the same month, January, he sent to Williams and Jane the poem described by Williams in his Journal as "some beautiful but too melancholy lines":

> When I return to my cold home, you ask
>   Why I am not as I have ever been.
>   *You* spoil me for the task
>   Of acting a forced part in life's dull scene,—
>   Of wearing on my brow the idle mask
>   Of author, great or mean,
>   In the world's carnival. I sought
> Peace thus, and but in you I found it not.

These lines, which begin "The serpent is shut out from paradise", are written to Emilia Viviani, not Jane, and the explanation of Mary's coldness is found not merely in her longing for society or her misunderstanding of her difficult husband, but in a long series of deaths and emotional complexities that go so far back that their source is to be found in the very earliest days of their association; at this particular moment, however, Mary had some reason to be cold, for Shelley's remarkable platonic passion for Emilia Viviani had recently been brought to an end.

To assume that while at San Terenzo Shelley was consumed by a self-pitying passion for Jane is to fail to see the depth and seriousness of his older and more complex passion for Mary. His views on the intercourse between a man and a woman were very different from those of men for whom it is the most natural thing in the world to debate, in face of Shelley's detestation of promiscuity, the baseless question of whether he seduced Jane or whether he wanted to do so. In his work, the deeper the emotion the greater the compression of language and poetic thought, as may be seen if the obscurities of *The Zucca,* and its poetical slackness, are compared with a poem dated by Mary 1822, in which Shelley's preoccupation seems to be with his marriage and the mysterious tensions that were destroying it, rather than with any outside object of sympathy:

>   When the lamp is shattered
> The light in the dust lies dead—
>   When the cloud is scattered
> The rainbow's glory is shed
>   When the lute is broken,
> Sweet tones are remembered not;
>   When the lips have spoken,
> Loved accents are soon forgot
>
> .   .   .   .
>
>   When hearts have once mingled
> Love first leaves the well-built nest;
>   The weak one is singled
> To endure what it once possessed.
>   O Love! who bewailest
> The frailty of all things here,
>   Why choose you the frailest
> For your cradle, your home, and your bier?
>
>   Its passions will rock thee
> As the storms rock the ravens on high;
>   Bright reason will mock thee
> Like the sun from a wintry sky.
>   From thy nest every rafter
> Will rot, and thine eagle home
>   Leave thee naked to laughter,
> When leaves fall and cold winds come.

If, therefore, the "Jane affair" is not torn from its context in the concluding months of the poet's life, if it is seen not merely in relation to a number of romantic lyrics, but against the background of a marriage, it becomes more difficult to assume that the two final autobiographical poems were written with Jane's image exclusively in the poet's mind.

The first of these poems, *Lines Written in the Bay of Lerici*, was undoubtedly composed at San Terenzo. It evokes the mood of a man left, very late at night, by a woman who has aroused in him worship of "the delusive flame" of love. The lines that refer to

> every tone
> Which, though silent to the ear,
> The enchanted heart could hear

suggest the guitarist yet may refer to speech, not music or song.

> Her presence had made weak and tame
> All passions, and I lived alone
> In the time which is our own;
> The past and future were forgot . . .

are lines that suggest Mary as much as they suggest Jane, if one remembers the tensions that had long existed between Shelley and his wife, and the wretched conditions in which they shared Casa Magni with their friends.

> Memory gave me all of her
> That even Fancy dares to claim

are lines that may be read in more of a bitter than a romantic meaning, particularly in view of the conclusion of the poem:

> And the fisher with his lamp
> And spear about the low rocks damp
> Crept, and struck the fish which came
> To worship the delusive flame.
> Too happy they, whose pleasure sought
> Extinguishes all sense and thought
> Of the regret that pleasure leaves,
> Destroying life alone, not peace!

The final analysis of the emotion in this poem is not simple. Shelley failed often enough to put into words the obscurities of his feelings; but if the lines are read in conjunction with *The Zucca* we are reminded that the poet's mind and heart are preoccupied not with one woman but with two women and a man; with discomfort and discontent, with the undercurrent of conflict present among friends who spend too much time together.

The favourite interpretation of the lines *We Meet Not As We Parted* is that they were written after Shelley had been refused permission to kiss Jane. This naïve interpretation does not entirely fit the personality of the "nonagenarian", however. Nor does such a romantic situation square with the friends' final communications. The poem is about a moment:

> That moment from time was singled
> As the first of a life of pain;
> The cup of its joy was mingled . . .

Applied to Jane Williams, the second of these lines is clearly an untruth; and Shelley was not addicted to romantic lies of that kind. The fourth stanza refers to the kiss that must continue to trouble commentators:

> Sweet lips, could my heart have hidden
> That its life was crushed by you,
> Ye would not have then forbidden
> The death which a heart so true
> Sought in your briny dew.

If this means that the moment, the first in Shelley's painful life, occurred while the poet was extracting Jane from the sea after a spill while boating, it seems ungallant to say, "If I could have concealed the fact that you had already broken my heart, you would cheerfully have allowed that kiss". That would have been tantamount to the poet's calling the lady light. The strange sentiment fits more closely Shelley's relationship with Mary, a facet of which he had reflected in the verses:

> When a lover clasps his fairest,
> Then be our dread sport the rarest;
> Their caresses were like chaff
> In the tempest, and be our laugh
> His despair—her epitaph.
>
> When a mother clasps her child,
> Watch till dusty Death has piled
> His cold ashes on the clay;
> She has loved it many a day,
> She remains—it fades away.

It was Mary who edited Shelley's poetry, beginning with the posthumous poems and fragments in 1824. Shelley's most painstaking biographer, Newman Ivey White, points out that her dating of individual poems is not always accurate; but it is not easy to establish errors in dating, whether accidental or deliberate, for Shelley was not in the habit of dating his MSS. Mary Shelley did not suppress any poems, it would appear, and it is her editing which results in the implication that *Lines Written in the Bay of Lerici* and *We Meet Not As We Parted* may be connected as far as the occasion of their writing is concerned. It is easy to assume that Mary saw most of Shelley's poems as they were produced because she singles out the melancholy poems of 1818 as being concealed from her. But it does not by any means follow that she saw all her husband's shorter poems during his lifetime—or that she fully understood their import when she found them among his papers. We, posterity, know more about several aspects of Shelley's life than his wife knew; so that her editing, well-intentioned as it undoubtedly was, is not necessarily the most accurate or revealing explanation of "time, place and circumstance" in the poet's imaginative or physical life.

Shelley's poetry abounds in what may be called sexual situations. They are rarely worked out in a naïve manner. *We Meet Not As We Parted* seems to me to be a comment on a quarrel (not a flirtation) in which the woman refused one moment's opportunity of reconciliation. The poem is often printed without its fragmentary final stanza, which has only two extant lines, the final ones:

> Methinks too little cost
> For a moment so found, so lost.[1]

Even when writing verses for a girl's album, Shelley was not naïve; which is why Sophia Stacey, whose heart fluttered when he lifted her into a carriage, received this:

> I fear thy kisses, gentle maiden,
> Thou needest not fear mine;
> My spirit is too deeply laden
> Ever to burthen thine.

There is more to be said in Chapter Six on the subject of physical expressions of love and the painful dissensions that existed between the poet and both his wives. Shortly before Jane and Edward came on to the scene the source of *Epipsychidion*, Shelley's passion for Emilia Viviani, had reached its mental climax. Here if anywhere is the "affair" that illustrates better than any other incident the composition of his emotions. The resultant poem is an autobiography—of the emotions.

In September, 1821, he wrote to Byron, possibly with a view to preventing the spread of too colourful gossip among the tourists:

> "They have made a great fuss at Pisa about my intimacy with this lady. Pray do not mention anything of what I told you; as the whole truth is not known and Mary might be very much annoyed at it. . . . I pronounce you secure against any of my female friends here. I will trust you with Mrs. W(illiams)."

Emilia, for whom for the time being no husband could be found, lived in a convent at Florence. Shelley became, with the full knowledge of his wife, Emilia's friend and adviser. Mary did not take the matter very seriously: she wrote acidly to a friend about Shelley's "platonics". The "nonagenarian" was ambivalent, too, in spite of the intensity of the verses he wrote

---

[1] One editor, Locock, dates the poem 1814.

to Emilia. When in due course negotiations for her marriage were being made, the less favoured of her two suitors became frantic, and Emilia handed him over to Shelley "to quiet and console". The poet wrote:

> "It seems that I am worthy to take my degree of M.A. in the art of love, for I have contrived to calm the despairing swain, much to the satisfaction of poor Emilia, who in that convent of hers sees everything as through a mist, ten times its natural size."

Emilia was married in September, a few days before Shelley wrote to Byron in the terms quoted above; but the removal of the object of platonic passion was not entirely a joke, as may be deduced from his comment four months later, "My convent friend . . . is married, and I (am) in a sort of morbid quietness."

The mature Shelley was, for his time, fairly reticent on the subject of his private feelings; they were a labyrinth demanding verse for expression. *Epipsychidion* was so true a guide to the history of his heart, indeed, that after publishing it anonymously he soon fell out of love with it, and withdrew the work. Furthermore it was the only one of his poems about love that Mary Shelley could not read without pain; a deeper pain, one suspects, than the pangs of jealousy. In June, 1822, on a day when death lay three weeks and thirty sea miles away, he explained why he could no longer look at the poem:

> "If you are curious, however, to hear what I am and have been, it will tell you something thereof. It is an idealized history of my life and feelings. I think one is always in love with something or other; the error—and I confess it is not easy for spirits cased in flesh and blood to avoid it—consists in seeking in a mortal image the likeness of what is, perhaps, eternal."

When one reflects that from the age of nineteen till his death Shelley was surrounded by women, oppressed by their anxieties, ills and humours, answering their need for protection and support, it is something of a miracle that he should ever have contrived to keep his thoughts on the idealism expressed in *Epipsychidion*. Needless to say it is a mysterious poem, as the writer ironically warns in his opening paraphrase of Dante:

> My Song, I fear that thou wilt find but few
> Who fitly shall conceive thy reasoning,
> Of such hard matter dost thou entertain.

It is a love-poem conceived on the scale not of a lyric but of a symphony; and like a symphony it is contrapuntal—that is, not to be understood as a bare chronological history but as a structure consisting of layers of emotional experience. This method of writing is repeatedly encountered in Shelley's work. It is a method clear to any creative writer but not always perfectly lucid to academic critics, who tend to rely too much on chronology and who therefore assume that if one morning a poet says that he is out of love, the poem he writes in the afternoon cannot possibly refer to the woman whose glories he was celebrating the day before. As an example of this type of criticism, consider the comment made on the following reminiscence of a youth's encounter with a wanton:

> One, whose voice was venomed melody
> Sate by a well, under blue nightshade bowers;
> The breath of her false mouth was like faint flowers,
> Her touch was as electric poison,—flame
> Out of her looks into my vitals came,
> And from her living cheeks and bosom flew
> A killing air, which pierced like honey-dew
> Into the core of my green heart, and lay
> Upon its leaves; until, as hair grown gray
> O'er a young brow, they hid its unblown prime
> With ruins of unseasonable time.

Professor W. E. Peck makes from these lines the deduction that when at Oxford, Shelley contracted a venereal disease. The only result of "interpretation" of this kind is to cause several other academic scholars to embark enthusiastically upon the task of proving beyond doubt that Shelley did *not* contract the disease. If any scholastic communications reach Shelley's corner of Elysium, the poet is probably writing off this one as another "pure anticipated cognition" of the *a priori* school.

There is not much to be gained by trying to guess the identities of all the women mentioned in *Epipsychidion*, or by attempting to establish whether the line

>   And One was true—oh! why not true to me?

refers to Harriet Grove, the sweetheart of his boyhood, or to Harriet Westbrook, his first wife. What dominates the early part of the poem, before the entrance of Emilia, the vision "sought through grief and shame" is the figure of Mary Shelley, characterized as in other poems as the Moon:

> That wandering shrine of soft yet icy flame
> Which ever is transformed, yet still the same,
> And warms not but illumines.

A few lines later Shelley writes as clearly as possible the history of his second marriage:

> And there I lay, within a chaste cold bed:
> Alas, I then was nor alive nor dead:—
> For at her silver voice came Death and Life,
> Unmindful each of their accustomed strife,
> Masked like twin babes, a sister and a brother,
> The wandering hopes of one abandoned mother
> And through the cavern without wings they flew,
> And cried "Away, he is not of our crew."

It is not difficult to see in these lines the references to the children Clara and William. The result of their death, not only on Shelley's feelings as a father but on his experience as a husband, is deliberately obscured in the lines that follow:

> What storms then shook the ocean of my sleep,
> Blotting that Moon, whose pale and waning lips
> Then shrank as in the sickness of eclipse;—

> And how my soul was as a lampless sea,
> And who was then its Tempest; and when She,
> The Planet of that hour, was quenched, what frost
> Crept o'er those waters, till from coast to coast
> The moving billows of my being fell
> Into a death of ice, immovable;—
> And then—what earthquakes made it gape and split,
> The white Moon smiling all the while on it,
> These words conceal.

If these lines are interpreted literally in spite of Shelley's warning in the last three words, and taken to be a chronological account of his experience, the reader must adopt the improbable conclusion that between June, 1819, when William died, and September, 1821, when Emilia was married, Shelley fell in love with three women, the last of whom was Emilia. Several short poems, expressing something of the bitterness of the line "The white Moon smiling all the while on it", and referring without concealment to Mary, belong to periods before 1821, and suggest that the break took place earlier—in 1818, the year of the "poems of despondency", and of *Julian and Maddalo*. Yet the lines need not be taken literally as Shelley's emotional farewell to Mary. Life does not fall into simple compartments in that way, and with men of Shelley's temperament love's good-bye is never a final one. Love can return, passing even through hatred, as Shelley stated in one of the rejected fragments of this very poem, *Epipsychidion*:

> Folly can season Wisdom, Hatred Love.

Undoubtedly death came to Shelley before there was a complete reconciliation. Faced with the plain fact that there occurred a deep emotional (more than sexual) breach between the Shelleys, some writers seek to prove that it was mended, others that the whole fault lay with Mary. Thus, unfortunately, Mary is sacrificed for the sake of a reputation Shelley would not have desired, damned as a cold, callous and nagging wife, all with conspicuous disregard for the fact that in real life such breaches are rarely to be blamed on one partner only. In the paper-world, either Shelley or Mary has to be in the right. In the real world, the private world of their marriage, grief and blame were no doubt shared. I shall have more to say about Shelley's marriages in Chapter Six.

When a marriage or a love affair between people as highly intelligent as the Shelleys turns to bitterness the cause is not usually found in the offence of the one and the innocence of the other: it is more likely to spring out of a grievance that both suffer, yet which is too overwhelming to be shared or even discussed. Such was Shelley's feeling that he was destined to have no posterity. Society and death had combined to rob him of five children; it was as if all those children had cried, "Away, he is not of our crew". That Mary was infected by this fear, while at San Terenzo, is beyond doubt. Her last letter to her husband was full of foreboding of evil: her unborn child had miscarried and she was afraid that the only living one, Percy Florence, would die in infancy. Perhaps after all posterity can find the reason for their unhappiness written in the statistics of infantile mortality of early nineteenth-century Italy. The death of children could turn love itself into a death's head symbol. Shelley had written two years before, on learning of the death of the child christened at Naples Elena Adelaide Shelley: "It seems as if the destruction that is consuming me were an atmosphere which wrapt and *infected* everything connected with me."

This obsession appears repeatedly in his poetry—even in an attempt in *Epipsychidion* to idealize love. Thus, before the reference to the "electric lady", these lines occur:

> I questioned every tongueless wind that flew
> Over my tower of mourning, if it knew
> Whither 'twas fled, this soul out of my soul;
> And murmured names and spells which have control
> Over the sightless tyrants of our fate;
> But neither prayer nor verse could dissipate
> The night which closed on her; nor uncreate
> That world within this Chaos, mine and me,
> Of which she was the veiled Divinity,
> The world I say of thoughts that worshipped her;
> And therefore I went forth, with hope and fear
> And every gentle passion sick to death,
> Feeding my course with expectation's breath,
> Into the wintry forest of our life.

Hope and Fear are forces that appear frequently;[1] they are mentioned again later in the poem in words addressed to Emilia Viviani:

> Adoring Even and Morn
> Will worship thee with incense of calm breath
> And lights and shadows; as the star of Death
> And Birth is worshipped by those sisters wild
> Called Hope and Fear.

Among the fragments of poetry written in 1821 is a reference to "that strong boy", Pleasure, near whom stand Love, Hope, Desire and Fear, "the regents ... Of the four elements that frame the heart". Probably the best-known expression of the obsession is to be found in the sonnet that begins:

> Lift not the painted veil which those who live
> Call Life: though unreal shapes be pictured there,
> And it but mimic all we would believe
> With colours idly spread,—behind, lurk Fear
> And Hope, twin Destinies; who ever weave
> Their shadows, o'er the chasm, sightless and drear.

The end of Shelley's life was overshadowed by this obsession, but since a creative mind cannot live entirely in the pit of Fear, Hope is the final freedom, as broad as the Italian sky, to which the poet turns. This Hope is not merely a consolation for the heavy blows that had fallen upon him ever since 1814, when he became estranged from Harriet. In his early work it takes the form of his idealistic picture of love. His youthful expressions of passion, and the earthly forms in which he enthusiastically sought "the idol of his thought", are often bound to appear a little absurd, as they did to Shelley himself, later. Yet the contrast in quality between his early, sentimental poems and the work of his maturity scarcely disturbs the average reader because of the extraordinary consistency of emotion expressed: consistency of emotion being, for a man of Shelley's temperament, an essential of life, whether or not it is viewed as an obsession.

[1] This image, in its Petrarchian significance, is discussed in Chapter **Eight**.

What troubles many readers of Shelley—both those who are well-disposed and those who are ill-disposed towards his view of life—is curiously enough the fact that all his love-poems were not written to his legal wives. The reputation of hardly any other major poet has been affected by this desire to know his full emotional history. There is some deep logic in the desire, however, because that history is written fairly plainly in Shelley's works. He would have been pleased by Donne's lines:

> Whoever guesses, thinks, or dreams he knows
> Who is my mistress, wither by this curse.

Shelley wrote something similar in the rejected drafts of *Epipsychidion*:

> If any should be curious to discover
> Whether to you I am a friend or lover,
> Let them read Shakespeare's sonnets, taking thence
> A whetstone for their dull intelligence.

What precisely did he ask of love, and who was his "mistress"? In the greenness of his youth he demanded discipleship above all else. When he eloped with Mary and took her half-sister Claire tramping over Europe with him, he spent a large amount of time superintending Claire's education and trying to combat her laziness and boredom by encouraging her to study. When domestic crises occurred, he put all his faith in improvement of the mind: whatever storms were about to burst over their heads, they must keep up their reading. It was a sensible enough attitude. He wanted women to liberate themselves from a tradition of concubinage. Half his adoration of Mary (whose mind he at first insisted was far superior to his own) arose out of his reverence for the memory of her mother, Mary Wollstonecraft. He wanted women to free themselves from

> Things whose trade is over ladies
>   To lean, and flirt and stare and simper,
> Till all that is divine in woman
> Grows cruel, courteous, smooth, inhuman,
>   Crucified 'twixt a smile and whimper.

No namby-pamby poet, he hated "mincing women mewing like cats of their own virtue", and he tried as English poets had not done for many a year to give worthy expression to physical love, as in *Rosalind and Helen*:

> We will have rites our faith to bind,
> But our church shall be the starry night,
> Our altar the grassy earth outspread,
> And our priest the muttering wind.

His contemporaries had largely misunderstood the freedom of his expression when he wrote on this subject, and the legend arose that he believed in promiscuous sharing, when all he was stating was that men and women should not be chained to one another when love died and its rites must become a caricature and a mutual offence. In this as in many other respects the remarkable modernity of his mind is seen. The world has accepted his views on separation and divorce but does not always recognize them in his words. Aware of the glee with which the reviewers would seize upon his ideas and distort them, he wrote:

> Free love has this, different from gold and clay,
> That to divide is not to take away,

and in the revision wrote:

> True Love in this differs from gold and clay,
> That to divide is not to take away,

He lived his life as if engaged in a race against death. How this assiduous traveller and voluminous letter-writer, constantly in an intellectual ferment, never without worries, and so impatient to read that he was once seen in Pisa carrying an encyclopaedia and reading as he walked—how this man could be tattled of in England as the most licentious and evil-hearted of men is difficult to understand. Perhaps he knew too much about women, about their tribulations and weaknesses and miseries: the Byronic attitude, which departed not a hair's breadth from the twin traditions of the concubinage of women and the animalism of men, caused none of the offence that Shelley's personality stirred up in the muddy backwaters of Press and Society.

When he tried to express his idea of love in prose he had to add that his words were "ineffectual and metaphorical". In writing of the human being's "thirst after its own likeness", he used the image he had employed in *Epipsychidion* ("soul of my soul") to express the mirror in which the lover sees the beloved, whose intellectual shape is no other than his own: "a soul within our own soul that describes a circle around its proper Paradise, which pain and sorrow and evil dare not overleap." Even his admirers found his view of love "inhuman"; but perhaps "superhuman" would be an apter word. They were teased by the thought that his ideal woman—sister, wife and mistress—had no corporeal form. She was alive in his imagination but not in the world: he had never touched her. It was as if he spent many years of his life preparing to be the bridegroom of this third wife. He tried to describe her in prose: "We are born into the world, and there is something within us, which from the instant that we live, more and more thirsts after its likeness." And in verse, at the end of *Epipsychidion*:

> One hope within two wills, one will beneath
> Two overshadowing minds, one life, one death
> One Heaven, one Hell, one immortality,
> And one annihilation.

In a fragment written soon after he had been at work on a translation of Plato's *Symposium,* he expressed very plainly the compound satisfaction that he sought in love:

> "a communion not merely of the senses, but of our whole nature, intellectual, imaginative, and sensitive. . . . This want grows more powerful in proportion to the development which our nature receives from civilization; for man never ceases to be a social being. The sexual impulse, which is only one, and often a small part of those claims, serves,

from its obvious and external nature, as a kind of type of expression of the rest, a common basis, an acknowledged and visible link."

Such was his expression of the mental and physical happiness he would find with that third wife. She led him to a dark dwelling place: her spirit lay over graveyards. She was death, yet at the same time she had the form of a woman. The ceremony of love was for Shelley very like the ceremony of death. It was not a new idea, but it had been forgotten for a long time when Shelley was writing poetry.

Three

WEIRD ARCHIMAGE

And here like some weird Archimage sit I,
Plotting dark spells, and devilish enginery.
Letter to Maria Gisborne

LATE ON 12 May, after Williams had returned from Lerici with Shelley and rain had fallen, with thunder rolling in the hills and distant lightning flickering, the long-awaited boat rounded Portovenere from Genoa. Shelley wanted to call it the *Ariel*, but painted across the mainsail was the name of Byron's success, *Don Juan*.

They had planned it, with Trelawny, the previous summer. Williams had the section of a boat as a model to work from. On the sands of the Arno they drew a full-scale plan, dividing off its compartments. Then, says Trelawny,

> "with a real chart of the Mediterranean spread out before them, and with faces as grave and anxious as those of Columbus and his companions, they held councils as to the islands to be visited, coasts explored, courses steered, the amount of armament, stores, water and provisions which would be necessary. . . . Byron, with the smile of a Mephistopheles standing by, asked me the amount of salvage we, the salvors, should be entitled to in the probable event of our picking up and towing Shelley's water-logged craft into port."

On the evening of 15 January, 1822, at Pisa, Shelley, Williams and Trelawny decided to build the boat, and

Trelawny at once wrote to his friend Daniel Roberts, in Genoa, giving the order. When the decision had been made, Mary remarked to Jane, "Our husbands decide without asking our consent, or having our concurrence; for, to tell you the truth, I hate this boat, though I say nothing." "So do I," Jane agreed, "but speaking would be useless, and only spoil their pleasure."

The *Don Juan* was an undecked schooner of Torbay rig, fast but, as Trelawny observed, "very crank in a breeze". She was twenty-four feet long, eight feet broad, and had a four-foot draft. Trelawny had sent her from Genoa with a Mr. Heslop, two seamen and a boy of eighteen named Charles Vivian. The two seamen, who were sent back by Shelley, reported at Genoa that during their rough voyage the vessel had worked well but was "ticklish to manage"; they had warned the owner that the boat should be manned by two good seamen. Williams was proud of his skill as a sailor and evidently considered himself and the boy a match for the *Don Juan*.

On that Sunday evening, Williams recorded: "S. and I walked to Lerici, and made a stretch off the land to try her,—and I find she fetches whatever she looks at. In short we have now a perfect plaything for the summer."

That night there was torrential rain. The inhabitants of Casi Magni felt as if they were on board ship. At four in the morning of the Monday, the gale was unabated and the surf was heavy. The men again walked to Lerici, where the *Don Juan* was at anchor, found the harbour-master, Signor Maglian, anxiously awaiting the birth of his third child, and went aboard the boat: but there was obviously no hope of a sail that day.

"In the evening," Williams noted, "an electric arch forming in the clouds that announce a heavy thunderstorm if the wind lulls. Distant thunder—gale increases—a circle of foam surrounds the bay—dark, rainy, and tempestuous, with flashes of lightning at intervals that give no promise of better weather. The learned in these things say it generally lasts three days when once it commences as this has done."

The *Don Juan* had certainly brought ominous weather from Genoa. But next morning Williams observed with satisfaction and a gibe at the gossips on the quayside at Lerici, "Clear weather, and the breeze greatly moderated, contrary to all the expectations and prophecies of these would be sailors, these weather wise landsmen." The boat came across the bay and soon Shelley and Williams were aboard and bound for nearby La Spezia. They kept close to land, for on the way back they were hailed by a servant of "a Count Széchenyi, a minister of the Emperor of Austria", who wished for a sail; "but before he could get on board, the wind had lulled into a perfect calm, and we only got into the swell and made him sick".

Thanking Captain Roberts for the vessel, Shelley wrote, "It was with some difficulty that we could persuade ourselves that you had not sent us the *Bolivar* by mistake." A great compliment, for Byron's *Bolivar* was to cost ten times as much as the *Don Juan*.

Shelley loved sailing, but such an inveterate reader was not of much use as a sailor. Even when steering he usually had a book in his hand. When asked to let go of the main-sheet all he lost was his hat; Williams rebuked him, so he put his Plato into his pocket, and listened with interest to the nautical terms his friends used. Witnessing such a sailing-lesson later, Trelawny advised Williams to heave the books and papers overboard, have Shelley's hair cut, and dip his arms up to the elbows in a tar-bucket. He also had some advice for Williams: "Dowse your frock coat and cavalry boots." He noticed that the boy was quick, but that Williams was out of practice. Unfortunately Williams liked to make it clear that he was a knowledgeable sailor; and his over-confidence did not pass unobserved.

On Wednesday, 15 May, Jane and Mary consented to take a sail and "The boat sailed like a witch. After the late gale the water is covered with purple nautili, or as the sailors call them Portuguese men of war." After dinner Jane went with them to the point of the Magra and "the boat went back in wonderful style".

By 16 May the boat had been put through its paces thoroughly, and Shelley was writing to Trelawny, who was soon to sail down the coast with Byron's vessel, the *Bolivar*.

Both Shelley and Mary were looking forward to seeing Trelawny again, though Shelley had cancelled the arrangement whereby he, Trelawny and Byron were to have been joint owners of the boat. He had no desire to enter into a business partnership with Byron, to separate from whom, indeed, he had been driven to take Casa Magni so hurriedly.

Shelley had his private joke at Byron in the opening of the letter:

> "The *Don Juan* has arrived, and nothing can exceed the admiration she has excited; for we must suppose the name to have been given her during the equivocation of sex which her godfather suffered in the harem. Williams declares her to be perfect, and I participate in his enthusiasm, inasmuch as would be decent in a landsman. We have been out now several days, although we have sought in vain for an opportunity of trying her against the feluccas or other large craft in the bay; she passes the small ones as a comet might pass the dullest planet of the heavens."

Painting the name on the sail had been Byron's idea, arising out of what Williams angrily termed his "contemptible vanity". There is a contrast between this judgment and Williams's first admiring impression of Byron. Probably, during these last days, Shelley revealed to his friend his private feelings about Byron—and the term "contemptible vanity" was a reflection of this. Had Williams lived long enough he might have become the most valuable of Shelley's memoirists, for Shelley trusted and liked him. On 17 May Williams took the mainsail to Maglian to see if the letters could be erased. For twenty-one days and twenty-one nights, Mary recorded, the men discussed whether they should change the name and wash off the words *Don Juan*. "Turpentine, spirits of wine, boccata, all were tried, and it became dappled, and no more. At length the piece has been taken out," she wrote on 2 June, "and reefs put, so that the sail does not look worse. I do not know what Lord Byron will say, but, lord and poet as he is, he could not be allowed to make a coal-barge of our boat."

While Williams was consulting Maglian, Shelley and Jane

went to Carrara. Mary was not keeping a diary, so there is no information about the reason for this journey. Since they had no business to transact there, since the boat was out of commission that day, in the harbour of Lerici, and since this was one of the first settled days since they had come to the Gulf of Spezia, the outing may have been for sightseeing. They must have gone by coach, for the twelve-mile walk to Carrara, across the River Magra and along a particularly exhausting road, would have been too much, in one day, even for Shelley. They returned at half past nine. There may have been business at Carrara, for the servants were troublesome, Mary was ill, and Carrara was nearer Tuscan territory, where the servants whom Mary preferred lived. The little town of Sarzana would not have yielded much in the form of domestic labour, and La Spezia would be full of the people Mary disliked and dubbed "Genoese". Four days later two of the servants, Beta and Domenico, left Mary's service.

Early next day, Saturday, 18 May, Williams and Shelley took advantage of a fresh breeze to sail the *Don Juan* beyond Portovenere, off which lay the substantial island called the Palmaria and beyond that the Tino. Venturing farther out, they found another small one beyond (its name is the Tinetto) and called it the Syren's Rock. The name was chosen, Williams explains,

> "in consequence of hearing, at the time we were beating to windward to weather it, a sort of low murmuring, which as if by magic seemed to proceed from all parts of our boat, now on the sea, now here now there. At length we found that a very small rope (or cord rather) had been fastened to steady the peak when the boat was at anchor, and being extremely tight with the weight of the sail, it vibrated as the wind freshened—being on the other tack when we approached the island it ceased, and again as we stood off it recommenced its song. The Syren's Island was well named, for standing in close to observe it, from a strong current setting towards it, the boat was actually attracted so close that we had only time to tack, and save ourselves from its alluring voice."

They returned to attempt once again to remove the paint from the mainsail.

Shelley had long been fascinated by the sea. One of his most appreciative critics, Leigh Hunt, condemned in his poetry the sameness of metaphor, especially metaphor drawn from the sea. From the earliest days his work supplies abundant examples of an obsession with the depths of the sea:

> Peopled with unimaginable shapes,
> Such as ghosts dream dwell in the lampless deep.

For the brief remainder of his life, after the arrival of the *Don Juan*, he was to spend most of his time during fine weather, including moonlit evenings, on the water, writing *The Triumph of Life*.

He had always loved being in the open air, and particularly writing in a place where four walls did not constrict him. Trelawny found Shelley one day in the pine forest near Pisa, working on a "frightful scrawl; words smeared out with his finger, and one upon the other, over and over in tiers", which turned out to be the poem beginning:

> Ariel to Miranda: Take
> This slave of music.

The poet explained his method of composition thus:

> "When my brain gets heated with thought, it soon boils, and throws off images and words faster than I can skim them off. In the morning, when cooled down, out of the rude sketch, as you justly call it, I shall attempt a drawing. If you ask me why I publish what few or none will care to read, it is that the spirits I have raised haunt me until they are sent to the devil of a printer. All authors are anxious to breech their bantlings."

There was not much writing to be done in a home where Mary was ill, Jane was fractious, and Claire was alternately grief-stricken and talkative; where there was only one common room (the central dining-room) for use and where three little children had to be restrained from falling from the balcony and tumbling into the surf a few yards from the house. Sophia Stacey (the girl who had had no need to fear his kisses) had observed with wonder that he and Mary kept writing materials at their bedsides in order to write at night; but in the Italian climate Shelley did little writing indoors. He composed very rapidly; like Byron, he possessed a virtuoso's command of verse forms, and naturally fell into some of the traps that virtuosity baits. When he had time, he revised exhaustively. After his death Mary Shelley and other patient editors assembled the text of his unfinished and unpublished poems from MSS. that were overlaid with afterthoughts. Byron habitually wrote under the stimulus of gin and water; Shelley took no stimulants, but needed the constant sedative effect of laudanum. Cold water was his usual drink, and he diluted his wine. His liking for tea was so strong that he punned, "I am no a-theist", but he would not take sugar because it was produced by slave labour. An unfriendly acquaintance declared that at Oxford Shelley lived on "arsenic, aquafortis, and half an hour's sleep in the night". As for eating, he had once been an enthusiastic vegetarian; now he took what was offered, and did not complain if it was plain fare—a piece of bread and a handful of raisins. During Shelley's first marriage Hogg, a frequent guest, complained bitterly of the poor meals he received.

Shelley's gluttony was for books; for he read day and night, when eating, boating, walking. He was constantly moving and therefore constantly having to replenish his library. In England he had frequently to raise money, by means of post-obit bonds, in order to obtain the books he wanted, so that his mental like his physical sustenance often cost him twice as much as it cost other men. He read avidly, as if he knew that his life was not to be a long one; Trelawny describes him standing for hours at a time, at a mantelpiece, absorbed in a book. When the sea took him one of his hands was clasped round a book.

Perhaps his dominant habit at the end of his life was a love of solitude, though all his friends portray him as a companionable man. In his youth he dashed from place to place, talking

Shelley's last home, Casa Magni. *Above:* after the addition of the third storey, but before the building of the coast road. *Below:* as it is today

Val di Magra, near Lerici. Based on an engraving in
The Tourist in Italy, by T. Roscoe (1833)

enthusiastically; soon men and women disillusioned him and he turned ever more from their company. "Mary is under the dominion of the mythical monster 'Everybody'. I tell her I am of the Nobodies. You have been everywhere; have you seen the ubiquitous monster Everybody?" he asked Trelawny. He might attempt to avoid people, yet he knew how to deal with them. In his early youth he quietly distinguished himself for his astute business dealings during repeated disputes with his father. The point at issue between father and son was that Shelley considered primogeniture to be wrong, though complete adherence to the entails of Sir Timothy Shelley's estate would have made him a rich man. He would not give up his point, but he handled the lawyers skilfully in spite of the disadvantage of his position. He made practically nothing out of his own works, but drove a hard bargain when placing Mary's novel *Frankenstein*—so firmly did he hold out, indeed, that John Murray lost the book, and in revenge lent his voice to the chorus of slander against Shelley. Perhaps the secret of his skill as a man of practical affairs lay in his quick grasp of detail. He mastered his grandfather's will, a document that confused even the family lawyers, in a few days. Trelawny noticed his outstanding gift—shared with Dr. Johnson—of tearing out the heart of a book and expressing its essence, however abstruse, in plain English.

His energy was too abundant to be canalized in even the stream of poetry and prose that he produced during the ten or eleven years of his career as a serious writer. He was always running about to help his friends, and even making and designing things. When he conceived the idea of a steam-boat service between Italy and France, he designed the steam-engine and, as if this were not enough, tactfully offered to coach his partner, Henry Reveley, in English by correspondence. Comparatively little is heard about his absorption with things mechanical and electrical after the Oxford days, but it persisted. When he was an undergraduate Hogg saw in Shelley's rooms phials, crucibles, pistols, clothes, an electrical machine, an air pump, a galvanic trough, a solar microscope, glass jars, and other apparatus mixed with letters, bundles of pens, bottles of soda water and food. Allowing for Hogg's exaggeration, we perceive that Shelley was no absent-minded, ethereal being. He sprang naturally out of the tradition of "natural philosophers" of the eighteenth century. He read Erasmus Darwin, but had more of the cast of Joseph Priestley in his make-up, and in his works he has left a portrait of this side of his nature:

> And here like some weird Archimage sit I,
> Plotting dark spells, and devilish enginery,
> The self-impelling steam-wheels of the mind
> Which pump up oaths from clergymen, and grind
> The gentle spirit of our meek reviews
> Into a powdery foam of salt abuse.

And in detail:

> A hollow screw with cogs—Henry will know
> The thing I mean and laugh at me . . .
>   Next
> Lie bills and calculations much perplexed,
> With steam-boats, frigates, and machinery quaint
> Traced over them in blue and yellow paint.
> Then comes a range of mathematical
> Instruments, for plans nautical and statical;
> A heap of rosin, a queer broken glass
> With ink in it;—a china cup that was
> What it will never be again, I think,—
> A thing from which sweet lips were wont to drink
> The liquor doctors rail at—and which I
> Will quaff in spite of them—and when we die
> We'll toss up who died first of drinking tea,
> And cry out,—"Heads or tails?" where'er we be.
> Near that a dusty paint-box, some odd hooks,
> A half-burnt match, an ivory block, three books,
> Where conic sections, spherics, logarithms,
> To great Laplace, from Saunderson and Sims,
> Lie heaped in their harmonious disarray
> Of figures,—disentangle them who may.

He never played games, but at one sport, target-shooting, he almost equalled Byron, and he could row a boat as tirelessly as any man. These were aspects of Shelley that nineteenth-century idealization overlooked; which may explain why Shelley entered the twentieth century as an effete, morbid Ariel.

He stayed awake as long as possible. As a youth he told a friend that he lingered late because he dreaded the dreams he had. But for many years he was unable to combat the deep sleep of exhaustion that descended on him during the evenings, when he might lie in a chair or on a hearthrug for two hours, untroubled by the conversation around him. He was in such a sleep one night in March, 1818, on the eve of his departure from England, when Leigh Hunt and his wife came to say good-bye, and they went away without waking him.

Shelley's poems suggest that his memory, deep and exact, had a hallucinatory quality. If the subject could be avoided, he would not speak of the past. Some of his most poignant short poems are on the theme of the past, memory, change and the undying things, grief and happiness; in these lie some of the plainest clues to his vision of life—as, perhaps, a little eternity, a painted veil for something hidden, but never a passing show. In his first poem, *Mutability*, he wrote, possibly in direct reference to the later days of his first marriage:

> We rest.—A dream has power to poison sleep;
>   We rise.—One wandering thought pollutes the day;
> We feel, conceive or reason, laugh or weep;
>   Embrace fond woe, or cast our cares away:
>
> It is the same!—For, be it joy or sorrow,
>   The path of its departure still is free:
> Man's yesterday may ne'er be like his morrow;
>   Nought may endure but Mutability.

And in his second poem of the same title:

> Virtue, how frail it is!
>   Friendship how rare!
> Love, how it sells poor bliss
>   For proud despair!
> But we, though soon they fall,
>   Survive their joy, and all
>   Which ours we call.

Delight, the brief "lightning that mocks the night", passes but is unforgotten. In other words, there is no remission from thought. One of his four-line fragments illustrates the extreme compression of his thought:

> And where is truth? On tombs? For such to thee
> Has been my heart—and thy dead memory
> Has lain from childhood, many a changeful year,
> Unchangingly preserved and buried there.

It is possible to paraphrase the lines in at least two ways, depending on the precise significance of the phrase "dead memory" and on whether the poet meant "your childhood" or "my childhood". The simpler (and doubtless erroneous) version would be: "Perhaps truth is written on tombs? Since my childhood, through years of change, the memory of you who are dead has been preserved in my heart, your grave." But like Petrarch, in whose words he steeped his mind, Shelley adopted a device which has since come to be regarded as a not artificial poetic shorthand; namely the compression of an elaborate idea in a phrase such as "dead memory", which might produce in the reader a subtler response, to be paraphrased thus: "Where is truth found? Probably on tombs. That part of your history which you yourself cannot recall, from childhood through your years of change, has been preserved unchanged in my heart, which is the grave of your personality." And if such an interpretation seems over-elaborate, too tortured and metaphysical a conception, consider the banality of deducing from the first paraphrase that what Shelley meant was, "I saw you when I was very young and have remembered you ever since."

Part of the difficulty of Shelley's verse, for the reader, is due to the fact that he so frequently attempted elaborations which, had he been a musician, would have demanded counterpoint, in contrast to simple progressive harmony.

On Sunday, 19 May, the day after the discovery of the Tinetto, there was apparently no sailing during daylight, though it was fine; but Williams could not resist the temptations of the bay and the boat, even though he had resolved to put in some more work on his drama. In the serenity of the evening the party went out in the *Don Juan*. Mary Shelley said that Shelley was happier than she had ever known him, during the last two months of his life; as for herself, "my only peaceful moments were those passed on board that unlucky boat, when, lying with my head upon his knees, I closed my eyes and felt only the breath of the wind and our swift motion".

On Monday, 20 May, Williams sailed with Jane to La Spezia to consult yet another sail-maker about the troublesome mainsail. There was nothing to be done. Next day it was necessary to make another journey to the port, this time in connection with the more important business of some of Shelley's books, which had arrived there from England, and had been redirected from Pisa. Maglian was taken there too—soon after half past five in the morning—presumably because it was he who had helped to sweeten the Customs officer there a month earlier, over the matter of the furniture.

"I called on the Inspector of Customs to request his interest in getting his (Shelley's) books on shore. . . . Having been forwarded to us here in the Piedmontese territories, it is necessary that they should be inspected at Genoa by certain persons appointed by the Governors of the Church in order to prevent any seditious or immoral publications from falling into the hands of this *free and pious people*—this is a tyranny that cannot last long. It signifies nothing to what port soever they may be consigned; they must be seen and examined at Genoa, and a permit given before any book, of any kind, even a prayer book or missal can be suffered to land. A ship for instance bound for Leghorn to[1] Marseilles—as the one who brought Shelley's books here really is—must touch at Genoa, however much out of her way, under a penalty of imprisonment for life.

S.'s application proved ineffective and with the curses of all parties away went the books for Genoa. Sent to Genoa for some canvass. Clare departs for Florence—and Beta and Domenico leave Mary's service."

---

[1] Williams meant *from* Marseilles.

Four

THE TOWERS OF THE FUTURE

> Vultures, who build your bowers
> High in the Future's towers,
> Withered hopes on hopes are spread;
> Dying joys, choked by the dead,
> Will serve your beaks for prey
>   Many a day.
>
> *Lines*

AFTER BREAKFAST on 22 May, Shelley and Williams set to work to try to make a boat of canvas and reeds, as light as possible. It was to be eight feet six long and four feet six broad, and in addition to its being useful as a ship's boat for the *Don Juan*, Shelley would be able to use it for paddling about the bay. The flat-bottomed boat with sails which was now stored beneath the arches of Casa Magni was heavy, and in any case not a sea-going craft.

On Sunday morning, 26 May, Maglian was taken by the friends for a sail down the coast to Massa, a distance of about fifteen miles. The ancient town is three miles inland, and its exposed beach presents a very different scene from the picturesque ruggedness of the Bay of Lerici. The coast is flat and uninteresting, fringed by trees similar to those described in *The Recollection*:

> We paused amid the pines that stood
>   The giants of the waste,
> Tortured by storms to shapes as rude
>   As serpents interlaced.

On the way Maglian told them the romantic story of his friend the Commandant of Massa, who had been *cavaliere servente* to a jealous lady who thrust upon him a poisoned bouquet of flowers, taking care that he should prick himself, so that he died before the day was over. The outward voyage took three hours, and they were able to bring the *Don Juan* close to the shore near a rocky shelf. They went inland to Massa, dined there, and returned towards four o'clock in the afternoon to battle for seven hours against the westerly wind. Williams noted: "This wind (the Ponente as it is called) always sends a sort of damp vapour from the sea, which gathers into watery clouds upon the mountain tops, and generally sinks with the sun, but strengthens as he declines."

During the whole of the following week, in fine weather, Williams was at work on the boat of reeds; towards the end of the week he made the odd discovery that he had made it double the size he intended, and on 1 June he lost patience, took it to pieces, and began again. It was not successfully completed till 12 June, when it was launched. In 1890, when Guido Biagi went to Lerici and Viareggio to look for people who might tell him something of the last days of Shelley, he found at San Terenzo those who remembered that the English poet, often against the advice of the sailors, used to paddle about the bay in what they called his *sandalino* and what Mary Shelley called his "little shallop". Because, as Williams records, the boat of reeds weighed 86 lb., Dr. Biagi deduced that this could not have been the one that Shelley used to carry down to the sea under his arm; but to carry a weight of 86 lb. a distance of about ten paces would be a trifling feat for a man of Shelley's physique. It would defeat only the imaginary effeminate Shelley of late nineteenth-century criticism, the "ineffectual angel" of Matthew Arnold and the "Titan in a virgin's form" of Giosuè Carducci. So we can dismiss the idea that there were two *sandalini*, particularly because Trelawny, paying a last sad visit to Casa Magni in October weather, found in the boat-shed no *sandalino* but only the flat-bottomed skiff that had been brought from Pisa, with masts and oars broken. The *sandalino*, in which while exploring the coves of the Bay of

Lerici Shelley wrote his last long poem, was in fact washed up at Viareggio after the wreck of the *Don Juan*.

While Williams was boat-building and continuing his attempts to expunge the name *Don Juan* from the mainsail, Shelley had plenty of time to think of the Byron difficulty and other pressing problems involving friends and acquaintances. There were two other matters of great concern to him at this time. One involved his friend Leigh Hunt who, financed by Shelley, was now on his way to Italy. The other concerned Mary's father, William Godwin, whose demands for money and repeated complaints had of late made Mary so ill that she had asked Shelley to intercept all letters from Godwin and pass on to her only the essential news about her father and his money difficulties.

Shelley was not a friendless person, but it had been more than self-pity which had prompted him to write in 1819:

"I am regarded by all who know or hear of me, except, I think, on the whole five individuals, as a rare prodigy of crime and pollution, whose look even might infect. This is a large computation," he added with caution, "and I don't think I could mention more than three. Such is the spirit of the English abroad as well as at home."

Just how accurate this intuition was he did not know till later, when he made the bitter discovery that even Byron, who as a poet he so wholeheartedly admired, had been helping to spread tattle about him. Now that Allegra was dead and Claire would never see Byron again, the friendship with Byron, which had long been so intellectually important to the younger poet, was about to be severed. Byron ruined Claire and cannot have been quite sure that he was not responsible for Allegra's death. There was no hope that he would make any provision for Claire. Shelley had already done so, in his will. While she stayed in Florence, however, and Byron was at Pisa, close by, it was important to avoid a complete break. There was also Leigh Hunt to think about.

Shelley had long admired Hunt. When as editor of the

Examiner he had been sent to prison for writing a libel on the Prince Regent, the youth Shelley had offered a large contribution towards his fine. Hunt had declined this, on the ground that his friends ought not to be taxed simply because he as an editor had fallen foul of the libel laws. Later, Hunt was one of the very few critics who had commendatory (and constructive) words to write about the "infidel poet's" work.

In the summer of 1821 Leigh Hunt was in poor health and spirits. Shelley went to work to gain Byron's interest in his friend, and in August he was able to write to England:

> "He proposes that you should come and go shares with him and me, in a periodical work, to be conducted here; in which each of the contracting parties should publish all their original compositions, and share the profits. . . . There can be no doubt that the *profits* of any scheme in which you and Lord Byron engage, must, from various yet cooperating reasons, be very great. As for myself, I am, for the present, only a sort of link between you and him, until you can know each other and effectuate the arrangement; since (to entrust you with a secret which, for your sake, I withhold from Lord Byron) nothing would induce me to share in the profits, and still less in the borrowed splendour, of such a partnership. You and he, in different manners, would be equal, and would bring, in a different manner, but in the same proportion, equal stocks of reputation and success; do not let my frankness with you, nor my belief that you deserve it more than Lord Byron, have the effect of deterring you from assuming a station in modern literature, which the universal voice of my contemporaries forbids me either to stoop or aspire to. I am, and I desire to be, nothing."

Shelley added that he would not ask Byron to pay the cost of Hunt's journey and that he himself had insufficient money, but that he would probably "make up an impudent face", and apply to Horace Smith, who had frequently out of friendship acted as his "banker" in London. The review was planned under the title of *Hesperides*, later changed to the *Liberal*. Hunt was to be the editor, and Shelley knew that if he could persuade Byron to allow even one of his works to appear in it for the first time, the success of the project would be certain, such was the reputation of the poet one of whose works had, according to his publisher, sold 14,000 copies in a single day, and who earned by them, in ten years, the sum of £75,000. Byron had shown much enthusiasm for the scheme, but his passions were short-lived, and since this one had been at its height, his personal affairs had taken a turn for the worse. A brawl at Pisa had resulted in the serious wounding of a dragoon, and there was a possibility that Byron would be ordered with his mistress and her party to leave Tuscany.

The two poets had first met in Switzerland in 1816. Shelley was anxious to meet the most famous poet of the day, and it may be that he was urged to decide on the journey by Claire, who unknown to him was at that time carrying Byron's child. Byron was not telling the truth when he wrote to England that the girl had travelled across Europe to unphilosophize him; the unphilosophizing had taken place months before in Dover Street, Piccadilly. Shelley's final journey abroad, in March, 1818, had been closely connected with Byron's affairs; one purpose was to soften Byron's hatred of Claire, if possible, and to deliver Allegra, whom Byron referred to as his "bastard", and ordered to be brought to him with tooth-powder and the latest novels. Shelley had made mistakes about people in his youth, but even in 1818 his admiration for Byron's literary work did not cause him to judge his character any the less shrewdly: "He has a certain degree of candour while you talk to him, but unfortunately it does not outlast your departure."

During 1818 there had been nonetheless a strong intellectual attraction between the two men. It is preserved in *Julian and Maddalo*, not only in verse but in the preface that Shelley wrote to introduce Maddalo (Byron) and Julian (himself). Of Maddalo he wrote, with penetration but not malice:

> "It is his weakness to be proud: he derives, from a comparison of his own extraordinary mind with the dwarfish intellects that surround him, an intense appre-

hension of the nothingness of human life. . . . I say that Maddalo is proud, because I can find no other word to express the concentered and impatient feelings which consume him; but it is on his own hopes and affections only that he seems to trample, for in social life no human being can be more gentle, patient, and unassuming than Maddalo."

His self-portrait as Julian has humour which is particularly noteworthy because *Julian and Maddalo* is a lacerating piece of poetic autobiography.

"Julian is an Englishman of good family, passionately attached to those philosophical notions which assert the power of man over his own mind, and the immense improvements of which, by the extinction of certain moral superstitions, human society may be yet susceptible. Without concealing the evil in the world, he is for ever speculating how good may be made superior. He is a complete infidel, and a scoffer at all things reputed holy; and Maddalo takes a wicked pleasure in drawing out his taunts against religion. What Maddalo thinks on these matters is not exactly known. Julian, in spite of his heterodox opinions, is conjectured by his friends to possess some good qualities. How far this is possible the pious reader will determine. Julian is rather serious."

In the intervening years the friendship appeared above ground to be a fair plant, but its roots were bitter. Speaking to those who were not Shelley's friends, and to several who pretended to be, Byron nicknamed him Shiloh the fanatic Joanna Southcott's promised Messiah. To his face, Byron called him the Serpent, a name not entirely unrelated to the agility of his mind. Shelley's regard for Byron's intellect was developed to an exaggerated degree; Byron's view of Shelley's mind was a jealous one, possibly because he preferred to surround himself with "dwarfish intellects". Shelley's name for Byron was affectionate and romantic—Albè, or the Albaneser.

For a year before the removal to Casa Magni, Shelley and

Byron had spent much time together, especially at Pisa. On Christmas Day, 1821, they entered into a wager whereby the one who first came into his inheritance should pay the other £1,000. Within a month, Shelley had won, for Lady Noel died and Byron became an exceedingly rich man, and at the same time miserly. Shelley did not mention the bet or comment on the fact that Byron had not honoured his word. Various people in the Pisa circle noticed the omission, however, not only at the time but a year later, when as a widow Mary Shelley lacked enough to pay even her fare to England. Shelley had already willed Byron £2,000.

The break between the poets threatened to happen not on account of a triviality such as this, but for graver reasons, not the least important of which was that the friendship had been murdered by Byron in 1820. In that year what is now known as "the Hoppner scandal" was brought to birth. Hoppner, a British consul, married to a Swiss, had been hospitable to Shelley and his wife in 1818, just after Clara Shelley's death. In 1820 he wrote to Byron to remark that in view of a story that his wife had heard from Elise, formerly nurse to the Shelley's children, he had formed a poor opinion of Shiloh. Byron replied that the story was doubtless true, and he promised to keep Hoppner's counsel. A year later, however, he showed Shelley the letter Hoppner had written. Mary Shelley wrote a letter in refutation of the slander; it was entrusted to Byron for forwarding to the Hoppners, but there is no evidence that it was ever sent to them, and it was found after Byron's death among his papers.

Hoppner's allegation was that Shelley had had a child by Claire Clairmont, that the infant had been born in the Shelley's apartment at Naples without Mary's knowledge, and that Shelley had had it spirited away to a foundling hospital, where it had died. The Hoppner story is connected with the brief life-story of Elena Adelaide Shelley, and it is discussed in greater detail in Chapter Seven.

In the summer of 1822 Shelley could not know all the facts about the slanderers, but he can have had little faith in the belief that Byron had dissociated himself from them. He had made up his mind even before Allegra's death, when he wrote to Claire:

"It is of vital importance both to me and to yourself, to Allegra even, that I should put a period to my intimacy with L.B., and that without *eclat*. No sentiments of honour or justice restrain him (as I strongly suspect) from the basest insinuations, and the only mode in which I could effectually silence him I am reluctant (even if I had proof) to employ during my father's life. But for your immediate feelings I would suddenly and irrevocably leave this country which he inhabits, nor ever enter it but as an enemy to determine our differences *without words*."

The last sentence was a recognition that if he left Italy, Claire would never again have even a hope of seeing her child or knowing how Byron was treating Allegra; the same would happen if Shelley challenged Byron to a duel, for Byron was the better shot, and he was the kind of man who would shoot to kill. In the preceding sentence Shelley means that he would challenge Byron if he had proof that he had slandered him—but not during Sir Timothy Shelley's lifetime and before Shelley had inherited the entailed estate, for that would mean, in the almost certain event of his being shot, that his family and Claire would be left in penury to await Sir Timothy's death. It remained for the Tyrrhenian Sea to do what Byron was not to be provoked into doing.

Thirteen years later, Claire wrote to Mary:

"From the continuation of that intimacy has arisen all we have suffered since, and ah! how much it is! What years of poverty and humiliation, of exile from all that is dear to us. . . . His genius extinct, the greatest that was ever known, and the noble system he would have established therewith fallen for many ages to the dust. All this for his ill-advised gentleness."

As a woman of over seventy she confided to Trelawny:

"Shelley as you know adored Genius—Lord Byron possessed it undoubtedly—at that period this was sufficient to decide Shelley to think no ill of him. Three years later he altered his opinion and became convinced that Lord Byron's genius was a fatal gift that developed in him inordinate pride and a dryness of heart and fierceness of feeling most dangerous in theory as in practice."

Gentle he might have been, but when death closed the quarrel the crisis in the affairs of Shelley and Byron was approaching. Of his calumniators in the reviews he had written in the summer of 1821:

"As yet I have laughed; but woe to these scoundrels if they should once make me lose my temper. I have discovered that my calumniator in the *Quarterly Review* was the Rev. Mr. Milman. Priests and eunuchs have their privilege."

Byron's views on friendship, as expressed to Trelawny, were simple:

"I don't feel friendship for anyone, not even for Shelley. . . . Moore is the best convivial companion, Hobhouse is a good man of business, and I am the worst. If we have a good balance at our banker's, we shan't want friends."

And when he declared that he had well looked after his reputation for posterity by writing his own life and entrusting it to Moore, he added, "I have good security—he always wants money; my memoirs will bring it." The irony of the outcome was that Moore found the autobiography of so little interest to him that he put it aside for a long time without reading it; and then he was quite content to hand it to the publisher Murray, who burnt it in his parlour grate.

Byron never compensated in actions for the considerable injury he did Shelley by accepting without question the Hoppners' slander, and withholding Mary Shelley's answer from the slanderers. The damage done was great because, as with so many charges against Shelley, the evil was spoken and became established as truth before the events that gave rise to it were clearly discussed by his biographers or personal friends. Much the same happened in connection with the failure of his first marriage, and the interpretation of Shelley's bitterest poem, *Julian and Maddalo*: the smoke was raised first and the fire sought only after the passage of many obscuring years.

But if Byron did no good action to make up for having helped to propagate a grave slander against his friend and the mother of Allegra, he did what he could in words on 3 August, 1822, when he wrote to John Murray:

> "You were all brutally mistaken about Shelley, who was, without exception, the *best* and least selfish man I ever knew. I never knew one who was not a beast in comparison."

It is envy that creates and nourishes literary cliques and cabals; in literary history, praise and calumny are too often merely matters of thoughtless imitation. Shelley was temperamentally unwilling to have anything to do with the puffing and reviling that characterized what passed as criticism in the Press of his day. To a reviewer, he wrote:

> Alas, good friend, what profit can you see
> In hating such a hateless thing as me?
> There is no sport in hate where all the rage
> Is on one side: in vain would you assuage
> Your frowns upon an unresisting smile,
> In which not even contempt lurks to beguile
> Your heart, by some faint sympathy of hate.
> Oh, conquer what you cannot satiate!

He had need of those lines when he was dead and only the words he had written could answer those who competed with one another in abusing him. His life and work have for over a hundred and thirty years created extraordinary interest, and it is a curious fact that the bitterest condemnations came from people who never met him; very few of the many who knew him spoke evil of him, and most of them recorded his good qualities. Of the acquaintances who spoke ill, Byron may be excused because he had the twin diseases of vanity and envy, and Hazlitt because it was his boast that he never altered his

opinion on anything after passing his sixteenth birthday. John
Murray, who described him as "the vilest wretch now living",
had lost *Frankenstein* because Shelley had been sensible enough
to stand out for a fair price for it; with Murray, as with many
of his kind, it was his purse and not his moral sense that was
affronted. Shelley hoped that his own publisher, Ollier, would
not be frightened by *The Cenci* into adopting an Albemarle
Street manner: "If Ollier is not turned Christian, Jew, or
become infected with *the Murrain*, he will publish it."

Southey, who had a brief acquaintance with Shelley during
the days of the first marriage, was among those who took pains
to speak harshly of him whenever an opportunity presented
itself. In 1830 he wrote, "With all his genius (and I think *most*
highly of it) he was a base, bad man." In an afterthought he
wrote that he meant Shelley was a liar and a cheat. In 1820
Shelley, having been persuaded that Southey was the author
of a malignant notice of *The Revolt of Islam* in the *Quarterly
Review*, wrote to ask Southey if this report was true, and gave
his former friend a taste of his fighting style:

> "That an unprincipled hireling, in default of what to
> answer in a published composition, should, without provo-
> cation, insult the domestic calamities of a writer of the
> adverse party—to which perhaps their victim dares scarcely
> advert in thought—that he should make those calamities
> the theme of the foulest and the falsest slander—that all
> this should be done by a calumniator without a name—
> with the cowardice, no less than the malignity, of an
> assassin—is too common a piece of charity among Christians
> (Christ would have taught them better), too common a
> violation of what is due from man to man among the
> pretended friends of social order, to have drawn one remark
> from me, but that I would have you observe the arts
> practised by that party for which you have abandoned the
> cause to which your early writings were devoted."

Southey denied his guilt, but wrote exhorting Shelley to
become a Christian and accusing him of ruining Harriet.

Of contemporaries who never met Shelley, Carlyle, the

The Castle and Bay of Lerici seen from the road to Sarzana.
From William Brockedon's *Italy*

La Spezia, seen from the road to Lerici. From *The Tourist in Italy*, by T. Roscoe (1833)

writer whose adulation of naked force in the character of Frederick the Great was Adolf Hitler's last literary consolation as he waited for death in a Berlin bunker, was perhaps the most vituperative. He said, "Yon man Shelley was just a scoundrel, and ought to have been hanged." Lest this conversational judgment should pass unrecorded, he put his opinion into writing, "Weak in genius, weak in character (for these two always go together); a poor, thin, spasmodic, hectic, shrill and pallid being;—one of those unfortunates, of whom I often speak, to whom 'the talent of *silence*', first of all, has been denied."

Charles Lamb's opinion was, "No one was ever the wiser or better for reading Shelley." In answer to this, no words of Shelley's could have hurt Lamb more than those the poet wrote in 1819 when thanking Leigh Hunt for a parcel of books, "When I think of such a mind as Lamb's,—when I see how unnoticed remain things of such exquisite and complete perfection, what should I hope for myself, if I had not higher objects in view than fame?"

Wordsworth, when asked by the impetuous Trelawny, who had not met Shelley but who had just read *Queen Mab*, to give his opinion on the work of his young contemporary, replied from the eminence of his fifty years, "Nothing." He added, "A poet who has not produced a good poem before he is twenty-five, we may conclude cannot, and never will, do so." Not to be daunted, Trelawny exclaimed, *"The Cenci!"* Wordsworth preceded his Scotch terrier into his coach with the words: "Won't do. . . . This hairy fellow is our flea-trap." He then drove away. Time revealed that when thus damning Shelley, Wordsworth had not read a line of his works; that necessary prelude to criticism was to come later. It so happened that a few months before, Shelley, who *had* read Wordsworth, and greatly admired his early work, had spent six or seven days composing a keen and neglected satire entitled *Peter Bell the Third*, in which he recorded the fate of poets who turn prosy:

>Peter Bell the First was Peter
>Smugger, milder, softer, neater,
>Like the soul before it is
>Born from *that* world into *this*.

F

There must be something in the personality of Shelley that excites poets as well as churchmen to malignant expression; for in our own time we have Mr. T. S. Eliot adding his contribution by describing Shelley as humourless, pedantic and something of a blackguard.

Shortly after Shelley's death three clergymen collaborated in what purported to be an obituary article, the purpose of which was to express the pious satisfaction of all right-minded followers of Christ's teachings, that the sea should have strangled so vile a creature before his thirtieth birthday. At least the England of the eighteen-twenties would not be menaced by the production of another *Prometheus Unbound*.

It is exceedingly difficult to prove that Shelley was a villain, but extremely easy to prove that he was a fool, if the word is used as what he called the "loud world" employed it. One aspect of his foolishness, taking the shape of William Godwin, his fallen idol, was casting a shadow over his last days at San Terenzo. Ever since Shelley had eloped with Mary, Godwin had extorted money from "the seducer", who, the moment Harriet's death permitted Shelley to marry Mary, became in the father-in-law's letters the young gentleman, son of a baronet, with whom his daughter had made a gratifying match. The irony of the situation was that the gratifying match was half due to Shelley's high regard for the man who had written *Political Justice*, and for Mary Wollstonecraft, who were Mary's father and mother. Through weary years, Shelley robbed his family to keep the author whose works are now almost forgotten, the publisher whose money-making schemes had, on the very day the Shelleys settled at Casa Magni, resulted in writs, one of which was for the possession of his house by his creditors.

Shelley's disillusionment took place slowly, for quite late in the day he wrote, "The author of *Mandeville* is one of the most illustrious examples of intellectual power of the present age." When William Shelley died, William Godwin wrote rebuking his daughter for excess of grief because a child of three years was dead. Shelley totted up what Godwin's demands had extracted from his sorely strained bank account and from his expectations, and wrote to Leigh Hunt:

"He heaps on her misery—still misery. I have not yet shown her the letter—but I must. I doubt whether I ought not to expose this solemn lie; for such and not a man is Godwin. . . . I have bought bitter knowledge with £4,700. I wish it were all yours now."

When Shelley paid his father-in-law money Godwin had a strange manner of acknowledging it. He once refused to cash a cheque written by Shelley to him in his name, and demanded:

"I hope you will send a duplicate of it by the post which will reach me on Saturday morning. You may make it payable to Joseph Hume or James Martin, or any other name in the whole directory."

In May, 1822, having on Mary's request intercepted Godwin's complaining letters to her, Shelley was trying to raise £400 for him, through Horace Smith. To Godwin he wrote, with patience but not purse exhausted:

"I have given you within a few years the amount of a considerable fortune, and have destituted myself for the purpose of realizing it of nearly four times the amount. Except for the *good will* which this transaction seems to have produced between you and me, this money, for any advantage it ever conferred on you, might as well have been thrown into the sea."

All the thanks Godwin could give was to tell his friends that Shelley was a lover of falsehood for its own sake.

During May, 1822, Shelley learned that Godwin's latest lawsuit had been decided against him, and that he had been adjudged to pay £900. In asking Horace Smith to advance £400 Shelley mentioned that Mary's latest novel had been sent to Godwin and that the copyright would probably bring him £300 or £400. On 29 May he wrote to Mary Jane Godwin:

"(Mary) imagined that her novel might be turned to immediate advantage for him; I am greatly interested in the fate of this production, which appears to me to possess a high degree of merit, and I regret that it is not Mr. Godwin's intention to publish it immediately. I am sure that Mary would be delighted to amend anything her father found imperfect in it."

During the last days of May, when the weather was becoming ever more settled and working up to the wave of oppressive heat the breaking of which was to destroy the two friends, Williams continued his boat-building and Shelley grappled with the troubles that beset him.

A friend in Pisa, Mrs. Mason (really Lady Mountcashell, but she had left her husband for a more congenial companion), wrote gloomily that she dreaded Claire's return to Casa Magni and that she wished the Williamses at least half a mile away; nevertheless Shelley wrote to Claire on 29 May:

"Tell me when we are to expect you, and the precise hour and day at which you arrive at Viareggio. . . . I think that, at least for the present, you would be happier here than anywhere else. . . . Mary still continues to suffer terribly from languor and hysterical affections; and things in every respect remain as they were when you left us."

He told her the story of the mainsail of the *Don Juan*.

"I sit within the whole morning and in the evening we sail about.—I write a little—I read and enjoy for the first time for these ten years something like health—I find, however, that I must neither think nor feel, or the pain returns to its old nest.

Williams seems happy and content, and we enjoy each other's society. Jane is by no means acquiescent in the system of things, and she pines after her own house and saucepans to which no one can have a claim except herself. It is a pity that any one so pretty should be so selfish.—But don't tell her this—and come soon yourself, I hope my best Claire, with tranquillised spirits and a settled mind."

Perhaps the letter was never posted. It reads like a draft of the one postmarked "Sarzana, 31 May, 1822", in which Shelley speaks of "a great gulph fixed" between himself and Byron, "which by the nature of things must daily become wider". He writes of a few mornings' composition which have

"somewhat shaken my nerves.—I have turned Maria's room into a study, and am in this respect comfortable.—What do you think about the situation of the G(odwin)s, and their pretensions upon our resources? This question you cannot answer in a letter, but I should be very glad to hear your opinion on it; meanwhile I do nothing. Mary has been very unwell; she is now better, and I suppose it will be necessary to make the Godwins a subject of conversation with her—at present I put off the evil day. . . . Jane the other day was very much discontented with her situation here, on account of some of our servants having taken something of hers, but now, as is the custom, calm has succeeded to storm, to yield to the latter in accustomed vicissitude. . . . I wish you could mark down some good cook for us—a man, of course.—If you could find another Betta without the disagreeable qualities of the last, it would do."

By 2 June Mary was feeling strong enough to write, and she reported to her friend Mrs. Gisborne the story of the stain on the mainsail of the boat, and how a piece had finally been cut out. The previous evening she had been sailing with the whole party.

Life passed with surface tranquillity until the evening of Thursday, 6 June, brought anxiety. At five in the morning Shelley and Williams set sail for Viareggio to meet Claire. Williams records: "At 8 the wind sprung up, baffling in all directions but the right one. At 11 we could steer our course, but at one it fell calm and left us like a log on the water, about four miles to windward of Massa." They remained becalmed for five hours, in excessive heat, watching the thunder-clouds gather on the peaks of the mountains beyond Massa. At seven, they rowed to the beach, but were confronted by the guard, who told them that the chief of the fort was at a *festa,* and they must wait till he returned, since he himself was unable to read their papers. After the long wait in the sun, Shelley resented this and showed his seigneur manner for once. When the guard produced two old muskets, Shelley and Williams primed their pistols. This show of determination frightened the guard, who called to the sailor boy Charles Vivian and had him hold the identification paper about a yard from him, while two men who were bathing on the beach explained who Shelley and Williams were. The guards were as troublesome and dilatory about *i documenti* as their descendants can be today.

Their identity established, Shelley and Williams and the boy were allowed to go to Massa—which probably meant walking. They slept there, while Mary and Jane waited at Casa Magni, and Claire looked for them in vain at Viareggio, about the same distance away. Next morning they left Massa early; the atmosphere was hot and oppressive. At eight o'clock a breeze enabled them to struggle to Magra Point, the eastern extremity of the Gulf of Spezia, and they reached home at half past two. In the evening Claire arrived, unexpectedly vivacious and talkative.

Five

OF KINGS, AND PRIESTS, AND SLAVES

> A thousand years the Earth cried, Where art thou?
>   And then the shadow of thy coming fell
> On Saxon Alfred's olive-cinctured brow:
>   And many a warrior-peopled citadel,
> Like rocks which fire lifts out of the flat deep,
>   Arose in sacred Italy,
>   Frowning o'er the tempestuous sea
> Of kings, and priests, and slaves, in tower-crowned majesty.
>
> *Ode to Liberty*

WHAT MOST of his contemporaries could not endure, of course, was his opinion of religion, and the means he adopted to express it. Trelawny asked Shelley: "Why do you call yourself an atheist? It annihilates you in this world." Shelley replied: "It is a word of abuse to stop discussion, a painted devil to frighten the foolish, a threat to intimidate the wise and good. I used it to express my abhorrence of superstition; I took up the word, as a knight took up a gauntlet, in defiance of injustice. The delusions of Christianity are fatal to genius and originality: they limit thought." This was said to a friend, in private conversation; in print Shelley said a great deal more on the subject. He did not know what expediency was: and that was what Trelawny meant by his annihilation.

The opinions that Shelley held on the subject of the monarchy did not in any similar degree contribute to the malignant hatred expressed against him. To assault Christianity was unforgivable; to criticize the monarchy was permitted, though you did it at risk of your goods and freedom.

as Leigh Hunt discovered. A cynical rather than adulatory attitude to Royalty was current among men and women of Shelley's class. Today it may be held that almost the reverse viewpoint represents popular opinion. When Shelley wrote

> O, that the free would stamp the impious name
> Of * * * * into the dust!

the four asterisks represented the word "king", but a critic quoted five in the hope that his readers would read "Christ" and thus share his impotent hatred for the poet whose work he was purporting to criticize. Radicalism drew curses on Shelley's head, but it was not the profession of his political views that "annihilated" him.

When as a youth he declared himself an atheist, he alienated his father, and his holding to that opinion caused his expulsion from Oxford. Today, if a young man's profession of disbelief in Christianity resulted in his making a bitter enemy of his father we should consider it an exception rather than an inevitable result. Sir Timothy acted as a gentleman of his time, and Shelley as a man somewhat in advance of his time. He would not be bribed to abandon his objection to either Christianity or primogeniture. Neither father nor son was ridiculous in this quarrel, the father for acting as if his son, a genius of eighteen, were a silly schoolboy, or the son for placing an intellectual principle above the interests of the family estate. Neither was ridiculous: they were merely persons of different epochs.

A similar view can scarcely be taken of the young Shelley's quarrel with the Master and Fellows of University College, Oxford. In justice to the University it must be recalled that their quarrel with him was not, as is often assumed, on the count of Shelley's atheism. It arose because he would not deny having written and printed *The Necessity of Atheism*. He wrote: "I was informed that in case I denied the publication, no more would be said. I refused, and was expelled." Shelley fell foul not of any intolerance in the University authorities, but of their sense of expediency and their assumption that a sensible young man would not object to telling a lie about his religious beliefs. It cannot be too strongly emphasized that Shelley's expression of religious scepticism gave rise to the gossip about his personal life and damned his chances as an author. Byron, a much more wide-awake man, kept on the leeward side of religious orthodoxy, and many another man did the same. A great deal of cant was talked about Shelley's attacks on marriage, and about his unfitness to be a husband and father—but who sincerely, in those days, cared if a man broke out against the institution of marriage, provided he confined his rebellion to betraying his wife discreetly and did not talk too much or print anything on the subject?

Shelley's atheism, the label for his dislike of churchiness and cant, and the vices that might be aproned by a cassock or a public profession of piety, was of a sincere but not solemn kind. About a year before his death he had occasion to debate part of the matter in a curious letter written to Taaffe, an acquaintance at Pisa. He began the letter:

> "I am not convinced,—if God damns me, even by making me my own hell (as indeed sometimes when I am in an ill humour he does in this life) it by no means follows that I *must* desire to be so damned. I may think it extremely disagreeable, as I do to be in an ill temper, and wish to God that God would not have damned me either in this or any other manner.—I confess I cannot understand how I should be necessitated to desire to be damned under any circumstances, although I can easily conceive that I should be necessitated to be damned; and if your argument is as lucid as my apprehension of it is obscure I am sure I deserve to be damned for my stupidity; though I cannot fancy how I should desire to be everlastingly tormented for that or any other of my numerous sins."

A solemn atheist did not write this, but a man humorously satisfying the Irishman Taaffe's insatiable desire for metaphysical debate.

Shelley joked about the things that were dearest and most hurtful to him. He joked about love, about his "platonics", about his ecstasies. He jested about his atheism. He laughed about the way people reviewed his works. He mistakenly assumed that if he discussed religious matters in print he would gain a hearing from men and women who had enough money to buy his books and the capacity to read them. Where simpler folk were concerned he did not affront them: when he felt impelled to designate himself an atheist in hotel registers in Europe, he took care to write in Greek; but even then, solemn travellers followed him, debated whether they ought to delete the word, and even cut it from the innkeepers' registers to transmit it to England and use it as evidence in the case against him. Again the contrast with our own times presents itself: nowadays there exist countries where if you do *not* state your beliefs you may be clapped into gaol.

Shelley did not joke about his beliefs because he held them lightly; the tension in his personality demanded some such release in jest. If anyone could be accused of humorlessness it was not even the adolescent Shelley, formulating schemes for the betterment of mankind, the abolition of the tyrannies of marriage, the whittling away of part of the influence of priests. Even before the age of twenty he could joke on these subjects, as the notes to the inflammatory *Queen Mab*, which caused him so much injury, reveal:

"Christianity was intended to reform the world: had an all-wise being planned it, nothing is more improbable than that it should have failed: omniscience would infallibly have foreseen the inutility of a scheme which experience demonstrates, to this age, to have been utterly unsuccessful."

His prose, even at this early age, has a wit and a polish and a *panache* that could not please his age. The notes to *Queen Mab* make entertaining reading, even today, when most of the issues they discuss cause little stir, Shelley having fulfilled his destiny among the poets as a not entirely unacknowledged legislator of mankind; and even the earnest *Address to the Irish People*, published in Dublin when he was twenty, contains between a few passages of tedium a remarkable amount of good prose and good sense. But always, when dealing with the affairs of government and religion, Shelley strove to make his meaning crystal-clear. He was never a satirist, and therefore he never shared the benefits defined by Jonathan Swift for such writers:

> "Satire is a sort of glass, wherein all beholders do generally discover everybody's face but their own; which is the chief reason for that kind reception it meets with in the world, and that so very few are offended with it."

In Shelley's portraits of mankind too many saw their own faces, too many were offended; and in that sense he was Ariel to the world's Caliban.

One of his graver mistakes was not so much attacking established religion as laughing at it. A modern critic may lightly suggest that probably God has the laugh on Shelley, who may have spent the last 130 years making himself a nuisance in the vicinity of the eternal throne, trying to bring the Deity round to his way of thinking—but it is still possible for such a pleasantry to be taken as blasphemy. Shelley disliked the concept of an entirely humourless God. Like Blake, and later Shaw, he liked occasionally to take a running kick at Nobodaddy. He lived in an intellectually dark age in which it was perilously easy to commit blasphemy, since the priests evidently did not consider God competent to punish such offences (if He thought fit) in His own way.

When a young man attacks the fortresses of government and religion he can scarcely avoid falling into ridiculous attitudes. At the end of his life, Shelley regretted his early broadside, *Queen Mab*. The poem was pirated, and he protested, disclaiming the immature production. He even directed his solicitor to apply to Chancery for an injunction to restrain the sale, or so he stated in a letter to the Press. This was a twist of his own peculiar humour, since during his former dealings with Chancery *Queen Mab* had been the chief (indeed only) witness against him.

A man's deep hates are like his deep loves: though they fester and do not fertilize his spirit they are equally important in an understanding of his work. Shelley's festering hatred of the Lord Chancellor was hatred of the system that it was that officer's duty to uphold. Atheism brought him in conflict with the state. At the University, the real issue had been brought about by his refusing to lie; in the Court of Chancery the issue was quite plainly whether as an atheist he was entitled to have custody of his children. A brief summary of the case shows why Shelley was embittered by the way certain laws were interpreted in England early in the nineteenth century.

Shortly after Harriet Shelley's death her family filed a bill in Chancery applying for the custody of his two children, on the grounds that he had published *Queen Mab* and avowed himself an atheist and a republican, that before Harriet's death he had lived with Mary Wollstonecraft Godwin, and that he was therefore unfit to have charge of his children. According to Chancery law, he must admit or deny these accusations on oath; it rested with the Lord Chancellor whether he was to be allowed custody of his children. He could prove that he had not in fact published *Queen Mab*, but that he had simply had a small number of copies privately printed to circulate among his friends. As he perforce viewed the matter, Chancery could decide that he had no right to his own children for the simple reason that he was an infidel. This was not the principal reason put forward against him, but it ranked foremost in his mind, and it cannot be said to have been put into the background by the Court. Whatever the outcome of the case, there was always the possibility that a criminal prosecution would follow. He argued, in vain, that if he had attacked religion he was punishable—but not by the loss of his children. The Lord Chancellor took his children from him and explained that he did not do so because the father held certain religious and moral opinions, or because he had lived in illicit union with Mary Godwin, but because he would certainly inculcate immoral opinions and conduct in his children. Shelley had a keen brain for legal niceties, and this particular nicety must have enraged him because it was a perfect example of judging a man on the strength of a hypothetical intention: in other words a violation of the letter of the law as well as of its spirit.

Lord Eldon was in fact in a difficult position. He had to

establish that he was not intolerant in religious matters, yet at the same time he had to satisfy the faction that would applaud the crushing of an infidel. Judgment given, he passed the whole matter to a Master in Chancery named William Alexander who, knowing that an appeal by Shelley's lawyer was bound to fail, at first reversed the Lord Chancellor's decision that though the father might not have the children, his nominee might be accepted as their guardian. Shelley's lawyers appealed to the Lord Chancellor, who directed his subordinate to reconsider the matter. Alexander naturally obeyed what was a virtual order, and Shelley's nominee was accepted. Shelley was given permission to see his children once a month; but by the time the lengthy proceedings ended he had gone to Italy, fearful lest William also might be taken from him:

> Come with me, thou delightful child,
> Come with me; though the wave is wild,
> And the winds are loose, we must not stay,
> Or the slaves of the law may rend thee away.

His atheism broke Shelley's reputation and it was only his friends who perceived that it was not quite the same as blasphemy. One day, when in her bitterness Claire drew up in her journal some ideas for caricatures of Byron, she grew tired of the effort and continued: "Caricature for poor dear S. He looking very sweet and smiling. A little Jesus Christ playing about the room. He says:

> 'Then grasping a small knife and looking mild
> I will quietly murder that little child.'"

Perhaps Shelley's most powerful utterance on the subject of "that little child" is to be found in *Prometheus Unbound*, where the words addressed by the shackled Prometheus to the youth nailed to a crucifix share the passion of a Dostoievsky in *The Grand Inquisitor*:

> I see, I see
> The wise, the mild, the lofty, and the just,
> Whom thy slaves hate for being like to thee,

> Some hunted by foul lies from their heart's home,
> An early-chosen, late-lamented home;
> As hooded ounces cling to the driven hind;
> Some linked to corpses in unwholesome cells:
> Some—hear I not the multitude laugh loud?—
> Impaled in lingering fire: and mighty realms
> Float by my feet, like sea-uprooted isles,
> Whose sons are kneaded down in common blood
> By the red light of their own burning homes.

In Shelley's day some people were as passionately attached to words, at the expense of ideas, as they are today. At his school, Eton, the boys gave the term "atheist" to anyone who rebelled against authority. When grown men called Shelley "atheist" they meant something very similar: that he believed in nothing. What he did not believe in was the Christian God and the right of certain men to grant a licence to God to receive the prayers of certain of His creatures: "How ridiculous in a foppish courtier not six feet high to direct the spirit of universal harmony in what manner to conduct the affairs of the universe!" All this reflected on his morals and caused men of standing to unite in maligning him; thus Southey, whom he had once sought out with deep respect but who he afterwards said was "corrupted by the world", spread the story in England that Shelley, his wife, Claire and Byron had "united in a League of Incest". His contemporaries would have preferred him to be a discreet rake, and it often seems that posterity would have preferred him to leave in some scrawled journal a catalogue of gutter lecheries, such as Boswell's. Mentally too energetic and physically too fastidious to engage the affection of posterity in this way, he was doomed for long years to be shuttled from critic to critic, now as a prig, now as a blackguard. Too eager a champion of man, he would not compromise with men by wearing the mask of virtue.

Many years after Shelley's death, Leigh Hunt wrote:

> "He had only to become a yea and nay man in the house of commons, to be one of the richest men in Sussex. . . . Had he now behaved himself pardonably in the eyes of the orthodox, he would have gone to London with the

resolution of sowing his wild oats, and becoming a decent member of society: that is to say, he would have seduced a few maid-servants, or at least haunted the lobbies, and then bestowed the remnant of his constitution upon some young lady of his own rank in life, and settled into a proper church-and-king man, perhaps a member of the (Society for the) Suppression of Vice."

When Shelley went to Italy he did not anticipate that he would always live away from England. Though he had rather more justification than Lord Byron for considering himself in exile, he frequently contemplated his return, which was repeatedly put off. Among the reasons he had for assuming that his Italian years were merely an interlude in his life was his belief that one day he would succeed to his father's seat in Parliament.

If Percy Bysshe Shelley had been able to write "M.P." after his name, English parliamentary history would undoubtably have contained a colourful chapter, even if it had dealt only with his attempts to gain admittance to the House of Commons despite his being an atheist. If he had lived out his natural span English political history might have borne an even stronger imprint than that which his poetry placed on literature. Unless one takes into account his political aspirations his brief life must be seen in false perspective.

He lived his formative years, till he was twenty-three, in a long drawn-out war, the righteousness and wisdom of which were doubted by many people who were far from sharing his Radical views on Church and State. He first went abroad shortly after the end of the war, and saw the desolation of Eastern France. It was not the sights he saw during the 1814 tour that prompted him to write such expressions as "the impious name of King"; his views were already well formed. He was a republican without faith in violence, who believed that England could be made a better place if superstition—all types of religious and secular idolatry—were destroyed. "Perhaps," he wrote, "you will say that my republicanism is proud; it certainly is far removed from pot-house democracy."

Shelley's roots were in the end of the eighteenth century. The sheer interest of his life has made it difficult for his biographers to give any but the most superficial attention to the time he lived in and the background of that time—the world in which his mother and father and schoolmasters grew up. Far more attention has been given to the influence his work had on nineteenth-century political thought and literature—a forgivable distortion, because that influence was so great. *Queen Mab* made many rebels during the century following Shelley's death—which was no bad thing for England, for its verse and prose have passion, clarity and idealism such as it might be difficult to find in a warehouse full of Radical squibs and pamphlets. Bernard Shaw described *Prometheus Unbound* as a modern epic, a judgment which no critic who has read the poem more than twice would care to quarrel with. *Prometheus* grows in stature and even Shelley's occasional lyrics can stand up to the corrosive test of being constantly anthologized in school books. We resuscitate his prose writings and admire his clear-sightedness. We think of such splendours as Demogorgon's final speech, and of other passages in *Prometheus* such as the prophetic words of the earth to the moon:

> All things confess his strength. Through the cold mass
> Of marble and of colour his dreams pass;
> Bright threads whence mothers weave the robes their children wear;
> Language is a perpetual Orphic song,
> Which rules with Daedal harmony a throng
> Of thoughts and forms, which else senseless and shapeless were.

> The lightning is his slave; Heaven's utmost deep
> Gives up her stars, and like a flock of sheep
> They pass before his eye, are numbered, and roll on!
> The tempest is his steed,—he strides the air;
> And the abyss shouts from her depth laid bare,
> "Heaven, has thou secrets? Man unveils me; I have none."

Yet for an understanding of Shelley a picture of the world that made him is as important as a knowledge of the world he helped to make. He is labelled in school books a Romantic poet, as if he were somehow associated with Lamartine and

Liszt, and to be linked with high-flown ideas about art for art's sake, and a Continental Romantic movement which was in fact quite foreign to him. He drew some of his romanticism from Wordsworth and, later, from Goethe. But he had little in common with his fellow "Romantics", Byron and Keats. Two great influences swayed him, the English and the Italian. The second was a literary interest and what hope he drew from Italy's coming struggle for freedom, which he foresaw, was based firmly on what he hoped for England. He did not rail against England as Byron did: by origin, education and taste Shelley was, indeed, the most English of poets, and when we need more anthems we might do worse than to draw on his works.

By an odd dislocation of time, the nineteenth century began, in England, in 1793, the year after Shelley's birth. It was a year that marked a great division in the English people. An intellectual awakening had taken place, the results of which were to be suppressed for about three decades, and it is to that period of savage repression that Shelley belongs. In May, 1793, several Members of Parliament in both Houses rose to declare warmly that the English Constitution was perfect. For several hours the debaters zealously sought to prove that their Parliament was in no need of reform; that, indeed, it was a model of legislative decorum; that the times were unsuitable for any electoral changes, and that to regard borough-mongering as an evil was a dangerous heresy of the lower classes—by which they did not mean the poor, but the educated middle classes. The House of Commons applauded the Member for Cockermouth when he declared, "The very advanced price at which seats are now represented to be sold in Parliament is not (if true) a proof of its corruption, but of the increasing wealth and prosperity of the country."

The Government faced a state of emergency. In France, the Terror had broken out, and at home there were commercial troubles, riots and discontents. The force feared most was not the mob, but the trading and professional middle class of liberal sentiments against which, indeed, the Government's *agents provocateurs* occasionally incited the mob. The dangerous class had formed societies for political debate, of which the younger Pitt and Fox had at one time been members. The names of the moving spirits in what became known as the English Jacobin movement are now for the most part forgotten: Horne Tooke, the parson and political philologist; Thomas Hardy, the retired shoemaker; Major Cartwright; Thomas Day; the Earl of Stanhope; Capel Lofft; Dr. Price and John Thelwall. Just as Shelley aroused the curiosity of the Pisans by walking in the street reading a volume of an encyclopaedia, so Thelwall had surprised people in the Strand by walking about with a book held close to his eyes; he even had a taper fitted up so that he could read while walking at night. He gave up the law for journalism, and tried his debating powers at Coachmaker's Hall in discussions which were considered by Authority to be harmless, till the French Revolution broke out. Government spies were employed to mark down the dangerous anti-Constitution men, among whom were Thelwall, member of the Society for Constitutional Information, and Horne Tooke, founder of a society for the protection of the Press. Many societies for electoral reform were founded, and the reformers were often blamed for the riots which Government agents instigated, among gangs of bullies, against them. In 1791 an intoxicated "Church and King" mob rioted in Birmingham, causing destruction that was visible ten years after the event; there were similar riots in the North, all part of a policy of using gin-drunk mobs against the Jacobins.

By 1792 the Jacobins were said to be in correspondence with the French National Assembly. In May the Proclamation against Sedition was issued, and troops were employed to disperse meetings; in December the Speech from the Throne "revealed" a sensational plot to destroy the Constitution, and Tom Paine was tried in his absence for sedition. One of the first victims was a bill-sticker, charged with pasting up seditious literature, though the poor man happened to be completely illiterate. Next the booksellers were attacked. In 1793 Thelwall and his friends organized a Convention, as a reprisal for which five Jacobins were transported. Thelwall delivered a series of lectures on William Godwin's works, to raise funds for the family of one of the men transported, who, in fact, died on the voyage out. He spoke so cautiously, in parable and satire, that Pitt's spies could not produce evidence of sedition.

In May, 1794, when Habeas Corpus was in suspension, Thelwall and others were arrested, cross-examined by Pitt, Dundas and the Privy Council, and finally cast into the Tower of London. They were not allowed writing materials or permitted to consult lawyers. Five months later they were indicted, and given ten days in which to prepare their defence at Newgate Gaol. When the Grand Jury retired to consider whether a True Bill could be pronounced against the prisoners, charging them with treason, the Attorney-General and the Solicitor for the Crown locked themselves in the jury room with them. At the trial, one of the Government spies admitted, while in a drunken stupor, that he had committed perjury.

The accused men were acquitted, but the Attorney-General referred to them as "the acquitted felons".

Many more examples of cynicism and tyranny could be given, but that of Thelwall, now almost forgotten, is typical. He was a member of the Godwin circle and knew Southey, to whom Shelley had poured out many expressions of youthful admiration.

The history of Thelwall and his associates is chiefly concentrated in the seventeen-nineties. This decade was what might be termed, without straining language or image, a little dark age. England found herself in a crisis, the sort of crisis which the most confident and skilful political physicians could not handle.

For any cultivated man, the times were dark and confusing. The generation before Shelley's saw the crumbling of a cultural tradition. The intellectual's new interest at that time was what was termed "philosophy". It was a mixture of arts and sciences of which we now have no experience. It presupposed a lively imagination; a classical education; an interest in the developing science of "œconomy", in letters, and in the teeming scientific advances of the age. It was that unique human culture which exalts the works of man and relegates to a discreetly sentimental but insignificant background the works of God and of Nature. The lesser part of life lay in violence. First there was the true violence: disease, sudden death, hanging, rioting, robbing and wenching. Secondly there was the incidental violence: eating, drinking and quarrelling were violent and eccentric—it was as if all the compulsions of a man of education and feeling led away from these ordinary human activities, causing him in reaction to throw himself into brawling, bibbing or gorging with determined savagery. This violent side of life was not the true eighteenth century, but merely a popularization of it, like "Victorian" prudery and "Elizabethan" chivalry. Barbarity often flourishes side by side with high culture. It was so in the state of these ingenious philosophers.

Liberal ideals grew on soil already fertilized by Dissent. Parliament may have been the "best club in London", the still impregnable fortress of the aristocracy, the landed gentry, and the leisured class; but where, for thousands of Englishmen, political dissent was forbidden, save as a fruitless social amusement, religious dissent offered to resolve the yearnings of multitudes who felt, amid all this activity and progress, that they were being cheated of some vital intellectual element of which they had recently become aware.

In the towns, a new class of men, small in numbers but destined to be important in influence later, were growing up. A fresh type of observant and inquiring artisan was born of the Industrial Revolution. Some founded mercantile families, thus helping to build a nineteenth-century bourgeoisie; families such as Shelley's formed part of this though their roots were in very different soil, and they would have resented the suggestion that they had any social aims in common with those of the new industrial rich of the second half of the nineteenth century. Some of these new artisans turned Radical, or more precisely Rationalist, and put some new blood into the artistic and literary world of the second half of the century. When Shelley was a boy they were beginning to realize that they were not circumscribed by the physical and mental narrowness of village life.

The many causes of the movement for reform which broke rudely upon the consciousness of men of property at the end of the century cannot be listed in a paragraph; but the movement of Dissent in religion aptly illustrates the forces at work.

The disciples whom the indefatigable John Wesley gathered to his bosom during a long life of itinerant preaching were chiefly drawn from this growing bourgeois class; drawn with difficulty, too, for the upper classes found no appeal in the movement and the lower classes used earth and stones to express their disapproval of it, in defence of the "Church and State" from which they received so little, and of the mechanism of which they were so ignorant. The real dilemma for the man of property who had some title to intellectual honesty was this: the cultural inheritance of his forebears, the dignity of academic learning, was deteriorating, and striving against his allegiance to this was a new allegiance to scientific progress. It was this progress in the mechanical arts—fully shared by Shelley—which was rapidly producing that radical change in the social order which necessitated reform.

But of the existence of the new class of "respectable mechanicks" and ambitious tradesmen the man of property remained, for a long time, oblivious. After the excesses of the French Revolution all reformers were associated, in his mind, with the "swinish multitude" of Burke's phrase.

Where the economics of literature are concerned this cleavage between the old order and the new idea was of great significance. In the early part of the century the system of patronage was unspoiled. A number of distinguished authors lived—and lived as befitted the honour of their profession—through either the direct patronage of a nobleman, or the indirect patronage of many who bought and subscribed to books. The background of the literary scene consisted of Grub Street. In Grub Street few wretches had any opportunities of advancement; they were men thrown by that folly which addiction to the printed word begets into the degradation and misery of literary hovels. At the end of the century a great change had taken place. There were—and always will be—cases of extreme distress among literary men and hacks; but the system of patronage had fallen. Johnson, who dealt it a heavy blow with his letter to Chesterfield on the subject of the Dictionary, was one of the first of the new literary order: an author who lived decently by virtue of his work, and not by the favour of a condescending nobleman. John Thelwall, in common with others, supported himself and his family during the greater part of his life on occasional literary earnings. The English poets were no longer necessarily drawn from the families of the rich. In 1795 John Keats was born the son of a groom. De Quincey, Hazlitt and Leigh Hunt were middle-class people. They began to work at a time when it was becoming possible for a journalist to live by his writing.

When social changes take place which have a wide influence, it is only too easy for posterity to view the metamorphosis from afar and, seeing cause and effect neatly arranged in history, to pass harsh judgment on those who while deep in the strife saw nothing or saw what was not there. This gravely important development in English history, round which the life of John Thelwall, Horne Tooke and their friends revolved, affords many spectacles which it appears difficult to believe true. First, there is the prospect of two intelligent Englishmen, Edmund Burke and Charles James Fox, remaining in apparent ignorance of the facts which made a popular movement for Parliamentary Reform inevitable in England after the Revolution in France. This catastrophe accelerated the movement, but had the French Revolution been postponed for twenty years it is probable that the nineteenth century would not have opened without some emphatic statement by the new reformers.

Burke, Fox and Pitt had all, in earlier years, been ardent for Parliamentary Reform. Yet when the determined cry arose, and the demagogues received punishment and glory, these three statesmen were not silent. Burke made his own impassioned statement against what he firmly and sincerely believed to be the machinations of opportunists and anarchists. Fox, feeling less alarm, perhaps, was reserved and sceptical. Pitt, the victim of the enormous pressure of public affairs, and the prey of consuming doubts, threw in his lot against the little band of men who had so suddenly become articulate, and organized against them the tremendous forces of corruption and tyranny.

In the light of ensuing events the history of the English Jacobin movement is a barbarous recital of almost unrelieved corruption and villainy, strewn with trumped-up libel actions, terrorism, bribery, espionage, forgery, the dereliction of duty and the undermining of justice.

It was in a world such as this that Shelley lived—a fact not to be forgotten when one reads his tremendous expression of faith in man, in *Prometheus Unbound*. He attacked that world unceasingly, yet there was invariably a note of hope in his political poems and letters, as at the end of his sonnet on England in 1819:

> Religion Christless, Godless—a book sealed;
> A Senate,—Time's worst statute unrepealed,—
> Are graves, from which a glorious Phantom may
> Burst, to illumine our tempestuous day.

It was in this year that—in *The Masque of Anarchy*—he stated his unchanged conviction that in face of the worst tyranny, liberty would be won if men united to face the bayonet

> With folded arms and looks which are
> Weapons of unvanquished war.

Some hints of what practical measures he might have tried to introduce had he entered Parliament are given in the unpublished MS. of *A Philosophical View of Reform* as quoted by Dowden: abolition of the National Debt, the disbanding of standing armies, the cessation of tithes (with due regard for vested interests), absolute freedom of speech, and the achievement of justice that would be cheap, speedy and secure. In 1817, when he published *A Proposal for Putting Reform to the Vote*, he stated his income, a thousand pounds a year, and offered to place one-tenth of that income in a fund to advance the cause of electoral reform; and how far-seeing he was in practical politics may be judged from this passage:

> "The consequences of the immediate extension of the elective franchise to every male adult, would be to place power in the hands of men who have been rendered brutal and torpid and ferocious by ages of slavery. It is to suppose that the qualities belonging to a demagogue are such as are sufficient to endow a legislator. I allow Major Cartwright's arguments to be unanswerable; abstractedly it is the right

of every human being to have a share in the government. But Mr. Paine's arguments are also unanswerable; a pure republic may be shown, by inferences the most obvious and irresistible, to be that system of social order the fittest to produce the happiness and promote the genuine eminence of man. Yet nothing can less consist with reason, or afford smaller hopes of any beneficial issue, than the plan which should abolish the regal and aristocratical branches of our constitution, before the public mind, through many gradations of improvement, shall have arrived at the maturity which can disregard these symbols of its childhood."

He was writing for the future, as he did when he prophesied:

"In spite of the low-thoughted envy which would undervalue contemporary merit, our own will be a memorable age in intellectual achievements, and we live among such philosophers and poets as surpass beyond comparison any who have appeared since the last national struggle for civil and religious liberty."

It was to verse that he turned in order to express his highest aspirations on behalf of man in search of political greatness:

> Man who man would be,
> Must rule the empire of himself; in it
> Must be supreme, establishing his throne
> On vanquished will, quelling the anarchy
> Of hopes and fears, being himself alone.

Literary society encourages all the passions: love, hatred, lust, anger, envy, the desire to kill and to drink and to worship. It breeds good and evil, idealism and cynicism. Shelley spent little time among the cliques. It is noteworthy that he lived in a time of literary as well as social change: the pursuit of literature was establishing itself as an art, not merely the toy of gentlemen of leisure and the ruin of penniless hacks capable, in the eyes of the fashionable world, of nothing better than scribbling. The age of the professional was soon to dawn. It is not enough to think of him merely as a poet, or merely as an eccentric gentleman who revolted against his compeers, disapproved of primogeniture, pitied the wretchedness of the poor, and scorned the pomp of priests, Court sycophants and lickspittle poets. He believed that literature as a force in life, drawing its subject-matter from the times as well as from mythology, was a topic worthy of discussion in the same breath as estate management, fox-hunting and regular attendance at church; he was in a way the squire who woke too soon.

Shelley left a country in which panic at the swift progress of events, combined with the bleeding process of a long war, had enthroned injustice and reaction. New generations do not spring into the world armed with bright new weapons; we have to learn to walk, then to read, then to think and judge, and if we are dissatisfied with the world of our fathers, we have to search family attics for old swords and bucklers to sharpen and polish and fight for the world we want. Our ideas, actions and reactions still demonstrate the truth that our minds are born, so to speak, a few decades before our bodies are. That is, we draw reasons for our first ideals, our first admiration and our first anger from the world our fathers knew. Shelley's father and grandfather may have been dull squires, more interested in food and drink and rents than anything else, but both were Whigs of the eighteenth century who saw as many swift changes and convulsions in history as we of the first half of the twentieth century have seen. Their talk would encompass, in international affairs alone, the breakaway of the American colonies, the French Revolution, the reaction in England and the Napoleonic Wars. If Shelley had been born a little over a century later he might have been submitted to similar influences. His father's talk might have dealt with the end of the nineteenth century and the twilight of the Victorian world of enterprise and empire; with religious doubts springing out of a reading of Darwin and Huxley instead of the "natural philosophers", Rousseau and Buffon; with the Kaiser and then Lenin instead of Napoleon; with the rise of Trades Unionism, not the writings of Tom Paine and William Cobbett. These are only rough comparisons, but they help us to see why

Shelley still has an impact as a modern writer, and how fully men of the twentieth century share some of his experiences. If it were possible to agree on a method of plotting in graphs the development of man's mental and material life between 1800 and 1850, and then between 1900 and 1950, we might well find that the curve of progress was much steeper in the first half of the nineteenth than in the first half of the twentieth century.

Shelley abandoned (but only temporarily, as he planned) the sepulchrous air of England to go to Italy. There he found no more justice or humanity but isolation of spirit and some hope on which to feed his ambition for poor benighted humankind.

Post-war Italy was, as a Sardinian minister of the time succinctly explained, "merely money which you pay for other things". The liberation of the Peninsula consisted of dividing it into areas of influence for the victorious allies. Three years after the Congress of Vienna, when Shelley made his home in Italy, the chief diplomatic concern of the English, Austrian and Russian ministers was to watch one another and seek means of increasing the usefulness of the princelings whom they had appointed as their catspaws in Genoa, Naples, Florence, Lucca and other parts of the Peninsula. This new kind of peninsular war was complicated by the fact that the subject people had aims quite different from those of the allies who had liberated them by defeating Napoleon. During Shelley's sojourn in Italy the secret societies which were later to provide the core for the movement of unification were proliferating. It is easy to laugh at the activities of these societies because, like many embryonic revolutionary movements, they fell into absurdities; Lord Castlereagh's correspondents in Italy did their best to assure the British Foreign Minister that all was well with the oxen beneath the Austrian yoke, until the Revolution of Naples revealed how inaccurate their comforting information had been.

It was Castlereagh, strangely enough, who summed up the Italian situation in a striking and accurate phrase, though he never visited Italy and was constantly misinformed about its affairs by his ministers abroad. On 20 October, 1820, after the Naples revolt had exposed to him the unreliability of the

Of Kings, and Priests, and Slaves 107

Foreign Office intelligence from Italy, he instructed his ministers on their attitude to the revolt in a dispatch marked "Most Secret" in which he spoke of the dastardly plan "to consolidate the whole of Italy into one common Hate". No phrase could have expressed more truly the simmering beneath the surface of Italian life during Shelley's years in that country. Abhorrence of the Austrian rule is modern Italy's deepest scar and even in our own times it has not been healed.

Castlereagh was one of Shelley's hates:

> I met Murder on the way—
> He had a mask like Castlereagh.

It was his unrelenting and oppressive policy which resulted in the "Peterloo" massacre and thus directly called forth *The Masque of Anarchy*, and when he killed himself, a few days after Shelley's remains were burnt at Viareggio, a large number of Londoners, united by one common hate, grimly cheered as his funeral cortège passed by.

Castlereagh became Foreign Secretary in 1812, about the time when Shelley was writing *Queen Mab*. The Foreign Office files of 1818 to 1822 help to show what kind of atmosphere surrounded the foreigner in Italy at that period. Daily life presented a picture of a bowed and broken people—"a miserable people, without sensibility, or imagination, or understanding" was Shelley's first impression, written to Godwin after a few months in Italy. The heavy blanket of superstition lay over the land, and the power of the Church depressed Shelley as much as that of the Austrians:

> Many-domèd Padua proud
> Stands, a peopled solitude,
> 'Mid the harvest-shining plain,
> Where the peasant heaps his grain
> In the garner of his foe,
> And the milk-white oxen slow
> With the purple vintage strain,
> Heaped upon the creaking wain,
> That the brutal Celt may swill
> Drunken sleep with savage will.

Lord Burghersh, the English minister in Florence, came home on leave in 1822, and therefore had not the embarrassment of having to apply to the Government of nearby Lucca to permit the cremation that the poet's wife and friends desired; and curiously enough the only official papers relating to his leave deal with the trouble he caused the Treasury through demanding to bring home an inordinate amount of red wine under diplomatic exemption from Customs duty.

The "brazen-gated temples" in the country of his adoption depressed Shelley as they may well have depressed many later travellers. The heart-rending natural beauty of Italy contrasted then as now with the squalor of some of the cities. Today there is at least one beggar outside every great church in Italy; in Shelley's times there were shackled convicts in the streets, too. Whereas he saw the peasant garnering his wheat and grapes for the occupying forces, the modern traveller may see the vintners doctoring and prinking up what should be their noble wines in order to compete with the popular taste for an American concoction of mineral water and syrup. When very near the end of his life, Shelley seriously planned to ride with friends into Lucca and rescue a priest who was condemned to be burnt alive for stealing from a church. Byron was suspected of having direct contact with the Carbonari, chief among the many political secret societies of the time. When the Naples Revolution broke out in 1820 the Neapolitan troops were under the command of a British general, and Lord Vane Stewart, in Vienna, was hastily insuring that certain Englishmen who applied for passports to Naples should be permitted to go as far as Florence only, in case they designed to take up arms against King Ferdinand's soldiers under their generalissimo Nugent. When Shelley was entertaining Prince Mavrocordato and dreaming of Greek independence, which cause later took Byron with the Prince to Greece, Dawkins, the Secretary of Legation at Florence, was carefully reporting Mavrocordato's movements and proclamations to Castlereagh. In the year of "Peterloo" Castlereagh was demanding of his correspondents in Italy news of the "diabolical spirit" of "Jacobinical principles but ill-concealed under the specious mask of attachment to the system of Representative Governments", and receiving news of the "violent incendiaries and revolutionaries who frequent the Coffee Houses" in Naples, and of a dangerous Frenchman in Bologna who was "in the habit of receiving, privately, all the disaffected, and those known to be hostile to the present order of things".

The air was heavy with suspicion in Italy, and the diplomatic bags were often weighted with complacent misinformation. Life as viewed from anywhere but the doors of an embassy or legation gave room for hope to people of Shelley's persuasion, however. Even Claire Clairmont, who had little enough time to take an interest in politics, wrote enthusiastically about the Naples Revolution, and the event which preceded and even precipitated this—the Revolution in Spain—resulted in Shelley's *Ode to Liberty*, a Miltonic hymn to the indignation and pity that shames men out of the torpor that dogma casts them into:

> Indignation
> Answered Pity from her cave;
> Death grew pale within the grave,
> And Desolation howled to the destroyer, Save!
>
> . . . . .
>
> Men started, staggering with glad surprise,
> Under the lightnings of thine unfamiliar eyes.

"I should like to be in Madrid now," he wrote to a friend in England.

Shelley wrote so much on the subject of love that his capacity for hatred is often either forgotten or concealed. His constant fight against corruption in public and private life made him no stranger to the emotion of hatred, and he knew it in its bitterest form, which assails a man when he is impotent to strike.

If there are readers who grow oppressed by the rarefied air of some of Shelley's pronouncements on love, there is refreshment for the palate to be had from the bitter springs of the poet's mind. There is a virile power in his curses. His personal hatreds could be intense. Dowden writes:

"We know how swiftly a fever of dislike could inflame Shelley's blood, could infect his whole nature, and, rising to detestation and abhorrence, could render every nerve a seat of throbbing anguish."

In such a mood he wrote of his sister-in-law Eliza Westbrook:

"I have sunk into a premature old age of exhaustion, which renders me dead to everything but the unenviable capacity of indulging the vanity of hope, and a terrible susceptibility to objects of disgust and hatred."

He once said to a friend, "Hunt, we have love-songs, why should we not have hate-songs?" He sang such songs with greatest power when writing of types of men, as in *Lines Written during the Castlereagh Administration*:

> Corpses are cold in the tomb;
> Stones on the pavement are dumb;
> Abortions are dead in the womb,
> And their mothers look pale—like the death-white shore
>   Of Albion, free no more.

.   .   .   .   .

> Ay, marry thy ghastly wife!
> Let Fear and Disquiet and Strife
> Spread thy couch in the chamber of Life!
> Marry Ruin, thou Tyrant! and Hell be thy guide
>   To the bed of the bride!

It was his belief that hatred could season love, and the sexual imagery which appears in much of his idealistic poetry is used also to give energy to his curses. Of "two political characters of 1819" he wrote:

> ... two vultures sick for battle,
> Two scorpions under one wet stone,
> Two bloodless wolves whose dry throats rattle,
> Two crows perched on the murrained cattle,
>   Two vipers tangled into one.

Claire Clairmont listed three things that Shelley hated most. They were: didactic poetry, institutional Christianity and Lord Eldon.

Peter Bell the Third, written in anger against a poet who Shelley considered had sold his creative power, is full of expressions of biting contempt, and not for Wordsworth alone. To lose ideals and to betray the spirit of youth in politics and morals was something that Shelley often forgave in human beings, but he made greater than human demands of poets, and delivered on them more bitter judgments than on the generality of "the loud world". What the poet in him could never forgive was the loss of creative power that could result from the atrophy of intellect or conscience. What ordinary men say may not be important; what they do matters. What poets say is always, for fellow-poets, of immense importance. Shelley must have known, when composing his "hate-songs", that in losing creative power the poet becomes a destroyer.

The spirit of hatred and destruction can produce great poetry, however; this is nowhere better shown, perhaps, than in *The Sensitive Plant*, that mysterious allegory about man, woman and love, written in 1820. In this poem Shelley employed a large amount of imagery quite different from that which characterized the style of his year of tremendous creation, 1819. The garden is choked:

> And plants, at whose names the verse feels loath,
> Filled the place with a monstrous undergrowth,
> Prickly, and pulpous, and blistering, and blue,
> Livid, and starred with a lurid dew.
>
> .   .   .   .   .
>
> Spawn, weeds, and filth, a leprous scum,
> Made the running rivulet thick and dumb,
> And at its outlet flags huge as stakes
> Dammed it up with roots knotted like water-snakes.

In the year of depression, 1818, he had succeeded in refining the expression of that hatred in terms of myth and humanity rather than those of weed and fungus:

> The world is full of Woodmen who expel
> Love's gentle Dryads from the haunts of life,
> And vex the nightingales in every dell.

Love, hatred and death were intertwined in Shelley's private mythology, and this linking of ideas is an important key to the understanding of the autobiography that he wrote into his verse. When Trelawny asked Medwin why Mary should not write her husband's life, Medwin replied:

> "No, women cannot write men's lives and characters—they don't know them: much less his—he was so different from ordinary men. She told me she could never get him to speak of the past. He disliked being questioned, was impatient, left the room whenever she attempted it; and never spoke of himself. She knows very little of his early life, except what I and others have told her."

His writings on the subjects of love, hatred, birth and death are an eternalizing torn out of his experience. Fighting its way out of his poetry, wriggling through the metaphysics that so annoy some readers, striving for expression through a maze of repeated images and frequently verbiage on the subject of Nature, is the sensation of an eternal moment: the idea that the heights of love and death in the mind are an eternalizing, and perhaps identical in themselves. Herein lay the strong appeal of Petrarch, whose *Trionfi* Shelley was reading again in the last few weeks of his life as the model for *The Triumph of Life*. Time was Shelley's unfathomable sea, and the past was ever present:

> Forget the dead, the past? Oh, yet
> There are ghosts that may take revenge for it,
> Memories that make the heart a tomb,
> Regrets which glide through the spirit's gloom,
>   And with ghastly whispers tell
>   That joy, once lost, is pain.

In a fragment on Keats, death is "The immortalizing winter".

It appears frequently in poems on love. It haunts many lines on marriage, for Shelley had discovered, in spite of his ideal of emotional freedom, that when a man takes a woman, not lightly, as wife or mistress, he binds himself not only to her present image but to her past and future.

Six

THE LAMP IN THE DUST

> When the lamp is shattered
> The light in the dust lies dead—
> When the cloud is scattered
> The rainbow's glory is shed.
> When the lute is broken,
> Sweet tones are remembered not;
> When the lips have spoken,
> Loved accents are soon forgot.
>
> *Lines: When the Lamp is Shattered*

THE STILL, oppressive weather that had caused Shelley and Williams to be becalmed on their way to Viareggio persisted on Sunday, 9 June. Williams went alone in the morning to the Tino and on his return found Mary unwell. He seems to have gathered from the others that she had a miscarriage, for what he wrote in his journal, word for word, was: "On my return found Mary had been alarmingly unwell—i.e. that she had —— 'tho I left her at breakfast perfectly well. Night, strangely better." The attack seems to have been a preliminary to the miscarriage, which actually took place, according to Mary's recollection, a week later. She kept to her room during the increasingly hot weather.

By Wednesday, 12 June, the *sandalino* had been completed and launched. That evening the men took Jane sailing, but were once again becalmed, "and left there with a long ground swell which made Jane little better than dead. Hoisted out our little boat, and brought her on shore—her landing attended by the whole village."

Thereafter, Shelley used the boat in the evenings, to seek

the tranquillity of the coves surrounding the bay. Mary wrote: "At night, when the unclouded moon shone on the calm sea, he often went out alone in his little shallop to the rocky caves that bordered it, and sitting beneath their shelter, wrote *The Triumph of Life*, the last of his productions."

On 13 June a visitor arrived to cheer them. At nine o'clock in the morning the *Don Juan* was sailing between Portovenere and the Palmaria when a vessel like a man-of-war brig was sighted in the direction of Genoa. It was the *Bolivar*, recently completed for Byron and being delivered by Daniel Roberts and Edward Trelawny to Leghorn. When the vessels met, Trelawny fired a salute of six guns, and later the two crews determined which was the faster boat. The *Bolivar*, which cost ten times the price of the *Don Juan*, won easily, and Williams noted wistfully, "She is the most beautiful craft I ever saw." The competition over, the *Bolivar* anchored off Lerici and Roberts and Trelawny arranged to stay at an inn there. Roberts was consulted about certain changes in the rigging of the *Don Juan*, and they must have been quite extensive, for three days later, when Trelawny took the *Bolivar* on to Leghorn, the Captain stayed at Lerici.

Trelawny's arrival must have cheered Mary. Three weeks after they first met, early in 1822, she wrote of him:

> "A kind of half-Arab Englishman, whose life has been as changeful as that of Anastasius, and who recounts the adventures of his youth as eloquently and well as the imagined Greek. He is clever; for his moral qualities I am yet in the dark; he is a strange web which I am endeavouring to unravel. I would fain learn if generosity is united to impetuousness, probity of spirit to his assumption of singularity and independence. He is six feet high; raven black hair, which curls thickly and shortly like a Moor's; dark-grey expressive eyes; overhanging brows; upturned lips, and a smile which expresses good-nature and kind heartedness. His shoulders are high, like an Oriental's; his voice is monotonous, yet emphatic; and his language, as he relates the events of his life, energetic and simple, whether the tale be one of blood and horror or of irresistible comedy."

Trelawny was an adventurous Cornishman. Even if his fame did not rest on his having written the liveliest and most entertaining book about Shelley and Byron as they talked, ate, wrote and amused themselves, he would probably not be a forgotten figure. He could not spell or punctuate and he had a poor head for dates and a liking for good yarns; yet he had a natural and energetic style and the capacity, uncommon among the many who wrote about Shelley and Byron, of setting down records that have the unmistakable ring of truth. He was the same age as Shelley. His morals were far more akin to Byron's than to Shelley's.

He preferred Shelley as a man, as a companion and as a poet, yet in his writings he did not play off one against the other. He was a good reporter, and his perception of the relations between the two poets, in 1822, was uncannily accurate in the light of later revelations; even though he could have no clear idea of the cause of their tension, even though the salient facts were probably never known to him, he reproduced it. This was because he penetrated the characters of both; there is scarcely a line in his account that is seriously inconsistent, or dull. He had a robust egoism which prevented his being fooled by the seeming characters of literary men, allied to a literary modesty which made him immune from envy:

> "I have seen Shelley and Byron in society, and the contrast was as marked as their characters. The former, not thinking of himself, was as much at ease as in his own home, omitting no occasion of obliging those whom he came in contact with, readily conversing with all or any who addressed him, irrespective of age or rank, dress or address. To the first party I went with Byron, as we were on our road, he said, 'It's so long since I have been in English society, you must tell me what are their present customs. Does rank lead the way, or does the ambassadress pair us off into the dining-room? Do they ask people to wine? Do we exit with the women, or stick to our claret?'
>
> On arriving, he was flushed, over-ceremonious, and ill at ease. He had learnt his manners, as I have said, during the

Regency, when society was more exclusive than even now, and consequently more vulgar.

To know an author, personally, is too often but to destroy the illusion created by his works; if you withdraw the veil of your idol's sanctuary, and see him in his nightcap, you discover a querulous old crone, a sour pedant, a supercilious coxcomb, a servile tuft hunter, a saucy snob, or, at best, an ordinary mortal. Instead of the high-minded seeker after truth and abstract knowledge, with a nature too refined to bear the vulgarities of life, as we had imagined, we find him full of egotism and vanity, and eternally fretting and fuming about trifles. As a general rule, therefore, it is wise to avoid writers whose works amuse or delight you, for when you see them they will delight you no more. Shelley was a grand exception to this rule. To form a just idea of his poetry, you should have witnessed his daily life; his words and actions best illustrated his writings. If his glorious conception of Gods and men constituted an atheist, I am afraid all that listened were little better. . . . The cynic Byron acknowledged him to be the best and ablest man he had ever known. The truth was, Shelley loved everything better than himself."

Trelawny it was who heard Byron talking, with "a knowing look", about the wisdom of cracking up the work of a popular author because he would invariably pay in the same coin, then adding that none of his friends had repaid such money lent. Trelawny reminded him, "By your own showing you are indebted to Shelley; some of his best verses are to express his admiration of your genius." Byron replied: "Ay, who reads them? If we puffed the Snake, it might not turn out a profitable investment. If he cast off the slough of his mystifying metaphysics, he would want no puffing."

If Trelawny was perceptive, so was Shelley. It is pleasant to reflect, however, that to the end of his long life Trelawny never suspected that during their brief friendship Shelley did not entirely trust him. He ended the partnership over the *Don Juan* by buying out Trelawny as well as Byron. He had several times been disillusioned on entering into a business partnership with a friend; perhaps he also wished to discover whether the liar in Trelawny was of the kind likely to produce complications. Trelawny never lied for gain or for reputation or for reflected glory; but he liked to romanticize his own exploits, some of which would have been concealed by a more calculating man. Trelawny saw in Shelley the finest human being he ever knew, and by an occasional and happy lack of perception he did not sense Shelley's withdrawal from him.

If Shelley never offended Trelawny, Mary was forced to, in later years, though she did so as tactfully as possible. He wrote to her suggesting, in his celebrated offhand manner, that they should marry. She turned him down in a lighthearted but not flippant letter, and explained herself thus: "He is full of fine feelings and has no principles. I am full of fine principles but never had a feeling; he receives all his impressions through his heart, I through my head." It was as if he lived the rest of his life remembering the last few weeks of Shelley's existence. Had he liked Jane Williams, and had not another man stepped in swiftly to take Williams's place, he would probably have proposed to her, too. He certainly wrote to Claire, many years later, offering marriage and, as an afterthought, the position of mistress—for his complex matrimonial affairs would probably have precluded legal marriage. She too turned him down.

During his brief stay, Trelawny heard much about the *Don Juan*.

> "They were hardly ever out of her, and talked of the Mediterranean as a lake too confined and tranquil to exhibit her sea-going excellence. They longed to be on the broad Atlantic, scudding under bare poles in a heavy sou'wester, with plenty of sea room."

He went out for a sail in her and witnessed Williams's attempts to make Shelley part company with his Plato while he was steering. He noticed Shelley's particular delight in the *sandalino*:

> "The Poet was delighted with this fragile toy, and toying with it on the water, it often capsized, and gave him

many a header. . . . By practice he learnt to mitigate its evils, and vaunted that he had mastered and could do anything with it, and recklessly went out in bad weather."

He liked to allow it to drift out to sea till the breeze lapped the water over the gunwale; he felt "independent and safe from land bores".

One sultry evening, Trelawny was called by Mary Shelley from the terrace: Shelley had upset his *sandalino* and was being buffeted by the waves; he was more anxious to save the boat than to save himself. Trelawny waded in and brought them both to safety through the surf. As if thwarted of its prey, the sea rose that night; the spray swept the terrace and dashed itself against the windows of Casa Magni. About this time, Williams also began to observe the almost sinister moods of the sea on that coast. Part of his entry for 19 June runs, "The swell continues, and I am now the more persuaded that the moon influences the tides here—particularly the new moon—on the first week before she makes her appearance."

Two of Trelawny's favourite stories about his short visit, which have frequently been repeated, appear to have little basis in fact. One anecdote relates how, on a day when a visitor from Genoa was expected (his name, curiously enough, is not recorded), Shelley went bathing, upset his clothes into the water, and tried to creep furtively across the dining-room, in which the three women were entertaining the guest. The story is told at great length, and introduces the Italian maid who, Trelawny says, tried to screen him from the company when he explained himself in a dignified way. The tale is decorated with two poetical quotations and references to "his blushing wife" and "the sensitive lady", and its preamble oddly shows Shelley causing "a considerable commotion" during the preparations for the visit, and in a most uncharacteristic style encouraging the women to indulge in a large amount of dressmaking. It is an absurd story, and a number of circumstances, including Mary's illness during that week, the fact that no visitor from Genoa is mentioned in the journals or correspondence of anyone at Casa Magni, and the obvious absurdity of walking into the dining-room naked when he could have wrung out at least one garment and worn it, make the untruth obvious. No doubt Trelawny saw Shelley take a ducking and slip into the house, or heard that he had done so, and embroidered the story. His Italian was of an embryonic kind, but Trelawny had no doubt heard the catch-phrase *se non è vero è ben trovato*.

The second story relates how Shelley took Jane and her two children for a row in the *sandalino* and, when in deep water, suggested that they should now solve the great mystery. Jane Williams's family preserved this story, and like many family legends it is not very trustworthy biography. It is told as if Shelley literally did propose that he and Jane should commit suicide and murder two infants. If Jane did in fact undergo such an alarming experience it would probably demonstrate no more than her lack of understanding of Shelley's curious sense of humour. But since Trelawny represents her as leaping awkwardly out of the boat before it was beached, and Edward Williams asking her why she did so, and being told the story, it seems curious that Edward did not note the circumstance in his journal. Furthermore, Trelawny points out himself that the *sandalino* was built to take one person only.

In his biography of the poet, Professor N. I. White pointed out the thinness of the first story, but unexpectedly overlooked the fact which shows that very little of interest happened during Trelawny's visit, and that this encouraged the Cornishman to fill in those few pages of his book with second-hand stories. Because Trelawny mentions a terrible nightmare which Shelley underwent on the night of 22–23 June, yet does not mention Mary's miscarriage on the morning of 16 June, Professor White assumed that Trelawny paid two visits to Casa Magni, leaving very early on the morning of 16 June. There is no warrant for this, however, for Trelawny's account of the nightmare is secondhand (probably told to him by Mary, or Claire, or Jane) and he does not state that the happening took place while he himself was at Lerici. Trelawny certainly arrived on 13 June, and Williams notes on the 16th, "Wind continuing strong and unfavourable for the *Bolivar*". Shelley's letter, which Trelawny himself prints, and which is dated 18 June, makes it clear that he left in the *Bolivar* for Leghorn on the morning of that day, when he was seen by Shelley "eight miles in the offing", in calm weather.

Trelawny's omitting to mention the events of 16 June, when, in miscarrying, Mary Shelley nearly lost her life, and Shelley acted as doctor, may be explained by the fact that Mary herself assisted him in the revision of his book. It was natural that she should not wish for a graphic account of her illness to be included in the narrative. When Shelley wrote on 18 June, his footnote made it quite clear that Trelawny knew of Mary's illness. Williams's note for this day is conclusive: "Fine. The *Bolivar* sailed for Leghorn."

Mary's condition must in these oppressive days have caused Shelley much anxiety. After Mary's death in 1851 Trelawny said that she was jealous—but admitted that he did not know this when he knew the couple. This does not quite fit with his keen way of looking at his friends, and it may have been a later elaboration, partly encouraged by the good-humoured refusal that he had encountered when he proposed marriage to Mary, and linked in his mind with a remark that Shelley had once made to him on the subject of jealousy. Perhaps this term, jealousy, was too crude a description to apply to the state which had arisen, on the evidence of Shelley's own works, between himself and his wife during the previous three or four years. This state must have recalled to his mind the wreck of his first marriage. To understand the second marriage, there is much to be said for reviewing the little—and that little mysterious—that is known about the emotional aspect of the first.

Shelley was expelled from Oxford when eighteen and a half years old. He married Harriet Westbrook on 28 August, 1811, when he was nineteen. Since this marriage, following their elopement, was a Scottish one, he remarried her on 22 March, 1814. There is little to be gained by trying to discover why he married her. He is supposed to have been still distressed by the marriage of his first love, his cousin Harriet Grove. He deeply loved his sister Elizabeth, and hoped that she would marry his best friend, Jefferson Hogg. He was disappointed in this desire as in his own love for Harriet Grove. Four days before he announced his intention to "rescue" Harriet Westbrook from her school, where her chatter about his infidel ideas made her unpopular, he wrote to Hogg, "If I know anything about love, I am *not* in love."

The marriage lasted two and a half years. Then, in 1814, soon after the remarriage, and while Harriet was carrying his second child, they separated. Some of their friends stated that the cause of separation was Harriet's sister, Eliza, a vindictive woman nearly twice as old as Harriet, in 1811. But escape from Eliza could not have been an impossibility to a man of Shelley's notable obstinacy. What is certain is that he did not love Harriet when he married her; it is easy to understand his romantic, chivalrous feelings, and his philosophical hopes of moulding a disciple to his way of thinking on the subject of religion, politics and the "new woman". What is in dispute is the cause of the separation, and notably whether Shelley left Harriet because he believed her to have been unfaithful, or whether she left him, after a number of quarrels, to live with Eliza.

The discussion of this point—word-war might be a more apt term—has been carried on up to the present day. The assertion was made that Shelley persuaded Mary to elope with him in the summer of 1814 by stating that his wife had betrayed him. Two years later, when Harriet was found drowned, apparently pregnant, the allegation was made that she was living with a groom. Godwin asserted that he had "unquestionable authority . . . that she had proved herself unfaithful to her husband before their separation" with a Colonel Maxwell. Claire Clairmont said that Mary believed that Shelley left Harriet because the father of their second child was a Major Ryan. Jefferson Hogg told the Shelley family later in the century that the villain of the piece was Thomas Love Peacock. These are secondhand opinions, quite valueless to the biographer; and Hogg's inspired contribution turned out later to be a cover for the truth, which was that he had once tried to seduce Harriet when Shelley was called away from home. On evidence such as this, the causes of the breakdown of any marriage cannot be established.

Some biographers championed Shelley and stamped Harriet as little better than a prostitute. Others depicted Harriet as innocent and Shelley as an unmitigated scoundrel. Trelawny, writing from hearsay but valiantly striving to be fair, wrote that some time before Harriet's death an Army captain "professed to be interested and to sympathize in her fate", was drafted abroad, and promised to correspond with her; but "her poverty compelled her to seek a refuge in a cheaper lodging" and her former landlady refused to forward letters. Though Trelawny produces no authority for his statements, and though we know that Shelley never spoke to him of the matter, his story of the Army captain may seem to those who have scrutinized the evidence to be a version of the truth, for it certainly fits in with the inference that Harriet drowned herself because she was pregnant. The Army captain's promise to correspond may have been Trelawny's delicate way of saying that the man had consoled her with somewhat more than friendship. Before their separation, Shelley and Harriet had entertained a Major Ryan.

What Trelawny hated was the attempt made by Lady Jane Shelley, wife of Percy Florence Shelley, to blacken Harriet's character completely; for he wrote when aged eighty-three, "Lady Shelley is anxious to assert that she (Harriet) was a prostitute to a stable-man—Shelley would not have permitted this wicked lie nor would I—but we shall pass away—and then there is none to stop her." He was writing to Claire. Professor White made a scarcely convincing suggestion that the body taken from the Serpentine after a month's immersion was not that of a pregnant woman, but a corpse naturally inflated. But such guesses surely have no result except to confuse the issue and embitter the controversy. Shelley himself, after all, had something to say on the subject.

The chief biographical question is whether Shelley sincerely believed that Harriet had betrayed him. As far as concrete statements go, controversy in this respect is focused on the letter he is alleged to have written on 16 December, 1816, reporting the circumstances of Harriet's presumed suicide to Mary. The salient passages are:

"I have spent a day, my beloved, of somewhat agonizing sensations; such as the contemplation of vice and folly and hardheartedness exceeding all conception must produce. . . .

It seems that this poor woman—the most innocent of her abhorred and unnatural family—was driven from her father's house, and descended the steps of prostitution until she lived with a groom by the name of Smith, who deserting her, she killed herself—There can be no question that the beastly viper her sister, unable to gain profit from her connexion with me—has secured to herself the fortune of the old man—who is now dying—by the murder of this poor creature. Everything tends to prove, however, that beyond the mere shock of so hideous a catastrophe having fallen on a human being once so nearly connected with me, there would, in any case have been little to regret. Hookham, Longdill—every one, does *me* full justice;—bears testimony to the upright spirit and liberality of my conduct towards her:—there is but one voice in condemnation of the detestable Westbrooks. If they should dare to bring it before Chancery, a scene of such fearful horror would be unfolded as would cover them with scorn and shame."

The emotions contained in this letter are pity, disgust, anger and coldness, and it suggests a hysterical writer. These are perhaps stronger arguments for its authenticity than any other: for the letter fits Shelley's character in 1816. In addition, the facts are verifiable elsewhere. (Shelley's hasty belief in Harriet's "prostitution" is *not* a fact; he afterwards made it clear that he did not accept the allegation, and it is worth noting that the calumniator he was confuting then was William Godwin.)

The fact that Mary Shelley answered the letter on 17 December, whereas its opening suggests that it was written late on 16 December, has caused a little confusion. The mail between Bath and London would permit this, provided Shelley caught the last coach. The letter would not arrive in Bath till late on 17 December. But the evidence of date is in any case given far too much significance by some writers, for it is possible that either or both of the correspondents misdated a letter. When troubled, one does not necessarily demonstrate the accuracy of an almanac.

The letter exists in several forgeries, the market for such productions, notably in America, having made their manufacture inevitable. If the British Museum holograph, or some other, is indeed the original behind the several forgeries, the conclusion is assumed to be that Shelley was justified in the separation because he once sincerely believed that he had been cuckolded. This is a sweeping assumption, leaving out of account the possibility of other dissensions in which neither Shelley nor Harriet could be blamed or exonerated by outsiders. If the letter is a pure fabrication, the equally sweeping conclusion is adopted that Shelley was entirely in the wrong to separate from Harriet.

The quarrel between Shelley's biographers has long since pushed into the background the quarrel between Shelley and his first wife; in some ways that is the best conclusion to the affair, since all the investigation overlooks the fact that when a husband and wife reach the emotional pitch that demands a separation, the causes of the break may be unknown not only to their friends and relatives, but to themselves. We can at least ask how Shelley recorded in his poetry the critical emotional situation of spring, 1814. Certain expressions indicate that having married Harriet (chivalrously or stupidly) in 1811 without love for her, by 1814 he had fallen in love and had found that as his love increased, so hers waned—an emotional situation not unknown to men and women, and likely to reach a critical state if there is a third person, in the form of Eliza, on the scene.

In *Stanzas*, dated April, 1814, he wrote:

Pause not! The time is past! Every voice cries, Away!
    Tempt not with one last tear thy friend's ungentle mood:
Thy lover's eye, so glazed and cold, dares not entreat thy stay:
    Duty and dereliction guide thee back to solitude.
Away, away! to thy sad and silent home;
    Pour bitter tears on its desolated hearth;
Watch the dim shades as like ghosts they go and come,
    And complicate strange webs of melancholy mirth.

And in the first poem *Mutability*, written in 1814, the following stanzas occur:

> We rest.—A dream has power to poison sleep;
>   We rise.—One wandering thought pollutes the day;
> We feel, conceive or reason, laugh or weep;
>   Embrace fond woe, or cast our cares away.
>
> It is the same!—For, be it joy or sorrow,
>   The path of its departure still is free:
> Man's yesterday may ne'er be like his morrow;
>   Nought may endure but Mutability.

There may be something of Harriet—not prescience of her lonely death but a representation of her failure to respond to him—in the following lines supposedly written in 1815:

> The moon made thy lips pale, beloved—
>   The wind made thy bosom chill—
> The night did shed on thy dear head
>   Its frozen dew, and thou didst lie
> Where the bitter breath of the naked sky
>   Might visit thee at will.

Six months after Harriet's death, in the summer of 1817, Shelley wrote another stanza, in the dedication to Mary attached to *The Revolt of Islam*, which may not be entirely without significance as autobiography:

> Alas, that love should be a blight and snare
>   To those who seek all sympathies in one!—
> Such once I sought in vain; then black despair,
>   The shadow of a starless night, was thrown
>   Over the world in which I moved alone:—
> Yet never found I one not false to me,
>   Hard hearts, and cold, like weights of icy stone
> Which crushed and withered mine, that could not be
> Aught but a lifeless clod, until revived by thee.

So much for autobiography in poetry. In practical matters the legend that Harriet was driven to seek the support of a groom or even of an Army officer is not consistent with facts for which there is a warrant in legal documents. During the separation, Shelley was dunned for Harriet's debts as well as his own. In 1815, when at last he came into an income of £1,000 a year, he at once sent her £200 to clear her immediate debts, and settled an annuity of £200 a year upon her. She had also an annuity of £200 a year from her father. In 1815 and 1816 a woman with an income of £400 a year was not driven to prostitution or even, as Trelawny would have it, "compelled to seek a refuge in a cheaper lodging". Details of the settlement were naturally established by the defence in the Chancery case after her death.

It is fruitless to attempt fake-lawyer methods in order to establish who was to blame for the broken marriage, or whether Shelley knew or believed Harriet to be unfaithful. The causes of emotional breakdown are rarely those which can be established definitely by lawyers' reasoning and evidence produced before a court, even when the two litigants appear and attempts are made to analyse the physical causes of dissension. As for the much-discussed letter of 16 December, 1816, a great deal of paper and ink has been expended in establishing that it exists in several forgeries; yet, on the assumption that it is entirely fabricated, no explanation has ever been advanced to show why the forger, who worked for money by producing imitations of genuine letters, should have been at pains to whitewash Shelley.

Shelley's second marriage is documented in far greater detail than his first, yet it presents equally impenetrable mysteries. It began on a note of ecstasy and was preluded by an elopement. For a description of its physical object, the offspring of Shelley's idols, Mary Wollstonecraft and William Godwin, we can go to Mary Shelley's harshest critic, Claire, who began a bitter note on her half-sister with this attractive word-picture:

> "Mary's hair is light brown, of a sunny and burnished brightness like the autumnal foliage when played upon by the rays of the setting sun; it sets in round her face and

falls upon her shoulders in gauzy wavings and is so fine it looks as if the wind had tangled it together into golden network."

The biographical mysteries involving Mary are two. A third mystery, which will be discussed, was more the concern of Mary and her husband than of biographers and critics, though it may have had a bearing on one of the problems that are to be briefly discussed now.

The first question is whether Mary was in full possession of the facts about Elena Adelaide Shelley, the child born in Naples and the source of the "Hoppner scandal". This question has been asked by the biographers in something more than a spirit of idle curiosity. The precise answer has a bearing on Shelley's biography in that the existence of Elena Adelaide must, whether Shelley told the truth about her or not, have influenced the marriage; and this answer has a bearing on the poetry because Shelley's work is so richly autobiographical.

The second question is what influence Mary had on the state of Shelley's mind which, beginning with the "poems of dejection" of 1818, continued intermittently till the end of his life.

Both questions have been prejudged in various ways by various writers. After Shelley's death Mary applied herself, not unnaturally, to editing his works and helping to establish among posterity the reputation that he had been denied during his life. The task of editing was no easy one, and might well have earned a scholar unconnected with Shelley the unquestioned gratitude of posterity. During her widowhood (between 1822 and 1851) Mary also bought a number of Shelley's letters, genuine and forged. She allied herself with her son's wife, Lady Jane Shelley, who later played the part of main villainess in the piece, impelled by her embarrassing desire to present Shelley as a kind of angel. In this she was as harmful to Shelley as Byron, who called him Shiloh the Messiah with very different motives from those of Lady Jane. Canonizing Shelley, in Lady Jane's mind, necessarily involved blackening Harriet Shelley. The inevitable shuttling of sympathy took place: there were those who decided that if Harriet was innocent of blame,

Shelley must have been a thorough blackguard; and there were those who decided that if Harriet was blameworthy in any degree, Shelley must be faultless.

Claire, Trelawny and others wrote unkind things about Mary, often for reasons having little relation to the eight years she spent with Shelley. Claire was angry because after Shelley's death Mary "sneaked in upon any terms she could get into society"; yet towards the end of one of the bitter passages she wrote about her half-sister, Claire added, "She is a mixture of vanity and good nature." Trelawny was irked by Mary's refusal to marry him, though in justice to him it must be added that this was not the sole reason; he seems to have felt that Mary ought to have answered with more vigour and directness the people who denigrated Shelley so long after his death. A mass of second-, third- and fourth-hand criticisms against Mary gained circulation, and Crabb Robinson's is worth quoting as an example not because it has any biographical value but because it illustrates the taste for tittle-tattle and the waspishness of certain chroniclers of society and literature:

"Lady Blessington says," he wrote in 1832, "that Byron's hatred of Southey originated in Southey's saying that Lord Byron was *the lover of two sisters*, Mrs. Shelley and Miss Clairmont—not that he was offended by the immorality imputed to him, but the bad taste of loving so vulgar a woman as Mrs. Shelley. . . . Lord Byron was enraged that to the very last Shelley could never be made conscious of the artificial character and worthlessness of his wife."

Thus Mary Shelley suffered at the hands of partisans on all sides, and when her own biography came to be written its sympathies naturally enraged her enemies the more. It is therefore more difficult to write about Mary than to write about her husband, for any attempt to portray her as she may very well have been—as a woman with remarkably conflicting weaknesses and strength—is certain to invoke the wrath of the two camps. Not least of all, it may invoke the posthumous curse of Mary herself, who wrote, when discussing the poems Shelley wrote in 1821, "The heart of the man, abhorred by the poet, who could

> 'peep and botanise
> Upon his mother's grave',

does not appear to me more inexplicably framed than that of one who can dissect and probe past woes."

When Shelley met her and fell in love with her he greatly exaggerated her intellectual power; but Mary can scarcely be blamed for the lover's error or for the disillusionment that inevitably followed. Not all his friends shared his high opinion of her in the early days. Leigh Hunt's son Thornton, a child in 1817, saw her as a harassed, sharp-tongued, carelessly dressed young woman not in the best of health. Peacock and she were so temperamentally opposed that he once refused to enter the house at Marlow when she was at home, and in later years he refrained from writing a biography of Shelley because of this incurable dislike. Some sympathy for Mary is deserved because during the association of eight years she bore four children, and because the marriage was a tumultuous affair of travelling and finding new lodgings and houses.

Before the task of editing his works and preserving his memory (more often by remaining silent than by recording facts) devolved upon Mary and in some degree thickened the mystery of her relationship with Shelley, she gave way to human grief and bitterness and wrote words that posterity is apt to place as a stamp on the whole association. For instance, she recorded on 4 August, 1819:

> "I begin my Journal on Shelley's birthday. We have now lived five years together; and if all the events of the five years were blotted out, I might be happy; but to have won, and then cruelly to have lost, the association of four years is not an accident to which the human mind can bend without much suffering."

It is easy to read this as a comment on the marriage, until

it is recalled that Mary was writing two months after the death of William, "the association of four years"—a curious mode of referring to one's son. The mysterious child Elena Adelaide was living at Naples when those words were written, and the entry is a minor though far from conclusive indication that Mary did not at that time know of her existence. This supposition, as will be seen, throws a little light on the question of whether the existence of Elena Adelaide had anything to do with the crisis which took place between Shelley and Mary in 1818 and 1819.

What event or emotional crisis, other than the death of their child Clara, clouded the happiness of Shelley and Mary at the end of 1818, the year of their arrival in Italy? That there was some grief in addition to that caused by the child's death seems probable, for Shelley referred to it in many fragments of which the following is typical:

> The world is dreary,
> And I am weary
> Of wandering on without thee, Mary;
> A joy was erstwhile
> In thy voice and thy smile,
> And now 'tis gone, when I should be gone too, Mary.

The lines were written in 1819, according to Mary's dating, but they are in the mood of despondency that set in during the year of disaster. Mary made no secret of the deeply gloomy nature of Shelley's 1818 poems, which, she wrote, "he hid from fear of wounding me". After a eulogy of his intellectual and moral qualities, his generosity and understanding, his learning and his prodigious memory, she concluded her note with three lines from Petrarch:

> *Ahi orbo mondo ingrato!*
> *Gran cagione ài di dever pianger meco;*
> *Chè quel ben ch'era in te, perduto ài seco.*

(Alas, ungrateful world! You have good cause to feel you must weep with me; for what good lay in you, you have lost in him.)

These lines, which occur in Petrarch's Canzone I on the death of Laura, are one of three quotations from Shelley's favourite poet which Mary Shelley put into print. What Mary Shelley was in fact saying about the year 1818 can be appreciated when the lines immediately preceding the quotation, and the sense Petrarch was expressing, are examined. The poet is addressing not "the ungrateful world", but Love:

> Amor, tu 'l senti, ond'io teco mi doglio,
> Quant'è 'l danno aspro e grave;
> E so che del mio mal ti pesa e dole,
> Anzi del nostro; perchè ad uno scoglio
> Avem rotto la nave,
> Ed in un punto n'è scurato il sole.
> Qual ingegno a parole
> Poria agguagliar il mio doglioso stato?

(Love, you feel how bitter and heavy is the loss I mourn with you; and I know that it is my misfortune rather than ours which weighs on you and grieves you; for we wrecked the ship on a rock, and in an instant the sun was darkened. What ingenuity with words can smooth my mournful state?)

This is precisely the mood of Mary's poem *The Choice*:

> Now fierce remorse and unreplying death
> Waken a chord within my heart, whose breath
> Thrilling and keen, in accents audible
> A tale of unrequited love doth tell.
> It was not anger,—while thy earthly dress
> Encompassed still thy soul's rare loveliness,
> All anger was atoned by many a kind
> Caress or tear, that spoke the softened mind. . . .
> My heart was all thine own,—but yet a shell
> Closed in its core, which seemed impenetrable.

The Shelleys travelled to Italy, taking Claire and Allegra, in March, 1818. Mary is referred to in terms of great affection in poems and letters written in the first eight months of the year. When, having concluded the difficult business of Allegra and Byron satisfactorily, as he thought, he asked Mary to join him at Este, he wrote in terms of considerable tenderness, and what may be the last couplet he wrote before her arrival, and the catastrophe, ran:

> O Mary dear, that you were here;
> The Castle echo whispers "Here!"

As a result of that journey in the heat of the first days of September the twelve-months-old baby Clara died. At this point the poems of dejection begin; but their theme is not the death of a child. Their key-note is sounded by such lines as:

> Forget the dead, the past? Oh, yet
> There are ghosts that may take revenge for it.
> (*The Past*)

> It lies on my abandoned breast
> And mocks the heart which yet is warm.
> (*On a Faded Violet*)

> Every little living nerve
> That from bitter words did swerve
> Round the tortured lips and brow,
> Are like sapless leaflets now
> Frozen upon December's bough.
> (*Lines Written Among the Euganean Hills*)

> And if I think, my thoughts come fast,
> I mix the present with the past,
> And each seems uglier than the last.
> (*Song for Tasso*)

To this year belong also the *Stanzas* written near Naples, the sonnet *Lift not the painted veil,* and *The Woodman and the Nightingale,* which describes the destruction of love, personified by the Nightingale, not by the Devil, or woman, or destiny, but by the Woodman.

The mood of these poems was one which persisted till the end of Shelley's life. It is reproduced in *Orpheus* (1820):

> Orpheus, seized and torn
> By the sharp fangs of an insatiate grief,
> Mænad-like waved his lyre in the bright air,
> And wildly shrieked "Where she is, it is dark!"

It reappears in the lines written in 1821:

> It were enough to feel, to see,
> Thy soft eyes gazing tenderly,
> And dream the rest—and burn and be
> The secret food of fires unseen,
> Couldst thou but be as thou hast been.

The catastrophe, greater even than the death of Clara (which did not leave Mary childless, for William still lived), was therefore written of plainly in Shelley's and Mary's poems. That it resulted in a dissension probably as great as that which had separated Harriet and Shelley, and that the dissension remained unresolved at the time of Shelley's death, is abundantly clear. Some forms of its expression have already been quoted from the poems written late in 1821 and in 1822. What was its cause?

The critic or biographer who gave a definite answer to this question would be as bold and ill-advised as any who have answered the similar question, "Why did Shelley and Harriet separate?" Yet there is much more definite information about the second catastrophe than about the first, so various possible answers may be briefly examined. The possibilities are (1) that Clara's death alone was rock on which, in Petrarch's words, they wrecked the ship; (2) that Shelley confessed an offence which Mary never forgave; (3) that Mary uttered some words that were terrible enough to destroy the heart of the marriage though not to separate them.

The first possibility seems unreal and untrue to the natures of both Mary and Shelley. Both were familiar with death, and they had lost their first child; William remained to console them; there was a possibility that Shelley might persuade Byron to allow them to adopt Allegra; here, though the children's death was a great sorrow, were not to be found the sources of complete emotional breakdown. Something else injected the poison.

The second possibility might involve Elena Adelaide, born at the end of 1818—but only if Shelley was the child's father. Shelley's poetry of the time contains no references to another love, an infidelity, or the mystery or menace of an unborn child for which he would be responsible; its dominant stress is on Mary's implacable coldness. In later poems there are no references that might be linked with the child's life or death. The second possibility, therefore, seems to have little substance.

The third possibility is not strengthened by the fact that the other two offer weak grounds for belief—that is an error too often made by those who apply fake-lawyer methods of reasoning to this and other episodes in Shelley's life. If it is to be more than an idle speculation, some evidence for it must be found in something that Shelley or Mary, or both, confided to friends or put into writing. There was no confiding in friends on this intimate matter, as far as we know. As for writings, there are Mary's *The Choice* and her selection of part of Petrarch's Canzone I, cited earlier; and there is Shelley's *Julian and Maddalo*.

The salient passages from this poem, which describes the visit paid by Maddalo (Byron) and Julian (Shelley) to the Madman on an island west of the Lido of Venice, belong to the lengthy, rambling and painful monologue of the Madman, about whom all that is known is that

> A lady came with him from France, and when
> She left him and returned, he wandered then
> About yon lonely isles of desert sand
> Till he grew wild.

The lady who caused the breakdown is represented as living, and returning to visit him later. Some commentators have assumed that Shelley was writing of nothing more than the parting between himself and Harriet. The passages which might be supposed to be tortured autobiography are:

> "Month after month," he cried, "to bear this load,
> And as a jade urged by the whip and goad
> To drag life on,—which like a heavy chain
> Lengthens behind with many a link of pain!—
> And not to speak my grief—O, not to dare
> To give a human voice to my despair,

> But live and move, and, wretched thing! smile on
> As if I never went aside to groan;
> And wear this mask of falsehood even to those
> Who are most dear; not for my own repose,—
> Alas, no scorn or pain or hate could be
> So heavy as that falsehood is to me,—
> But that I cannot bear more altered faces
> Than needs must be, more changed and cold embraces
> More misery, disappointment and mistrust,
> To own me for their father. . . .
>
> *(Lines* 300–315)

> "What power delights to torture us? I know
> That to myself I do not wholly owe
> What now I suffer, though in part I may.
> Alas! none strewed sweet flowers upon the way
> Where wandering heedlessly, I met pale Pain,
> My shadow, which will leave me not again.—
> If I have erred, there was no joy in error,
> But pain and insult and unrest and terror;
> I have not as some do, bought penitence
> With pleasure, and a dark yet sweet offence;
> For then,—if love and tenderness and truth
> Had overlived hope's momentary youth,
> My creed should have redeemed me from repenting;
> But loathèd scorn and outrage unrelenting
> Met love excited by far other seeming,
> Until the end was gained . . . As one from dreaming
> Of sweetest peace, I woke, and found my state
> Such as it is.—
>   "O Thou, my spirit's mate,
> Who, for thou art compassionate and wise,
> Wouldst pity me from thy most gentle eyes
> If this sad writing thou shouldst ever see—
> My secret groans must be unheard by thee;
> Thou wouldst weep tears bitter as blood to know
> Thy lost friend's incommunicable woe.
>
> *(Lines* 320–343)

> "As some perverted beings think to find
> In scorn or hate a medicine for the mind
> Which scorn or hate have wounded.—O, how vain!

The dagger heals not but may rend again . . .
Believe that I am ever still the same
In creed as in resolve; and what may tame
My heart, must leave the understanding free,
Or all would sink in this keen agony.—
Nor dream that I will join the vulgar cry,
Or with my silence sanction tyranny,
Or seek a moment's shelter from my pain
In any madness which the world calls gain;
Ambition or revenge or thoughts as stern
As those which make me what I am, or turn
To avarice or misanthropy or lust . . .
                              (*Lines* 354-368)

                    "I must remove
A veil from my pent mind. 'Tis torn aside!
O, pallid as Death's dedicated bride,
Thou mockery which art sitting by my side,
Am I not wan like thee? At the grave's call
I haste, invited to thy wedding-ball
To greet the ghastly paramour, for whom
Thou hast deserted me . . . and made the tomb
Thy bridal bed . . . But I beside your feet
Will lie and watch ye from my winding sheet
Thus . . . wide awake though dead . . . Yet stay, O, stay!
Go not so soon—I know not what I say—
Hear but my reasons . . . I am mad, I fear,—
My fancy is o'erwrought . . . thou art not here . . .
Pale art thou, 'tis most true . . . but thou art gone,
Thy work is finished . . . I am left alone!—

    "Nay, was it I who wooed thee to this breast
Which, like a serpent thou envenomest
As in repayment of the warmth it lent?
Didst thou not seek me for thine own content?
Did not thy love awaken mine? I thought
That thou wert she who said, 'You kiss me not
Ever; I fear you do not love me now.'
In truth I loved even to my overthrow
Her, who would fain forget these words: but they
Cling to her mind, and cannot pass away.

"You say that I am proud—that when I speak
My lip is tortured with the wrongs which break
The spirit it expresses . . . Never one
Humbled himself before, as I have done!
Even the instinctive worm on which we tread
Turns, tho' it wound not—then with prostrate head,
Sinks in the dust and writhes like me—and dies?
No: wears a living death of agonies!
As the slow shadows of the pointed grass
Mark the eternal periods, his pangs pass
Slow, ever-moving,—making moments be
As mine seem—each an immortality!

"That you had never seen me—never heard
My voice, and more than all, had ne'er endured
The deep pollution of my loathed embrace:
That your eyes ne'er had lied love in my face:
That, like some maniac monk, I had torn out
The nerves of manhood by their bleeding root
With mine own quivering fingers, so that ne'er
Our hearts had for a moment mingled there
To disunite in horror:—these were not
With thee, like some suppressed and hideous thought
Which flits athwart our musings, but can find
No rest within a pure and gentle mind;
Thou sealedst them with many a bare broad word,
And searedst my memory o'er them,—for I heard
And can forget not;—they were ministered
One after one, those curses. Mix them up
Like self-destroying poisons in one cup,
And they will make one blessing which thou ne'er
Didst imprecate for, on me,—death.

"It were
A cruel punishment for one most cruel,
If such can love, to make that love the fuel
Of the mind's hell—hate, scorn, remorse, despair:
But *me*—whose heart a stranger's tear might wear,
As water-drops the sandy fountain-stone;
Who loved and pitied all things, and could moan
For woes which others hear not, and could see
The absent with the glance of phantasy,

And with the poor and trampled sit and weep,
Following the captive to his dungeon deep;
Me—who am as a nerve o'er which do creep
The else unfelt oppressions of this earth,
And was to thee the flame upon thy hearth,
When all beside was cold:—that thou on me
Shouldst rain these plagues of blistering agony . . .
(Lines 383–453)

"Thou wilt tell,
With the grimace of hate, how horrible
It was to meet my love when thine grew less;
Thou wilt admire how I could e'er address
Such features to love's work . . . This taunt, though true,
(For indeed Nature nor in form nor hue
Bestowed on me her choicest workmanship)
Shall not be thy defence . . . for since thy lip
Met mine first, years long past—since thine eye kindled
With soft fire under mine, I have not dwindled
Nor changed in mind or body, or in aught
But as love changes what it loveth not
After long years and many trials.

"How vain
Are words! I thought never to speak again,
Not even in secret,—not to my own heart;
But from my lips the unwilling accents start,
And from my pen the words flow as I write,
Dazzling my eyes with scalding tears . . . my sight
Is dim to see that charactered in vain
On this unfeeling leaf, which burns the brain
And eats into it . . . blotting all things fair
And wise and good which Time had written there.

"Those who inflict must suffer, for they see
The work of their own hearts, and this must be
Our chastisement or recompense,—O child!
I would that thine were like to be more mild
For both our wretched sakes,—for thine the most,
Who feel'st already all that thou hast lost,
Without the power to wish it thine again;
And as slow years pass, a funereal train

Each with the ghost of some lost hope or friend
Following it like its shadow, wilt thou bend
No thought on my dead memory?

(Lines 461-492)

"I give thee tears for scorn, and love for hate;
And that thy lot may be less desolate
Than his on whom thou tramplest, I refrain
From that sweet sleep which medicines all pain.
Then, when thou speakest of me, never say
'He could forgive not.' Here I cast away
All human passions, all revenge, all pride;
I think, speak, act no ill; I do but hide
Under these words, like embers, every spark
Of that which has consumed me."

(Lines 496-505)

After listening to this searing accusation, confession or analysis, Julian and Maddalo

agreed his was some dreadful ill
Wrought on him boldly, yet unspeakable,
By a dear friend; some deadly change in love
Of one vowed deeply, which he dreamed not of;
For whose sake he, it seemed, had fixed a blot
Of falsehood on his mind which flourished not
But in the light of all-beholding truth;
And having stamped this canker on his youth
She had abandoned him.

(Lines 525-533)

The poet then relates how Julian leaves Venice, to return after many years and meet Maddalo's daughter (Allegra), now grown to womanhood, who reports that the "lady" returned to the Madman in remorse, but left him after all; and in reply to Julian's questions she says:

"Ask me no more, but let the silent years
Be closed and cered over their memory,
As yon mute marble where their corpses lie."
I urged and questioned still, she told me how
All happened—but the cold world shall not know.

(Line 613—end)

These extracts have been quoted at length because they form the most emphatic and tortured, and in some ways the most unguarded, pieces of autobiography in Shelley's poetry, and because they tell the story of the crisis of 1818 which continued till Shelley's death and afterwards prompted Mary to edit even his most bitter and despairing poems honestly, to write *The Choice* and choose tributes from Petrarch, and to refrain from writing his life or her own.

She eschewed both biography and autobiography, it may be, because she wanted neither to lie nor to tell the truth—and she could not have written without doing one or the other.

The passages quoted have always remained obscure for lack of the right biographical key, the answer to the question, "What was the lady's crime?" After the implausible suggestion that the lady was Harriet had been dismissed, a few critics tried without success to interpret the poem in the light of a confession of error by the Madman.

The "third possibility" of explaining the crisis of 1818, based on the idea that the "bare broad words" spoken by Mary caused a kind of earthquake in Shelley's spirit, may be simply this: that Mary told Shelley, in a moment of intense grief following Clara's death, and when William Shelley was the only link, "the association" between them, that she had once taken another lover.

At this stage I do not intend to annotate the preceding extracts, but I ask the reader—and in particular the reader who has a sound knowledge of the Shelley texts and is hence familiar with his idiom—to re-read the passages in the light of the supposition that the Madman, an avowed rebel and a believer in unfettered love free of the "mask of falsehood", has been told of his betrayal during a moment of anguish and revulsion, "some deadly change in love", by the woman who has abandoned him. All I claim for the present is that even the punctuation and syntax—and these are often the heart of the matter in Shelley—are clarified by the hypothesis I have put forward.

If the hypothesis is to be considered, the biographer must ask who could have been the supposed lover of Mary Shelley.

For the curious, some of the undercurrents in Shelley's two marriages are revealed by a careful consideration of the part played in his life by Thomas Jefferson Hogg.

Hogg was the young man Shelley met at Oxford, and who was sent down with him for refusing to admit to the authorship of *The Necessity of Atheism*. He was chosen by Shelley's son, Sir Percy, as official biographer, since he knew Shelley so well during the formative years—that is, till 1818; but the tone of the first two volumes of the biography prompted Sir Percy to apply for an injunction to restrain him from publishing more. Several people who knew Shelley approved of this drastic action, for they considered Hogg's presentation of the poet when young to be a caricature. There are some readers who find the biography entertaining, as indeed it is until one sees its subject through the eyes of other men and women, and begins to perceive its subtle distortion.

A deep envy runs through what Hogg wrote about Shelley; the writer may not have been quite conscious of it himself. Setting out to depict the character of the genius when young, he creates the character of an eccentric, the kind of fantastic who is produced by every university and soon forgotten. He deliberately picks out the foolish enthusiasms, the sentimentality, the youthful showing-off, making these the main colours in the portrait. He does not balance his account by giving proper weight to the other facts about the astounding youth who wrote such things as the notes to *Queen Mab*, which though out of date in parts can still make good reading and can surprise, by their wit and penetration and prose mastery, the reader who approaches them confirmed in the Hogg view that the youth was all enthusiasms and palpitations. It was in these notes that the boy who was to be regarded as the enemy of the sanctity of marriage commented:

> "Solomon kept a thousand concubines, and owned in despair that all was vanity. The man whose happiness is constituted by the society of one amiable woman would find some difficulty in sympathizing with the disappointment of this venerable debauchee."

The envy and mockery which could not be allowed open

expression in Hogg's biography and which worked their way through the account in the form of the lines of caricature possibly had their origin in sexual jealousy. Some of Shelley's letters, printed by Hogg, were falsified, and one of them, printed as if it were part of a novel, was in fact Shelley's reproach against Hogg for attempting to seduce Harriet Shelley. The forgiveness that Shelley extended to Hogg after this incident has tended to obscure the importance played in Shelley's life by Hogg's sexual activities, not all of which were known to the poet.

Hogg was a cynic, and he appears to have formed a plan to seduce Harriet almost as soon as Shelley introduced them. The couple had been married only a few weeks when Shelley, called away on business in Sussex, left Harriet in Hogg's care in York. Hogg interpreted Shelley's view, that human beings should freely seek their partners and should not be shackled by legal chains, as permission given to him to lay siege to Harriet; notable for prudence, he carefully waited till Shelley was absent from York before attempting the seduction. The story came out when Shelley, on his return, noticed a change in Harriet's attitude to Hogg.

The effect on Shelley was shattering, and should not be underrated as an emotional influence. It was not so much raw sexual resentment that worked in him as the knowledge that the betrayer was the man he considered his best friend. To his friend Elizabeth Hitchener he wrote, "This stroke almost withered my being." He spoke and wrote bitterly to Hogg, telling him that it was his vice, not Hogg, that he found horrible. Hogg made suitable gestures of remorse, tried to persuade the philosopher that to lust after Harriet was no vice, and begged to be allowed to live with the Shelleys as a pure friend. Shelley was not such a fool as Hogg made out in other terms when the biography came to be written; soon he left York without telling Hogg of his intention, for he did not believe that Hogg's professed platonics would resist the temptations of proximity. The incident was not closed in Shelley's consciousness as promptly as appears when one reads biography wholly according to chronology; later he wrote to Hogg, "Consider what havoc one year, the last of our lives, has made in memory", and he was referring to the seduction attempt as well as to their expulsion from Oxford. And "You a female Hogg!" he wrote indignantly to Elizabeth Hitchener when the gossips went to work on his friendship with her.

All that needs to be added is that long afterwards, when Harriet and Shelley were dead and it was in the interest of Lady Jane Shelley to establish that Harriet was wholly to blame for the separation, Hogg came valiantly to Lady Jane's assistance, though he was embarrassed by the fact that he could not cast himself in the role of Harriet's seducer. He got out of the difficulty by declaring that Thomas Love Peacock had seduced Harriet; incidentally, he assured Trelawny that Harriet was guilty of all offence.

In disentangling the emotional threads that went to the weaving of Shelley's poetry we must remember that many of the facts known to posterity were unknown to him. He knew of Hogg's offence against Harriet and himself and forgave it, but there is no indication that he knew of Hogg's offence, in 1815, against Mary and himself. A brief examination of this incident, unpalatable as it is, must be made for two reasons. The first is that if Mary did indeed destroy Shelley's peace of mind in 1818 by confessing to an infidelity without naming the man, Hogg may have been the person she was thinking of, and therefore the shadow across the pages of *Julian and Maddalo* may, unknown to the poet, have been that of Hogg; the second is that the letters which tell part of the story have not been discussed as evidence of anything more than a sentimental friendship.

By November, 1814, three months after Shelley's elopement with Mary, the friendship with Hogg was only superficially on its old footing. Hogg's cynicism had not abated, judging from the remarks he made on 7 November, which Shelley reported to Claire next day: "Hogg had been with him the evening before and asked him after his *two wives*." "I am disappointed in him," Shelley wrote, "though my expectations were very moderate." Later, a less icy comment, "Perhaps he still may be my friend, in spite of the radical differences of sympathy between us; he was pleased with Mary; this was the test by which I had previously determined to judge his

A page from a Shelley notebook, with his drawing of a labyrinth (Bodleian Library)

Lerici seen from Casa Magni. (Nineteenth-century photograph)

Carrara. From William Brockedon's *Italy*

character." The comment is made in the diary kept jointly by Shelley and Mary: Shelley was not concealing from Mary the coldness of his feelings towards Hogg, a fact which has quite an important bearing on what happened a few weeks later.

Hogg's prudence, however, was if anything greater than before. On 1 January, 1815, when Shelley had known Mary six months, and she was carrying his child, Hogg protested his love to Mary but did not risk Shelley's discovering that his friend now proposed to seduce his mistress as three years before he had attempted to become the lover of his wife. The affair is recorded in Mary's letters to Hogg, which she scrawled hastily, assuming that he would destroy them; his letters to her were presumably destroyed immediately after reading.

Mary's first letter—"prattle", as she called it—sets the sentimental tone. She wishes that she could return his love "with the passion you deserve", and promises to "use every effort to promote your happiness". By 4 January she is reporting that Shelley and Claire have gone out "and from the number and distance of the places they are going to I do not expect them till very late" so "perhaps you can come and console a solitary lady". She now considers Hogg so good and disinterested that she loves him more and more. Doubtless aware of his prudence, she adds, "By the bye when Shelley is in the country we shall never be alone so perhaps this is the last opportunity for a long time—but still I do not wish to persuade you to do that which you ought not." After writing "With one kiss", she adds a postscript in which she asks that if he cannot come "now", he should come earlier that evening.

By 7 January her ardour has progressed beyond one kiss, for she sends a lock of her hair and writes:

"I sincerely believe that we shall all be happy! My affection for you although it is not now exactly as you would wish will I think dayly become more so—then what can you have to add to your happiness—I ask but for time—time which for other causes besides this—physical causes—that must be given—Shelley will be subject to these also—and this dear Hogg will give time for that love to spring up which you deserve and will one day have.

K

All this—you know is sweet hope but we need not be
prudent now—for I will try to make you happy and you
say it is in my power."

The letter shows that the ardour is on Hogg's side, the
sentimental response on Mary's. There is still no indication
that Shelley has been consulted about the means she proposes
to make them "all" happy.

On 23 January Mary writes promising Hogg "joy and
delight" in the summer when she has her baby (expected
presumably in April), and she adds that they will have great
happiness in Shelley himself because Mary's "whole soul is
entirely wrapt up in him" and Hogg has "so sincere a friendship for him". The idea seems to be that the love affair on
coming to maturity will delight Shelley, who is still apparently
in ignorance of the surprise arranged for him; the letter ends,
"Shelley and Cl. are talking beside me which is not a very good
accompaniment when one is writing a letter to one, one loves."

During February Mary gave birth to a seven-months child,
who died on 6 March. On 28 February Shelley, seriously ill,
consulted a doctor who gave the opinion that abcesses were
forming on his lungs and that he was rapidly dying of consumption. That Mary knew of this diagnosis is made clear by
her notes to his poems for that period. For some time (until
17 April) Hogg appears to have lodged with the Shelleys,
though early in March there is correspondence which shows
that Hogg is encouraged to use the pet names Shelley had
given to Mary—"The Maië", "Pecksie" and "The Dormouse".
She writes to tell him, among other things, to bring back her
garters. By April Hogg's passion seems to be waning, but
Mary's is waxing, even adopting a demanding tone. There is a
significant postscript to one letter:

"I will write Lawrence[1] and you must go to A. Row for
the letter as I shall send it by coach. You must not (tell)
Clare of the invitation.
You can write direct as C. shall direct."

[1] Shelley's doctor. The following year, Claire used an address in Arabella
Row, Pimlico, during her secret communication with Byron.

Shelley was on the run from creditors at this time, but he had to make sorties to lawyers' offices as well as doctors' surgeries, for the death of his grandfather, in January, produced legal tangles the unravelling of which demanded his presence. Whether the invitation that must be kept secret from Claire refers to the doctor or to Hogg is not clear, but evidently she is being used to communicate to Hogg the address at which he can write to Mary.

The friend has now become "Dear Jefferson"; Mary is in the country and Hogg remains prudently in town, where in any case he has his own law business to attend to. The attentions of bailiffs had caused Shelley to move out to the country. The affair appears to have reached its climax at the end of April or the beginning of May. On 25 April Mary writes in a vein of coquettishness:

"Remember nothing take(s) away my maiëishness.
    For Maië girls are Maië girls
    Wherever they're found
    In air or in water
    Or in the ground."

Next day she writes:

"How are you amusing yourself with the Pecksie away very doleful no doubt but my poor Jefferson I shall soon be up again and you may remember that even if we had staid you would not have seen much of me as you must have been with me—
Do you mean to come down to us—I suppose not Prince Prudent well as you please but remember I should be *very* happy to see you."

Entries for the days between 24 April and 5 May are torn out of her journal. On 26 April she writes to Hogg, "You must not go to courts very early to-morrow as it is very likely we shall be with you about nine." She then speaks of the danger of Shelley's remaining in London with the bailiffs' spies looking for him.

"The Dormouse is going to take a long ramble today among green fields and solitary lanes as happy as any little animal could be in finding herself in her nature nests again —I shudder to think of breathing the air of London again —Jefferson Jefferson it is your duty not (to) keep any creature away from its home so come—I shall expect you tonight and if you do not come I am off—not to London I promise you—

But dear Jefferson all things considered the danger of Shelley remaining in London and my hatred of it do you not think you ought to come to Salt Hill *incontinently*—Remember I shall believe that your love is all a farce if you do not—so I expect you."

The "we" in this letter appears to refer to Mary and Claire, and the expressions used suggest that Shelley was in London.

So much for the available letters. Another part of the picture—the part known to Shelley—may be constructed from the following facts. In addition to being weighed down by legal troubles, debts and the doctor's verdict, Shelley was worried about Harriet's future and the debts she was contracting and for which he was responsible. By June, when his income was settled, he was able to send her £200 to pay off these debts, and settle on her the £200 which she could add to the similar annual amount she received from her family. Mary quarrelled with Claire, who frequently accompanied Shelley on his outings. The notes made by Mary in her journal on this side of their life express irritation and contempt for Claire, rather than jealousy. Claire's letter to her half-sister Fanny, written after she had gone to live elsewhere, makes no secret of the squabbles and does not read like the letter of a girl who wished to filch Shelley from Mary, and who had been driven ignominiously from his home:

"After so much discontent, such violent scenes, such a turmoil of passion and hatred, you will hardly believe how enraptured I am with this dear little quiet spot."

The possibility that Mary flirted with Hogg in order to play off the "dear friend" against Claire is faintly suggested by her note on the day Claire left, 13 May, "I begin a new Journal with our regeneration."

That Mary resented Claire is made clear by words such as these, written in her journal on 12 May:

> "Shelley goes out with his friend; he returns first. . . . Read over the Ovid to Jefferson and construe about ten lines more. Read Spenser. . . . Shelley and the lady walk out. After tea, talk; write Greek characters. Shelley and his friend have a last conversation."

This does not read like well-grounded sexual jealousy; it is the resentful expression of a woman envious of the sympathy that Shelley was expending on someone else; and read in conjunction with the letters to Hogg it creates a picture of a woman not above assuaging her physical loneliness by accepting Hogg as a lover.

Whatever happened between Mary and Hogg between 24 April and 5 May, there is strong evidence for the fact that Shelley knew nothing of the affair or of Mary's promise to Hogg that in the summer he should become her lover. At least two statements of his own indicate what Shelley's feelings would have been had Mary confided to him the summer scheme that she was planning. On 14 November, 1814, a few days after Hogg had inquired after his "two wives", Shelley wrote:

> "Perhaps he may still be my friend in spite of the radical differences of sympathy between us; he was pleased with Mary; this was the test by which I had previously determined to judge his character."

And when he reviewed the novel Hogg had written, his bid to join the ranks of the facetious school which was to succeed only when, much later, he wrote Shelley's biography, the poet praised *The Memoirs of Prince Alexey Haimatoff* with the following qualification:

"We cannot regard his commendation to his pupil to indulge in promiscuous concubinage without horror and detestation. The author appears to deem the loveless intercourse of brutal appetite, a venial offence against delicacy and virtue! he asserts that a transient connection with a cultivated female may contribute to form the heart without essentially vitiating the sensibilities. It is our duty to protest against so pernicious and disgusting an opinion."

Shelley's review is a puff for his friend's book, but the following words from the notice have a not unexpected resemblance to his mysterious poem *The Sensitive Plant*:

"It is an unweeded garden where nightshade is interwoven with sweet jessamine, and the most delicate spices of the east, peep over struggling stalks of rank and poisonous hemlock."

Of Hogg's amatory preoccupations Shelley writes further:

"We think that the interesting subject of sexual relations requires for its successful development the application of a mind thus organized and endowed. Yet even here how great the deficiencies; this mind must be pure from the fashionable superstition of gallantry, must be exempt from the sordid feelings which with blind idolatry worship the image and blaspheme the deity, reverence the type, and degrade the reality of which it is an emblem."

Were these words written by a man who, as some writers have stated, was at that time agreeing to the proposal that T. J. Hogg should become Mary's lover? It looks as if she is the exponent of free love, and Shelley the idealist. If Mary ever spoke to him about the suggestion that Hogg should live with them permanently, it may be that he understood her to mean that Hogg should live with them as a friend or brother. There is no warrant for believing that Shelley knew the true circumstances: that before the birth of the child, Mary had without equivocation promised Hogg that she would be his mistress;

that two months after the birth and death of the child she was addressing him coquettish invitations; that the day after a doctor told Shelley that he was dying of consumption, Mary was writing to Hogg, requesting him to return her garters.

However much or little Shelley knew, the aftermath was curiously like that of the Harriet affair. In June, Shelley took Mary to the West Country to look for a house. Between June and July he was absent from Mary for a month, leaving her at Clifton, whence she wrote him tearful pleas not to stay away from her. Thereafter Hogg did not enjoy the confidence of either Mary or Shelley, as formerly. On her return from the summer visit to Switzerland, 1816, Mary writes to Leigh Hunt describing Hogg as "more disagreeable than ever". She adds, "I would not have him come every week to disturb our peace by his ill humour and noise for all the world." Perhaps he was not quite so disagreeable as she says; it is likely that her glancing occasionally into Shelley's eyes, and reading there a trust which discomfited her, prompted her to wish to break off the association.

A poetic version of what Shelley had written in the *Haimatoff* review on Hogg's view of sexual conduct appears in his summer task for 1817, that rich but neglected poem *The Revolt of Islam*, where he writes of lust:

> what a loathsome agony
> Is that when selfishness mocks love's delight,
> Foul as in dream's most fearful imagery
> To dally with the mowing dead.

If between 24 April and 5 May, 1815, Mary Shelley was led into what she later termed "erroneous conduct" in relation to Hogg, and if the paternity of William Shelley (born 24 January, 1816) is thus placed in doubt, the sixth line in the third stanza of Shelley's poem to the child he so deeply loved may be meaningful and not (as would appear if it were read in any other light) merely weak:

> Come thou, beloved as thou art;
>   Another sleepeth still
> Near thy sweet mother's anxious heart,
>   Which thou with joy shalt fill,

> With fairest smiles of wonder thrown
> On that which is indeed our own,
> And which in distant lands will be
> The dearest playmate unto thee.

In this poem, *To William Shelley,* the reference to the unborn Clara (born 2 September, 1817) bears out Mary's dating of the work as 1817, and the theme—an imagined flight with William from "the slaves of the law"—tallies with the words that Shelley wrote to Byron on 9 July of that year:

> "It is possible that the interference exercised by Chancery in the instance of my two other children might be attempted to be extended to William. Should this be the case, I shall depart."

The point is not an unimportant one, because the lines were included in Mary's edition *Posthumous Poems,* and the accuracy of her dates in relation to certain poems dealing with Shelley's deepest feelings has already been questioned by Professor N. I. White. The sixth line might, of course, have been added later during revision: possibly when on the death of William in June, 1819, Shelley wrote the second poem *To William Shelley*:

> But beneath this pyramid
> Thou art not—if a thing divine
> Like thee can die, thy funeral shrine
> Is thy mother's grief and mine.

It will be remembered that this poem, which describes the Roman cemetery where William was buried, is prefaced by the curious comment:

> With what truth may I say—
> Roma! Roma! Roma!
> *Non è più come era prima.*[1]

If on that day in September, 1818, when Clara, whose

---

[1] "It is no longer as it was before." The line occurs in a popular song that Shelley heard in Rome.

resemblance to Shelley Mary noted, died and left Mary the mother of a son whose father might not be Shelley, something of her bitterness and regret might be understood, something of her "fierce remorse"; and the emotional crisis and her grief recorded on William's death might become clearer . . .

> "If all the events of the five years were blotted out, I might be happy; but to have won, and then cruelly to have lost, the association of four years is not an accident to which the human mind can bend without much suffering."

The remainder of Hogg's story may be told briefly. On 28 February, 1823, the widow Mary Shelley wrote him a long letter from Genoa. On Shelley's death, Hogg had not written to her; he had sent a message through Jane Williams, then in England, to state that he had not the heart to write to her. Mary was lonely and poor; she was so unsure of herself that, as her letters to Byron reveal, she repeatedly applied for permission to see that poet, and swallowed the humiliation of not being permitted free access to him: "I would come down, but I have found that there is small chance of seeing you when I do." Mary wrote to Hogg not to beg money, but to ask advice about returning to England. In the long, pathetic letter she wrote:

> "Although our connection was marked by storms; and circumstances led often into erroneous conduct with regard to you, yet now bereft of all, I willingly turn to my Shelley's dearest friend, and to one whom I am persuaded notwithstanding all thinks kindly of me."

She expresses her terror of the future and writes:

> "I think even to madness and torture of the past." In study "I find an opiate which at least adds nothing to the pain of regret that must necessarily be mine forever."

These are strong expressions of remorse. She feared not only poverty (she would not come into her inheritance till Sir

Timothy Shelley died) but the possibility that "they" would take her child from her if she returned to England. She feared, too, becoming dependant on her friends.

To this letter Hogg made no reply. Through Jane Williams he used arguments to persuade Mary to remain in Italy. He hoped that Byron and Trelawny would not give her the money to travel to England. He wrote to Jane:

> "Her want of conduct will injure her cause; she has not discretion enough to make the tribute, which the world demands in England (and I suppose in all other places) from the natives light and easy, that is *to appear* to live like other people."

Hogg was a lawyer, and prudence was his star; he even named his daughter Prudentia. Possibly one of his motives for wishing Mary Shelley to remain outside England was uncovered by Mary herself when in 1847, four years before her death, she wrote to a friend:

> "When I think of my melancholy return to England in 23 and the natural interest one would suppose a young widow with an infant son—the heir to a good fortune might have inspired—and the solitude and friendlessness of my position."

He feared, perhaps, being drawn into marriage with Shelley's widow; he certainly feared her indiscretion.

Trelawny met him, wrote some flattering things about him for publication, but referred to him elsewhere as "a thoroughbred hog". Sir Percy Florence had to restrain Hogg by writ from publishing the third volume of his life of Shelley, though in the course of composition of the first two volumes Sir Percy's wife, Lady Jane Shelley, was on excellent terms with Hogg.

Hogg died in 1862. His ambition to become a popular novelist of the comic school had been thwarted, and sadly, he had become a comic figure himself, for he was so fat that a visitor recorded her firm belief that he could not clasp his hands in front of his stomach. Whether he wrote the third volume of the biography is doubtful; Jane Williams told William Rossetti, ten years after Hogg's death, that he had completed the book but that she had not read the manuscript.

His amorous excursions had not ceased to touch the Shelley circle on Shelley's death. Scarcely nine months after the drowning of Shelley and Edward Williams, Hogg was writing in his characteristic epistolary style to Jane Williams:

> "How I long, dearest Jane, to add a few more chapters to our secret history and surprising adventures and to taste once more as much happiness as is consistent with discretion."

As in connection with the Harriet affair eleven years earlier, he evidently held to the lawyer's definition of the term seduction, as distinct from that which is adopted by modern psychologists.

If all the facts are examined, there can remain little basis for the belief accepted by certain biographers that Shelley knew and approved of the situation between Mary and Hogg during the first four months of 1815; even the fact that he was seriously ill and anticipated death cannot lead to this conclusion, which fits at no point with his views on the ceremonial aspect of physical love or with the sentiments he expressed on the subject of promiscuity. If Mary had wished to fall in with Shelley's ideas about love, she would have told Shelley about Hogg's protestations of love and her promise of fulfilment to him, and would perhaps have left the poet for the lawyer, who in any case could have married her at once. He was never able to marry Jane Williams, with whom he lived, for the same reason that had made it impossible for Edward Ellerker Williams to do so—the existence of her husband. Mary's conduct was clearly dishonest; though she was a girl of eighteen when she permitted Hogg's advances, she had the mind of a woman of thirty, unlike Harriet, who had left school only six months when Hogg offered her felicity consistent with discretion.

The part played by Hogg in Shelley's life after the days of trust and affection at Oxford cannot be briefly written off if any of the threads picked up in this chapter run through the obscure fabric of Shelley's second marriage. That Hogg scarred Shelley's mind needs no proof; the greater questions are how deep and enduring the scars were, and how much Shelley knew about the man who administered the wounds.

Half-way through Trelawny's visit—on 15 June—he and Jane were standing in the drawing-room at Casa Magni when Jane saw Shelley pass without a coat along the balcony. A few moments later she saw him pass a second time in the same direction, and since there is no way of walking round the house —both ends of the terrace lead to a twenty-foot drop—the level-headed Jane realized that she had seen a fantasm, for Trelawny had seen nothing, and Shelley was nowhere near.

Next morning there occurred the disaster which Mary may have asked Trelawny to omit from his reminiscences of the visit. At eight o'clock the illness of the previous week attacked her again, culminating this time in a miscarriage. The women— Jane, Claire and the servants—could do nothing to stop the haemorrhage which threatened to put an end to Mary's life, and when finally some ice was obtained, before a doctor could be rowed over the bay from Lerici, they were afraid to apply it. Shelley took the decision upon himself, applied the ice, and by the time the doctor arrived, Mary was out of danger.

> "I was so ill," Mary wrote afterwards, "that for seven hours I lay nearly lifeless—kept from fainting by brandy, vinegar, eau-de-Cologne, etc. At length, ice was brought to our solitude; it came before the doctor, so Claire and Jane were afraid of using it; but Shelley over-ruled them, and by an unsparing application of it I was restored. They all thought, and so did I at one time, that I was about to die."

It may have been this emergency, in addition to bad weather, which caused Trelawny to put off for a few days his departure for Leghorn, where he was to deliver Byron's *Bolivar*. When he did leave on the morning of the 18th, Shelley and Williams accompanied him out of the bay in the *Don Juan*, and though Shelley doubted whether he would do so, he made Leghorn that evening. Shelley went home and later that day he was busy writing letters, including one to Trelawny which shows him setting his affairs in order and contains a perfectly clear indication of his preoccupation with death:

"I have written to Guebhard, to pay you 154 Tuscan crowns, the amount of the balance against me according to Roberts's calculation, which I keep for your satisfaction, deducting sixty, which I paid the aubergiste at Pisa, in all 214. We saw you about eight miles in the offing this morning; but the abatement of the breeze leaves us little hope that you can have made Leghorn this evening. Pray write us a full, true, and particular account of your proceedings, etc.—how Lord Byron likes the vessel; what are your arrangements and intentions for the summer; and when we may expect to see you or him in this region again; and especially whether there is any news of Hunt.

Roberts and Williams are busy in refitting the *Don Juan*; they seem determined that she shall enter Leghorn in style. I am no great judge of these matters; but am excessively obliged to the former, and delighted that the latter should find amusement, like the sparrow, in educating the cuckoo's young.

You, of course, enter into society at Leghorn: should you meet with any scientific person capable of preparing the *Prussic Acid, or essential oil of bitter almonds*, I should regard it as a great kindness if you could procure me a small quantity. It requires the greatest caution in preparation, and ought to be highly concentrated; I would give any price for this medicine; you remember we talked of it the other night, and we both expressed a wish to possess it; my wish was serious, and sprang from the desire of avoiding needless suffering. I need not tell you I have no intention of suicide at present, but I confess it would be a comfort to me to hold in my possession that golden key to the chamber of perpetual rest. The Prussic Acid is used in medicine in infinitely minute doses; but that preparation is weak, and has not the concentration necessary to medicine all ills infallibly. A single drop, even less, is a dose, and it acts by paralysis.

I am curious to hear of this publication about Lord Byron and the Pisa circle. I hope it will not annoy him; as to me, I am supremely indifferent. If you have not shown the letter I sent you, don't, until Hunt's arrival, when we shall certainly meet."

He adds a footnote: "Mary is better, though still excessively weak."

Williams, meanwhile, was making a framework on the stern of the *Don Juan*. He then towed the vessel across to San Terenzo and began refitting.

Seven

THE CHANGEFUL YEAR

And where is truth? On tombs? For such to thee
Has been my heart—and thy dead memory
Has lain from childhood, many a changeful year,
Unchangingly preserved and buried there.
Fragment

ON TUESDAY, 18 June, Shelley wrote another letter. He sent his friend John Gisborne money for postage, "as I intend to indulge myself in plenty of paper and no crossings". He promised that Mary would write soon, described her recent illness and reported his own doctoring, adding, "She is now doing well, and the sea baths will soon restore her." Then he mentioned his poems, and after expressing a hope that *Adonais* would not meet the fate of the rest of his work, if only because it was a serious tribute to a poet of genius, he spoke of *Epipsychidion* in the regretful words already quoted in Chapter Two.

"Hunt is not yet arrived," he continued, "but I expect him every day. I shall see little of Lord Byron, nor shall I permit Hunt to form the intermediate link between him and me. I detest all society—almost all, at least—and Lord Byron is the nucleus of all that is hateful and tiresome in it. He will be half mad to hear of these memoirs. As to me, you know my supreme indifference to such affairs, except that I must confess that I am sometimes amused by the ridiculous mistakes of these writers. Tell me a little of what they say of me besides my being an atheist. One thing I regret in it, I dread lest it should injure Hunt's prospects in the establishment of the journal, for Lord Byron is so mentally capricious that the least impulse drives him from his anchorage."

Shelley was referring to a book by one John Watkins, *Memoirs of the Life and Writings of Lord Byron.* Gisborne had told him that the work contained references to him, and though Shelley never saw it, he remained curious and mentioned it a fortnight later in the last letter that he wrote at San Terenzo.

He turned to personal gossip:

"I like Jane more and more, and I find Williams the most amiable of companions. She has a taste for music, and an elegance of form and motions that compensates in some degree for lack of literary refinement. You know my gross ideas of music, and will forgive me when I say that I listen the whole evening on our terrace to the simple melodies with excessive delight. I have a boat here. It cost me £80, and reduced me to some difficulty in point of money. However, it is swift and beautiful, and appears quite a vessel. Williams is captain, and, we drive along this delightful bay in the evening wind under the summer moon until earth appears another world. Jane brings her guitar, and if the past and future could be obliterated, the present would content me so well that I could say with Faust to the passing moment 'Remain thou, thou art so beautiful'."

He wrote of Claire, "vivacious and talkative", and of Trelawny and the *Bolivar.*

"I write little now. It is impossible to compose except under the strong assurance of finding sympathy in what you write. Imagine Demosthenes reciting a Philippic to the waves of the Atlantic. Lord Byron is in this respect fortunate. He touched a chord to which a million hearts responded, and the coarse music which he produced to please them, disciplined him to the perfection to which he now approaches. I do not go on with 'Charles the First,' I feel too little certainty of the future, and too little satisfaction with regard to the past to undertake any subject seriously and deeply. I stand, as it were, upon a precipice, which I have ascended with great, and cannot descend without greater peril, and I am passing content if the heaven above me is calm for the passing moment."

Shelley then complained that Gisborne had not told him his opinion of Byron's *Cain*—"You send me the opinion of the populace, which you know I do not esteem." He reported that he was reading the plays of Calderon. "I read Greek and think about writing." He commented on a censorious young person who could not admire Metastasio: "The *nil admirari*, however justly applied, seems to me a bad sign in a young person"; he had rather that she conceived some admiration, for by that means she would become a better critic. It was one of the last general comments made by Shelley, that critic-harried poet, at whose heels so many small dogs yapped.

Shelley wrote the above letter to John Gisborne. As far as posterity knows, Gisborne and his wife were the only people, outside the poet's household and possibly a lawyer, who were ever informed, in speech or writing, about the greatest mystery in Shelley's life—the brief story of a child born in Naples and christened Elena Adelaide Shelley.

Shelley's life had a heroic sweep, and the mysteries it presents are those of birth, love and death. The circumstances of his death, which are to be discussed later, present a not insoluble mystery. The mysteries of love in his life are dark enough, for it is likely that no documents will explain to inquisitive posterity exactly why his two marriages failed. The mystery of birth—of the Neapolitan charge, as he called her—may yet yield to research.

The single unassailable fact—and it is possibly the sole basis of the maid Elise's gossip to the Hoppners—is that on 27 February, 1819, Shelley registered, as the child of his wife and himself born two months earlier, a child who on the same day was christened Elena Adelaide Shelley. On that day the Shelleys, Claire and their servants left Naples, where the

L

registration had been made. Some years later, Shelley told his cousin Thomas Medwin that when leaving Naples (on the afternoon of 27 February, 1819) he had been in danger of arrest. He did not conceal the existence of the child from his friends; in 1820, writing to the Gisbornes (who were particularly intimate with Mary) he mentioned the child, calling her "my Neapolitan", "my Neapolitan charge", and "my poor Neapolitan". He looked forward to the time when the little girl could join him and Mary in Pisa. He referred to "my situation at Naples in December, 1818", when reporting the attempt at blackmail made by Paolo Foggi, their servant at that time, who had been dismissed while at Naples after seducing Elise, and whose story, presumably, was eventually elaborated by Elise for the delectation of the Hoppners.

Richard Belgrave Hoppner was British Consul in Venice. He and his wife, a Swiss, knew Byron better than they knew the Shelleys. They knew Byron so well, indeed, that when Allegra was brought from England and given into Byron's care, the Hoppners had the child in their house for a time; they disliked her. On 16 September, 1820, Hoppner wrote to Byron exhorting him to have nothing further to do with the Shelleys, on account of a scandal that had been reported to his wife by one of their former servants. This servant, Elise, had been dismissed by the Shelleys at Naples in the winter of 1818–19, since she had conceived a child by Paolo Foggi. Elise had found her way to the Hoppners and earned their protection in return for the extraordinary story that she told them about the Shelleys. The story was that while in Naples, Claire Clairmont had, unknown to Mary, given birth to a child, the father of which was Shelley, who had secretly consigned it to the Foundling Hospital in the town, where the child had died. For some time after this, added Elise (forgetting that she had been dismissed very soon after the Shelleys arrived in Naples), the unspeakable pair had treated Mary with cruelty and abuse. The Hoppners were most anxious that Byron should know this story, but that he should not tell it to Mary, who was ignorant of the whole affair and even, Hoppner added, of the existence of the child.

Byron accepted the story as true and replied promptly: "The Shiloh story is true no doubt.... Of the facts... there can be little doubt; it is just like them. You may be sure that I keep your counsel." He wrote not a single word in defence of Shelley; in the same letter he enclosed "an epistle from Shiloh". All that can be said in Byron's defence is surely that it was his implacable, vengeful hatred of Claire that predisposed him to believe the scandal, or at least to help to spread it. He lowered himself to the level of the Hoppners with cowardly vulgarity: some time later, having received a pleading letter from Claire on the subject of Allegra, he sent it on to the Hoppners, writing across it a sneering reference to the alleged *ménage* of poet, wife and mistress and to the child-murder.

Almost a year later, on 6 August, 1821, Shelley visited Byron at Ravenna. He arrived at ten o'clock at night and talked enthusiastically with Byron till five o'clock in the morning. Some time during that night Byron's conscience pained him, or possibly he drank too much: he told Shelley about the Hoppners' allegations and showed him R. B. Hoppner's accusing letter. The accusation itself may have astounded Shelley, who was already used to calumny, but its original source cannot have afforded him much surprise. Elise's alleged lover, Paolo Foggi, had already attempted to make money out of similar allegations, and in self-defence Shelley had had to put the blackmailing letters into the hands of Del Rosso, a lawyer at Leghorn. Mary was aware of this blackmail, for she mentioned Foggi's activities in her diary and letters. She was also aware of the fact that Shelley had adopted a child in Naples, since he made no secret of the matter in his letters to their friends the Gisbornes.

Shelley left Byron, slept for a few hours, then wrote a letter to Mary, who was in Pisa, reporting what he had been told; he asked her to write to the Hoppners, for anything that he wrote in defence of Claire or himself would obviously bear no weight at all.

"As to what Reviews and the world says," he commented, "I do not care a jot, but when persons who have known me are capable of conceiving of me—not that I have fallen into a great error and impudence (*sic*), as would have been the living with Claire as my mistress—but that I have committed such unutterable crimes as destroying or abandoning a child, and that my own—imagine my despair of good, imagine how it is possible that one of so weak and sensitive a nature as mine can run further the gauntlet through this hellish society of men."

Mary at once wrote a letter to Mrs. Hoppner declaring that Elise's was an "infamous" tale, and pointing out that she herself must have known if Claire had had a child, since the whole party were in lodgings together and she, Mary, had access to all rooms. The pain and shock demonstrated by the first part of this letter in particular, in which the nature of the accusation had to be defined, could scarcely have been dissimulated; and this suggests that Elise had decorated the story previously used by Paolo in his attempt to blackmail Shelley.

Mary does not say anything about Shelley's adopted Neapolitan or indicate that the slander is not a new one. Because of this, biographers who favour the idea that the servant was telling the truth assume that Shelley and his wife laid a deep plot to conceal the guilt of Shelley and Claire. It is an untenable assumption for several reasons. The tone of Mary's letter suggests that Elise's most startling elaboration of the gossip lay in her naming Shelley as the father of the child. It is not known precisely what story Foggi threatened to spread, but a fair deduction is that he named Shelley or Claire (not both) as the parent. It is more likely that he named Claire, because if Mary's letter is not a complete fabrication, it shows that her horror arises from the accusation that her husband was the father. In the letter she wrote to Shelley, enclosing her letter to Mrs. Hoppner, there are two significant phrases. The following words indicate clearly that, though she knew of Elena Adelaide's existence in 1820, and though she knew that Foggi had tried to blackmail her husband on the strength of his "situation at Naples" in 1818, Mary had not previously heard the accusation that the child's parents were Shelley and Claire: "The shock for me is over, and I now despise the slander; but it must not pass uncontradicted. I sincerely thank Lord Byron for his kind unbelief." The second significant comment is in the postscript to this letter:

"Do not think me imprudent in mentioning Claire's illness at Naples. It is well to meet facts. They are as cunning as wicked. I have read over my letter; it is written in haste; but it were as well that the first burst of feeling should be expressed."

These words suggest that the chief practical consideration in Mary's mind was to defend Claire against the calumny by deliberately "meeting facts" and pointing out that she was, in fact, ill while at Naples.

Mary writes with, apparently, complete faith in Shelley. Of Claire she writes much less emotionally. If any implication may be drawn from this, it is surely that Claire had been the chief object of Paolo Foggi's earlier accusations and that, since the couple knew of Claire's illness, it would be unwise to pretend that she had been in normal health throughout the stay at Naples.

Two other facts have a bearing on the illness. Earlier in the year 1818, Claire had consulted a doctor. This in itself would ordinarily have no significance, for this was at the time of her first experience of an Italian summer at its height. In view of the Hoppner story it is often linked with the second fact—that during the summer Shelley wrote two short notes to his publisher asking him to pay in London, on his behalf, certain small sums to a person who would call to collect them. One interpretation of these notes is that Shelley had obtained abortifacients for Claire. A strange deduction which smells of the library rather than real life: for parcels often took many months to travel between England and Italy[1] and any Italian doctor would have supplied what was required, with advice thrown in, for a few lire.

On the accusers' side there are these facts. On 27 December, 1818, Mary noted in her journal that Claire was ill. This day was the alleged date of birth of Elena Adelaide Shelley, the date Shelley set down on the birth certificate; had he wished to confuse the matter he could easily have declared another date,

---

[1] When thanking Leigh Hunt for a parcel containing his portrait, some books and some letters, sent from London to Italy, Shelley wrote, "This parcel, you know, and all its letters, are now a year old; some older."

for he was making the declaration in February, exactly two months later. During that December, Claire went sightseeing with the Shelleys, and was carried in a litter, the reason for her indisposition being that she had twice fallen from a horse. If Claire had been able to establish that she had indeed fallen while riding, her accusers would inevitably have said that she did so purposely in order to procure an abortion!

All the facts were no doubt in Mary Shelley's mind when she wrote her letter to the Hoppners in August, 1821. The words in her defence show her belief that her husband had not betrayed her with Claire; the reading between the lines suggests that she and Shelley were defending someone else, whether Claire or another woman must be guessed. The idea that the letters that passed between Shelley and Mary were entirely fabrications, part of a cunning plot, is absurd, because in this case each could have written plainly to the other, the letters being immediately destroyed after they were answered; neither had a duty to posterity to preserve the correspondence.

Mary's silence on the matter after Shelley's death is also significant. The story was still going the rounds: in 1834 Mrs. Hoppner was regaling Crabb Robinson with it. If the widow Mary Shelley was engaged for twenty-nine years (as some people have suggested) in whitewashing her infidel husband, this matter must have engaged her earnest attention. The calumny had appeared in print. She and Shelley had discussed Elena Adelaide, the Neapolitan "charge", not only between themselves but with their friends the Gisbornes. Mary and Claire probably knew the facts, and two other people, the Gisbornes, knew the truth or a version of the matter. The child's birth and death had been registered in Naples and Elena Adelaide had been baptized in a church there. These four people maintained silence, though all knew that the story would be discussed. None of them troubled to invent an explanation, as they would surely have wished to do if the Claire-Shelley parentage had been a fact.

Having written her letter to Mrs. Hoppner, Mary sent it to Shelley; she had not the heart to make a copy, and wished him to do so. Evidently misunderstanding the purpose of this request, he wrote:

"I have not recopied your letter; such a measure would necessarily destroy its authenticity; but have given it to Lord Byron, who has engaged to send it with his own comments to the Hoppners."

Not knowing the Hoppners' address, Shelley unwisely took the letter to Byron, who found himself in an embarrassing situation: he had broken the Hoppners' confidence. Shelley quite understood what a humiliating position this was, and readily agreed that Byron should take charge of the letter, to send it to the Hoppners with his explanation or to hand it to them in a gentlemanly manner.

Shelley explained to Mary:

"People do not hesitate it seems to make themselves panderers and accomplices to slander, for the Hoppners had extracted from Lord Byron that these accusations should be concealed from *me*. Lord Byron is not a man to keep a secret good or bad—but in openly confessing that he has not done so he must observe a certain delicacy, and therefore he wishes to send the letter himself, and indeed this adds weight to our recommendations. Have you seen the article of the Literary Gazette on me? They evidently allude to some story of this kind."

Shelley left himself "naked to laughter" by entrusting the letter to Byron, though admittedly it might not have mended the situation had he insisted on sending it himself. The letter never reached the Hoppners; it was found among Byron's papers, with the seal broken, after his death. Whether Shelley opened the letter for him, or whether he did so himself, out of curiosity, cannot be known. Unless Mrs. Hoppner was completely heartless and malignant, the fact of her spreading the story in London Society thirteen years later suggests that she did not see what Mary Shelley had written. Byron's self-conceit had done the damage: it is folly to refuse to acknowledge that even so proud a man and so talented a poet could be meansouled and cowardly.

Later, Claire was enabled to talk to Elise, the maid, and she caused her to write two letters, which were sent to Mary. One, to Mary, denied that she had spread the scandal; the other, to Mrs. Hoppner, declared that the whole story was a lie. Mary sent the second letter to Mrs. Hoppner, but there was no reply. There was, of course, nothing that she could say.

It was his biographers, not Shelley, who made a deep mystery of the "Neapolitan". Shelley mentioned her in his letters to the Gisbornes, and Mary, writing to them, promised that she would tell them about the Foggi disturbance; it was naturally a matter that she preferred to talk about rather than to discuss in a letter. For over a century after Shelley's death the only fact the biographers could link with the references to the Neapolitan charge was Medwin's statement of what Shelley had told him: a romantic story about a woman of standing who came to him on the night before he sailed for Calais and placed her fortune and herself at his disposal. She followed him to Switzerland and watched his movements through a spyglass. Later she followed him to Italy. She was once for one night in the same hotel. She talked to him in Naples, and died there. So much for the story reported by Medwin, in which he may have somewhat confused Shelley's three journeys to Europe—in 1814, 1816 and 1818.

Whatever the truth of this story, it gave rise to the theory that Elena Adelaide was the daughter of this woman, entrusted to him before she died and adopted by him. The story has been dismissed as a romantic fabrication; too lightly, it may be, for Medwin received the story in 1820, and in that year, when Foggi was blackmailing Shelley and the "Hoppner scandal" was doubtless taking its form thanks to the gossip of Foggi or another, Shelley is little likely to have spread any such stories about his "situation at Naples". If, anticipating scandal, he wished to hint that the child had been adopted, he would have told not Medwin, who was his loyal friend, but someone calculated to spread the evidence—possibly Byron.

Turning from legend or reported speech to documentary fact, the birth and baptismal certificates of Elena Adelaide, both drawn up on 27 February, 1819, were discovered in the State Archives at Naples in 1936 by Professor Alberto

Tortiglione, who had been requested by Shelley's biographer Professor N. I. White to search the birth and death records of Naples for the salient period. The birth certificate stated the date of birth as 27 December, 1818; the place of birth as 250, Riviera di Chiaia, where the Shelleys and Claire were lodging; and the parents as Shelley and his wife Mary Godwin or Gadwin. (The name "Padurin", transcribed in Professor White's account, is a slip resulting from unfamiliarity with the Italian script used in the certificate.)

Elena died on 9 June, 1820, at 45, Vico Canale. In the certificate her age is given as fifteen months and twelve days—which is counting from 27 February, 1819. If the deposition made by Shelley in the birth certificate is correct, she must have been two months older. There is no certainty that Elena's birthday was 27 December, of course, since the only authority for the statement is Shelley's admittedly false statement, witnessed by Francesco Florimonte, a cheesemonger, and Antonio Di Lorenzo, a barber living near the Shelley's lodging in Riviera di Chiaia.

Paternity is much more difficult to establish than maternity, particularly after over a century has passed. Among putative mothers in the Shelley circle, only one may be confidently dismissed: Mary Shelley. Her son Percy Florence was born later in 1819—in November—and if she had been expecting a child eleven months before that month, nothing short of mental derangement could have explained her concealing the birth and never, before or after, mentioning it to a friend. On 27 December, 1818, supposedly the date of the child's birth, Mary was placidly filling in her journal, noting among other commonplace details that Claire was ill. On 27 February, 1819, she recorded the "great fuss" of last-minute preparations for departure from Naples.

What of Claire, accused by the Hoppners of having secretly given birth to a child in Naples? The evidence against her appears to be heavy, though circumstantial, if one is predisposed, as the Hoppners were, to believe that Elise's smoke was not without fire. In the summer she had been ill and had consulted a doctor. On 16 December, when she went with the Shelleys to see Vesuvius, she was not strong enough to walk, and Shelley writes, "Mary and I mounted mules, and Claire was carried in a chair on the shoulders of four men, much like a member of parliament after he has gained his election, and looking, with less reason, quite as frightened." The party returned at ten o'clock at night, by torchlight, having been on the move all day. Climbing Vesuvius and lingering to look into the crater till after nightfall is not precisely the kind of outing one expects a woman shortly expecting a confinement to undertake; if Claire had been within ten days of that confinement it would have been only reasonable for her to cry off such a trip by saying that she was unwell. But if we are to believe that Claire was Elena Adelaide's mother, we must also believe that before and after the birth Claire indulged in a tiring round of sightseeing tours on the longest of which, on 23 February, the party travelled sixty miles south of Naples and, on the first day's journey, walked five or six miles over a marshy road where the carriage could not travel.

Claire had twice fallen from a horse while at Bagni di Lucca. She was ill on 27 December. Ordinarily, such details would lead to simple conclusions: that her first experience of Italian heat had made her indisposed; that she did not ride very well; and that she had a trifling indisposition two days after Christmas. In reference to the illness, Mary Shelley wrote in the letter to Mrs. Hoppner that was entrusted to Byron:

"I now remember that Claire did keep her bed there for two days—but I attended on her—I saw the physician—her illness was one that she had been accustomed to for years—and the same remedies were employed as I had before ministered to her in England."

The third putative mother is the romantic lady of position supposed to have followed Shelley to Italy and to have talked to him in Naples and died shortly afterwards. She sounds like the answer to the riddle, if only because unlike Claire she would not have to be supposed capable of secretly giving birth to a child and pursuing her normal life a day or two later. It is not impossible that her existence may yet be established by a document in the Naples Archives.

It is reasonable to assume that the name "Adelaide" contains the clue to the paternity of the Naples child that has eluded research for so long. There is no record of Shelley's ever having known a woman named Adelaide. The name was not common at that time: it became fashionable later in the century. Professor White's suggestion that the name "Adelaide" was adapted from "Adeline", the name of a character in a novel that Shelley admired as a youth, seems extravagant. The name "Elena" is not so difficult to trace, for it is simply the Italian form of "Helen", the name by which Mary Shelley is personified in *Rosalind and Helen*.

The legend of the Englishwoman of family alleged to have died in Naples is dismissed largely on the negative evidence that the archives of the British Minister in Naples at the time contain no reference to any such death or to a woman bearing the Christian name Adelaide.

An examination of these archives, however, shows that they are fragmentary. The only record that I have ever found of a woman named Adelaide known to have been in or near Naples in the winter of 1818–19 relates to Adelaide Constance Campbell, daughter of Lady Charlotte Campbell. Lady Charlotte did, as a matter of interest, enter Shelley's life in an indirect way. She read his juvenile romance *St. Irvyne*. A friend of hers at Oxford informed her of the publication of *The Necessity of Atheism*, and of Shelley's expulsion.

You may find in the Foreign Office archives relating to the Italian States plenty of evidence which seems to suggest that they are complete—for instance, there are records of Lady Campbell's marriage to her chaplain in Florence in March, 1818; documents signed by Shelley and Byron giving their version of the Masi affair at Pisa; records of the christening of Sophia Stacey's first child and of Tom Medwin's daughter; Hoppner's report on the plague at Venice which broke out in the Lazzaretto almost on the day when the Shelleys left that city in November, 1818. But there are many gaps in the papers in spite of the survival of these records of minor interest. There is, for instance, no record of the marriage of Paolo Foggi and Elise, which Mary Shelley, in her letter to Mme Hoppner that Byron apparently failed to send on, declared to have taken place at Sir William à Court's, the British Minister's. By an order of Castlereagh's (7 May, 1816) all records of weddings celebrated at British Residences abroad were to be sent to the Bishop of London for entry in the book kept at his London Registry Office. This book exists, but it contains no record of the Foggi marriage.

The significance of this is that negative evidence cannot establish that the Foggis were not married at the British Residency in Naples, or that Mary Shelley was lying when she declared that they were. (She would scarcely have lied to the Hoppners, in any case, for as British Consul Hoppner could easily check this type of information.) It would be helpful to know when the Foggis married, and to trace their movements during 1819 and 1820, but the fact that we cannot find documents bearing on the matter is no indication at all that the event did not take place, but merely a reminder of the carelessness of Residency clerks at that time (of which there is abundant evidence in the Foreign Office records now kept at the Public Record Office) and furthermore of the incompleteness of the records themselves. If, therefore, the alleged death of the mysterious lady of quality is not mentioned in official documents, that is no evidence at all that she never existed and never died in Naples. Unfortunately the acceptance of similar negative evidence continues to bedevil much Shelley scholarship.

The other potential mothers are numerous and beyond tracing, if one takes Shelley's description of Elena Adelaide literally and assumes her to have been a foundling child, of Italian parents, adopted by Shelley with the added security that in official records she was described as his daughter born in wedlock.

Putative fathers are numerous, too, but Shelley is naturally the only one whose case can be examined. The possibility that the child was his by Claire or by another woman takes the inquirer back to an examination of the early months of 1818, where he finds no hint, much less evidence, of a liaison. On 11 March the Shelleys, Claire, William and Clara Shelley, Allegra, Elise and Milly, a servant brought from Marlow, left England to begin a long exhausting journey through France to Moncenisio and so on to Turin and Milan. Shelley was ill and depressed. Claire was taking her fourteen-months-old child to Byron in Italy, where she knew that a cold reception awaited her. Undoubtedly to the reasonable mind, not quite blinded by the dust of library research to the realities of life and a knowledge of the inns along the Chambéry route that was taken, this setting is not propitious to the idea of a brief affair involving Shelley and an unknown woman, Claire and an unknown man, or Shelley and Claire in conspiracy together. The unreliability of the date 27 December reminds us, furthermore, that the child may have been conceived before 10 March.

The party reached Milan on 4 April, and on 13 April Shelley was writing to Byron with a message from Claire, asking whether he had received a lock of Allegra's hair which she had sent during the winter. In his letter of 22 April Shelley has something to say about Claire's preoccupations as a mother:

> "Claire will write to you herself a detail of her motives and feelings relating to Allegra's being absent as you desire. Her interference as the mother of course supersedes *mine*, which was never undertaken but from the deep interest I have ever felt for all the parties concerned. Here my letter might well close, but that I would not the affair should finish so.
>
> You write as if from the instant of its departure all future intercourse were to cease between Claire and her child. This I cannot think you ought to have expected, or even to have desired. Let us estimate our own sensations, and consider, if those of a father be acute, what must be those of a mother? What should we think of a woman who should resign her infant child with no prospect of ever seeing it again, even to a father in whose tenderness she entirely confided?"

The letter continues in a strain of firm pleading for Claire, which runs through all Shelley's letters to Byron on the subject, and as in earlier letters there is an indication of Shelley's treatment of the scandals attached to Byron's name which contrasts strongly with Byron's almost eager acceptance of the Hoppner story about "Shiloh":

> "You can have no idea of the absurd stories which the multitude believe of you; but which every person of sense, and indeed every enlightened circle of our own countrymen, laugh at. This is the common lot of all who have distinguished themselves among men."

In a letter written eight days later he mentions his own poor health, Claire's wretchedness at having no assurance of being able to see Allegra after handing her over to Byron, and Elise the nurse, "in whom Mrs. S. entirely confides, and who even quits us somewhat unwillingly", to conduct Allegra to Venice.

It will be seen that fake-lawyer methods can establish no reliable conclusion at all. But a little common sense produces the evidence that virtually establishes Claire's innocence, for it reminds us that if she had been pregnant in December, 1818, she, Shelley or Mary would have made arrangements for a move to a remote country place, or at least a part of Italy less infested by English tourists than Naples. Each was well aware of the situation that had arisen after Allegra's birth in January, 1817, when the villagers of Marlow had assumed Shelley to be the child's father, and of the scandals spread by tourists in 1816, when Southey's accusation against Shelley and Byron, of forming a "league of incest", had caught the popular imagination. For the party to have remained in Naples with Claire expecting to become a mother, and for them to have hoped to succeed in spiriting away the child, would have been worse than folly.

A study of the records of the time and place shows repeatedly that the Riviera di Chiaia was the place where the English congregated. And they were many. A memorandum of 1822, containing a list of British residents in Naples from the Duke and Duchess of Leeds to the Misses Haggerstone, includes over fifty people. The Shelleys must have been closely watched during their three months in Naples. A dispatch written on 4 February, 1819, in Naples, contains the words:

"The numerous arrests which have taken place at Ferrara and the neighbourhood have again excited a great deal of attention throughout Italy to the proceedings of the sect of *Carbonari*."

Members of secret societies were plentiful in the North and in the Roman States, and

"we are not without a due proportion of these dangerous sectaries here. Amongst the persons arrested at Ferrara, are several persons of distinction, principally lawyers".

On 18 January, 1819, the Naples Government informed the Consul-General that foreigners were arriving without having their passports visa-ed by the Neapolitan Consul in the place where they came from; in future they would be refused permission to disembark at any port in the Kingdom of the Two Sicilies.

The more the facts are reviewed the more they appear to lead to the supposition that the child was Claire's, even if the father was not Shelley: but the flaw in this reasoning is that it is not the most satisfactory conclusion, but the least unsatisfactory on the basis of the evidence. That evidence is so thin that it would sustain no case in a court: hence the fallaciousness of the fake-lawyer method of judging the case. As in so many instances in the biography of Shelley, suggestion or supposition colours the picture: the hint takes root in the mind before the fact that confutes it is brought to light.

The hint which took root in regard to the Naples mystery appeared in the form of the Hoppner letter; yet this letter establishes very little. It states that there was a child; indeed, it is on this single fact that the whole accusation is founded. It declares that Claire was the mother; though the evidence against this is far heavier than the evidence for the supposition. It states that the child was taken to the Foundling Hospital; but the house in which Elena Adelaide died was certainly not a foundling hospital.

In 1818 the house where the birth is alleged to have taken place offered the Shelleys, in the poet's own words:

"a lodging divided from the sea by the royal gardens, and from our windows we see perpetually the blue waters of the bay, forever changing, yet forever the same".

At present, 250 Riviera di Chiaia does not exist, but information gathered in the district shows that it must have been a large palazzo, similar to those of that epoch which are still standing.

Vico Canale, where the child died and where, presumably, she passed her brief life, is still in existence; so is the house No. 45, given in the death certificate as Elena Adelaide's domicile. It is not certain whether the actual building is the one that existed in 1818, but the district is now a rather poor one, and in such quarters of all Italian towns the houses are built to last. Like the inhabitants, they are susceptible to little change.

The Sezione Montecalvario today houses families whose ancestors have lived there as long as the old people can remember. No. 45, which like its neighbours is on the level of the street (this type of house belongs to the category termed *bassi*), is now rented by a stone-breaker. There is no record of the inhabitants in 1822, but if the house had been a foundling hospital it is obvious that the custodians would have had to make an appearance and register the death. Instead, the death certificate was signed by Antonio Liguori, of 48, Vico Canale, and Pasquale Fiorenzano, of 59, Vico Lungo Trinità dei Spagnuoli. No. 48 is now a dwelling-house. Traces of the family named Liguori or Liquori, of Sicilian origin, still exist; they lived in an alley off the Vico Canale early in this century, and left Naples about 1920, according to a ninety-year-old woman of the quarter questioned in 1951.

It is by no means unlikely that more documentary evidence, throwing light on the Naples mystery, will come to light. The death of a child of English parents, in Naples, is likely to have been recorded in more than a mere death certificate. Shelley may have sent remittances to Naples during the eighteen months that Elena Adelaide lived there, and in some Naples bank vault the name of the payee may yet be preserved. One reasonably sound assumption is that whatever light bank or consular records may throw on the matter, nothing further written by Shelley or Mary, on this subject, is likely to come to light. This is not necessarily because the Shelleys had something shameful to conceal—there was no obligation upon them to tell the Gisbornes about the Neapolitan ward, yet they did so. Some information may yet be found in Leghorn, where Shelley consulted the lawyer Del Rosso when Paolo Foggi attempted to blackmail him.

But of letters sent to people outside Italy there are likely to be none, because in 1818 the postal convention cleverly imposed on the Italian States by Metternich, the Austrian Chancellor, was solely devised so that foreign mail from Italy would pass through the bureau set up in Vienna for opening, copying, decoding and re-sealing all correspondence. The arrangement worked against Metternich's interest in May, 1819, for he then complained that all his private communications with the French Government, particularly those relating to exiles under the surveillance of the Austrians, had been made public.

Byron, who was well aware of this censorship, included in a letter of 1820 the following passage for the edification of any Austrian who might pry into his correspondence:

"The police at present is under the Germans, or rather the Austrians, who do not merit the name of Germans, who open all letters it is supposed. I have no objection, so that they see how I hate and utterly despise and detest those *Hun brutes* . . ."

The Revolution at Naples had broken out in June, 1820. Byron's sources of revolutionary information were good. So were those of Shelley, whose association with Byron was carefully noted by the Italian police. In 1818 the Austrian troops were withdrawn from Naples and a militia was formed; and if Shelley flirted with any revolutionary elements there early in 1819, his statement that when he left he was in fear of arrest needs no explanation.

We know that at the time Foggi began to blackmail Shelley, Mary knew of the "situation at Naples in 1818", and at this time or later it is certain that Claire knew, for it was she who, after the "Hoppner scandal", caused Elise to write the two letters confuting the allegations ascribed to her by Mrs. Hoppner. Did all three know of the birth registration at the time it was made? It has been argued that Mary did not know— on the evidence that she did not record the event in her diary or circulate the news among her friends! The Foggis evidently knew, and a barber living in Riviera di Chiaia was one of the two witnesses who signed the birth certificate. That Shelley had plotted to keep the truth from his wife by confiding it to servants, tradesmen and the midwife, Gaetana Musto (named on the certificate of baptism), hardly appears rational. Flight from Naples would be no protection, because Shelley clearly remained in communication with Elena Adelaide's guardians.

If, as is possible, Shelley quixotically adopted a child of unknown Italian parents in an attempt to assuage Mary's depression, caused by Clara's death late in the previous summer, or if he took charge of a child born to the mysterious lady of position who he alleged talked to him there just before her death, Mary's reaction may explain the mystery. She may have reacted with disgust to a decision taken in a moment of dejection; or she may have coolly pointed out that experience over Allegra should have shown Shelley the foolishness of suddenly producing an infant whose mother would indubitably be assumed to be Claire. There is, therefore, no definite evidence for assuming Mary's ignorance of Shelley's false declaration on 27 February, 1819; indeed, the misery of their relations in that year may have been increased by this cause of dissension.

Finally, there is one possible line of investigation that has never before been put forward. It is simply that the child was the illegitimate infant of Paolo Foggi and Elise. This is not quite so fantastic a hypothesis as at first appears, and certainly no more unconvincing than many of the theories already examined. Elise, according to Mary Shelley, was carrying a child in the winter of 1818-19. If she gave birth to this child at 250, Riviera di Chiaia or 45, Vico Canale, it is not improbable that Shelley helped her to keep the matter quiet. He might even have decided, perhaps without telling Mary, who was still mourning the loss of Clara, to register the child as his and Mary's in order later to have the opportunity to produce her as his ward. Later he would be open to blackmail by Paolo Foggi, for he would have removed all evidence that the child was not his own.

It is significant that we hear nothing from the Hoppners about Elise's child. We do not know where the infant was born, or when; or whether it survived. In other words, there is one child, who we might expect would bear the name of Foggi, who is missing from the whole plot. If it were possible to trace the movements of Elise, who later appeared in Florence, considerable light might be thrown on the whole Naples episode and the subsequent blackmail. The hypothesis that Elena Adelaide was Elena Adelaide Foggi might explain why no documentary evidence of Shelley's payments for the support of the girl are in existence. He would have had to send instructions and funds by messenger or by post from the State of Tuscany to the Kingdom of the Two Sicilies, across a Customs barrier. But suppose, following the departure of the Shelleys from Naples, in haste, and with Shelley "in fear of arrest", on 27 February, 1819, Elise remained in Naples *at* 45, *Vico Canale*?

In May Shelley planned to return to Naples, and the plan was changed owing to the death of William Shelley. One of the few documentary references to the Naples expenses belongs to 8 March, 1820, when Shelley wrote to the Gisbornes:

"I inclose an outside calculation of the expenses at Naples calculated in ducats. I think it is as well to put into the hands of Del Rosso, or whoever engages to do the business 150 ducats—or more, as you see occasion—but on this you will favour me so far (as to) allow your judgment to regulate mine."

On 23 January, 1820, in Florence, the Shelleys received Elise as a caller, and even recommended Paolo as a servant to their friend Henry Reveley.

If the missing Foggi child is the solution to the mystery and Shelley fell innocently into a perfect trap by a blackmailer (who did not at the time of the birth, and for a long time afterwards, see the golden opportunity before him), the secrecy of the Shelleys afterwards is to some degree explicable. It would be useless to attempt to establish the truth and the only practical course of action would be to attempt to silence the Foggis.

On 30 June, 1820, Shelley wrote to the Gisbornes:

"My poor Neapolitan, I hear has a fever of dentition. I suppose she will die and leave another memory to these which already torture me. I am waiting the next post with anxiety but without much hope."

A postscript added on 2 July states:

"I have later news of my Neapolitan. I have taken every possible precaution for her, and hope that they will succeed. She is to come to us as soon as she recovers."

She had in fact died on 9 June. On learning of Elena Adelaide's death Shelley wrote:

"My Neapolitan charge is dead. It seems as if the destruction that is consuming me were an atmosphere which wrapt and *infected* everything connected with me."

And of Paolo he wrote:

"The rascal Paolo has been taking advantage of my situation at Naples in December 1818 to attempt to extort money by threatening to charge me with the most horrible crimes. He is connected with some English here who hate me with a fervour that almost does credit to their phlegmatic brains, and listen and vent the most prodigious falsehoods. An ounce of civet good apothecary to sweeten this dunghill of a world."

Neither Mary nor Claire left any known explanation of the episode; from which it may be deduced that they considered the folly best left in obscurity, or that to reveal what they knew might injure someone's reputation. It would have been easy for

Mary to establish for the benefit of Medwin, Hunt, Peacock, Hogg and anyone else interested in writing about Shelley that he had adopted a child; it might indeed have been assumed to be essential, if she wished to protect the posthumous reputation of Shelley and the living reputation of Claire, for sundry people in Italy, the Gisbornes and the Hoppners, had been told various accounts of the matter. But Mary Shelley preserved silence. Perhaps she found truth in the fragment she published in Shelley's posthumous poems:

> And who feels discord now or sorrow?
> Love is the universe today—
> These are the slaves of dim tomorrow,
> Darkening Life's labyrinthine way.

On Wednesday, 19 June, Williams went to work in earnest on the *Don Juan* with the help of Captain Roberts. The ballast was removed and the boat was hauled on to the beach, where it was cleaned and greased. The ballast consisted of the pigs of iron with which (Shelley had told Trelawny while sailing a few days before) he would go down to the sea-bed if the vessel ever capsized. While these repairs were being made, Shelley had more important matters to think of. He had at last received, on 20 June, news that Leigh Hunt had reached Genoa with his family. Hunt had arrived at Genoa, after a month's buffeting at sea, on 13 June, and had sent his news to Shelley at Pisa, whence the letter had to be redirected. Had the letter arrived earlier, Shelley would have gone to Genoa, where Hunt remained till 28 June. As it was, Hunt was instructed to look out, on the voyage from Genoa to Leghorn, for the white house in the Bay of Lerici, and if possible to arrange with the captain to fire a gun or send up a rocket, when the *Don Juan* "would instantly come alongside".

Though he was by no means confident of the arrangements for the publication of the new review, and though he foresaw friction between Byron and Hunt, he expressed happiness at the meeting with a man for whom he had always felt deep affection, and whom he had not seen for over four years—since the evening of 11 March, 1818, when he fell into an exhausted sleep and the Hunts, rather than wake him on the eve of the journey, went home without saying good-bye.

"A thousand welcomes, my best friend, to this divine country; high mountains and seas no longer divide those whose affections are united. We have much to think of and talk of when we meet at Leghorn; but the final result of our plans will be peace to you, and to me a greater degree of consolation than has been permitted since we met."

The week dragged on, the heat increasing daily, and giving little comfort to Mary Shelley as she recuperated from the miscarriage. Her spirits were low. Shelley planned to sail for Leghorn the following Monday, and she saw no reason for thinking with pleasure or even consolation of the journey he was about to make. Saturday, 22 June, brought overpowering heat. The ballast was stowed back in the *Don Juan* and the boat was launched. "She floats 3 inches lighter than before," Williams wrote. "This difference is caused, I imagine, by her planks having dried while on shore." The overhaul may have had something to do with the loss of the *Don Juan* a fortnight later.

Shelley wrote to Byron on Sunday, 23 June, to announce Leigh Hunt's arrival in Italy, and to insure that he would be met at Leghorn—a courtesy which Byron neglected.

"I hear," Shelley wrote with irony directed more at Byron than at the Americans, "that the Americans are tempting you to migrate, in hopes, perhaps, that when Time, who blots out scutcheons and patents of nobility, shall have made the title-page of *Cain* and *Childe Harold* still brighter, the Homeric doubt shall be renewed about your birthplace throughout all the regions in which English will be spoken. It will be curious enough to hear the academies of New Holland and Labrador disputing on such a subject."

Shelley returned to the subject of the Masi affair: "What

news of your process? I hear that Antonio is treated with more mildness, and likely to be released." Antonio was Byron's servant, whom the Tuscan Government had imprisoned following the incident.

"They say, too, that Masi is to be degraded and severely punished. This would be a pity, and I think you would do well, as soon as our own points are gained, to intercede for the poor devil, whom it would not be right to confound with his government, or rather with the popular prejudice of the Pisans, to the suggestions of which the government conformed itself.

Clare desires to send you the enclosed packet, and to request that her letters may be returned to her.

I hear nothing of your Schooner: Williams is on the look out for her all day, and has hoisted his flags at least ten times in honour of the approach of her phantom."

The *Bolivar* was to appear shortly; and so was her phantom, later—but not to Shelley.

That day Williams noted, "S. sees *spirits*, and alarms the whole house." In the middle of the night Shelley had a nightmare, and ran screaming into his wife's room. She recorded:

"I was sure that he was asleep, and tried to waken him by calling on him, but he continued to scream, which inspired me with such a panic that I jumped out of bed and ran across the hall to Mrs. Williams's room, where I fell through weakness, though I was so frightened that I got up again immediately; she let me in, and Williams went to Shelley, who had been wakened by my getting out of bed. He said that he had not been asleep, and that it was a vision that he saw that had frightened him. But as he declared that he had not screamed, it was certainly a dream and no waking vision. What had frightened him was this. He dreamt that, lying as he did in bed, Edward and Jane came in to him; they were in the most horrible condition—their bodies lacerated, their bones starting through their skin, the faces pale yet stained with blood; they could hardly walk, but

Edward was the weakest and Jane was supporting him. Edward said, 'Get up, Shelley; the sea is flooding the house, and it is all coming down.' Shelley got up, he thought, and went to his window that looked on the terrace and the sea, and thought he saw the sea rushing in. Suddenly his vision changed, and he saw the figure of himself strangling me, that had made him rush into my room; yet, fearful of frightening me, he dared not approach the bed, when my jumping out awoke him, or, as he phrased it, caused his vision to vanish."

The following morning, as the dream was discussed, Shelley sought to explain the second part of it, in which he had seen his own double. He told his friends that he had lately had many visions, and that recently he had seen the figure of himself, on the terrace, approaching him to demand, "How long do you mean to be content?" The "double" idea must have revived in Jane the memory of her own vision of Shelley on the terrace, on the evening before the day of Mary's illness. In 1830 Thomas Moore recorded the story that the figure of Shelley had once been seen walking in the woods near the house, when he was in fact far away.

Whether these happenings were merely the result of heat and imagination, Shelley's screams that night caused Mary a relapse, and on 24 June, when the *Don Juan* was ready for the voyage to Leghorn and Williams was about to weigh anchor, she was so ill that they had to abandon the idea of the journey for a week. The ominous double haunted not only Casa Magni but Shelley's imagination; he had written about self-seeing in 1819, in *Prometheus Unbound*:

> Ere Babylon was dust,
> The Magus Zoroaster, my dead child,
> Met his own image walking in the garden.
> That apparition, sole of men, he saw.
> For know there are two worlds of life and death:
> One that which thou beholdest; but the other
> Is underneath the grave, where do inhabit
> The shadows of all forms that think and live

Till death unite them and they part no more;
Dreams and the light imaginings of men,
And all that faith creates or love desires,
Terrible, strange, sublime and beauteous shapes.

The "shadows of all forms" had been Shelley's mental companions for a long time. His sisters recalled that once, when a child, he set a fagot-stack on fire, and when asked to explain himself, replied that he wanted a little hell of his own. There is no doubt that during his brief life he succeeded in creating and living in that private inferno. His life as reported by others, his letters, his poetry—the last most of all—contain abundant evidence of the state, as between sleeping and waking, in which he pursued the life of his imagination. He drifted on a sea of nightmare, in the fog of disappointment and regret; and in his verse, too much given, as Hunt pointed out, to metaphors of the sea, he yet contrived to write of the ocean as a bringer of peace as well as terror. It is worth noting that though he was temperamentally given to nightmares—so much so that during periods of his life he was reluctant to sleep—he managed to keep the "fringe-world" out of his poetry, or to refine its expression, to bring the ghosts into the daylight. In early youth, in the days of *Zastrozzi*, he had made fun, in rumbustious schoolboy manner, of Gothic romances. His private hell was a desolation of the spirit, again best expressed in *Prometheus Unbound* during that creative year which had begun with "some deadly change in love":

> Desolation is a delicate thing:
> It walks not on the earth, it floats not on the air,
> But treads with lulling footsteps, and fans with silent wing
> The tender hopes which in their hearts the best and gentlest bear:
> Who, soothed to false repose by the fanning plumes above
> And the music-stirring motion of its soft and busy feet,
> Dream visions of aëreal joy, and call the monster, Love,
> And wake, and find the shadow Pain, as he whom now we greet.

Though the expression of his hell is not Dante-esque, its principal idea—the betrayal of those who love—has in it something of the deepest circle of Dante's arrangement of the inferno, the fourth zone of the ninth circle, called the Giudecca, where Judas, Brutus and Cassius were gnawed in the three mouths of Lucifer. It is possible that it was the island of the Giudecca at Venice, towards which Shelley and Byron were rowed from the Lido, which suggested the building in which the Maniac in *Julian and Maddalo* was to be found:

> I looked, and saw between us and the sun
> A building on an island; such a one
> As age to age might add, for uses vile,
> A windowless, deformed and dreary pile.

But there is a way out of Dante's Giudecca, which his guide Virgil knew:

> *Lo duca ed io per quel cammino ascoso*
> *entrammo a ritornar nel chiaro mondo;*
> *e, sanza cura aver d'alcun riposo,*
> *salimmo su, ei primo ed io secondo,*
> *tanto ch'io vidi delle cose belle*
> *che porta il ciel, per un pertugio tondo;*
> *e quindi uscimmo a riveder le stelle.*

(The guide and I entered that underground way to return to the bright world; and without pausing to rest, climbed up, he leading, I following, till I saw the beauties that the sky presented through a round opening; and through it we came out to see the stars again.)

Eight

THE QUENCHLESS LAMP

> As the love from Petrarch's urn
> Yet amid yon hills doth burn,
> A quenchless lamp by which the heart
> Sees things unearthly . . .
> *Lines Written Among the Euganean Hills*

THERE REMAINED a week of summer weather in the Bay of Lerici—for Shelley, the last week of all. In this bright heat and stillness the enchantment which made Shelley, in the last words he wrote there, call the bay "divine", is produced by an alchemy of colour and sound. The sky on such days is the broad Italian roof of whose colour there is no imitation except the pigment which, four centuries ago, Italian painters themselves devised to express it; but the bay is shallow, and there is as much green as blue in its sparkling reflections.

The mountains that embrace the bay are dark green. When the midday haze descends, making Portovenere purple and smudging the horizon towards Corsica, the very houses seem magnified; even when standing many hundreds of yards away, in the hills, or high up in the courtyard of the grey and black castle, you are able to pick out the detail of their flaking walls of pink and ochre, terra-cotta and deeper red, and to distinguish every ancient red tile from its neighbour.

If towards evening the sirocco blows up a grey sky the voices of the people and the cracked bells of Lerici's churches, San Martino and San Francesco, are muted. Lethargy enwraps the bay, and you are quite likely to meet a San Terenzese strolling near Casa Magni in search of coolness, greeting his friends with the hopeful prediction, *"Pioverà domani sicuro"* ("It's sure to rain tomorrow"), and receiving no reply except a shrug of the shoulders, though he repeats his assertion in a loud voice as if making it for the first time, and he yawns uneasily. The humid heat, which Italians greatly dislike, subdues the people, but at midday it does not silence the cicadas in the olive groves above the graveyard of San Terenzo; their hysterical creaking may drive you down to the shore, where the surf rises and hisses as the afternoon draws on.

By the middle of the week Williams was writing (27 June):

> "The heat increases daily, and prayers are offering for rain. At Parma it is now so excessive that the labourers are forbidden to work in the fields after 10 and before 5, fearful of an epidemic."

Knowing that he was soon to meet Leigh Hunt again, Shelley probably thought with pleasure of his few loyal friends during that week, and towards its end he was writing to one of the most loyal. He had calculated at three the number of people who did not consider him a monster of evil, and made the calculation in no moment of intense dejection, for in the rejected fragments for *Epipsychidion* he wrote:

> If I had but a friend! Why, I have three,
> Even by my own confession; there may be
> Some more, for what I know; for 'tis my mind
> To call my friends all who are wise and kind,—
> And these, Heaven knows, at best are very few.

He had changed his mind, perhaps, since writing of his friends in *Letter to Maria Gisborne*, "Oh that Hunt, Hogg, Peacock and Smith were there." Peacock he always valued, and wrote to him most of his well-known "pictorial letters" on Italy, though Mary did not share his liking. Hunt's friendship was never clouded. Horace Smith, author with his brother of *Rejected Addresses*, was his friend and, unofficially, banker. Leigh Hunt, who wholeheartedly shared Shelley's affection for the parodist, wrote in his *Autobiography*, "A finer nature than Horace Smith's, except in the single instance of Shelley, I never met with in man," and he quoted Shelley's lines:

> Wit and sense,
> Virtue and human knowledge,—all that might
> Make this dull world a business of delight,
> Are all combined in Horace Smith.

Hunt adds something that Shelley once said to him about Smith:

> "I know not what Horace Smith must take me for sometimes: I am afraid he must think me a strange fellow: but is it not odd, that the only truly generous person I ever knew, who had money to be generous with, should be a stockbroker? And he writes poetry too—he writes poetry and pastoral dramas, and yet knows how to make money, and does make it, and is still generous!"

Recalling his first meeting with Shelley at Hampstead in 1816, when he already considered him a "grievously over-punished man", Horace Smith used expressions no less friendly:

> "I beheld a fair, freckled, blue-eyed, light-haired, delicate-looking person, whose countenance was serious and thoughtful, whose stature would have been rather tall had he carried himself upright; whose earnest voice, though never loud, was somewhat unmusical. Manifest as it was that his preoccupied mind had no thought to spare for the modish adjustment of his fashionably made clothes, it was impossible to doubt even for a moment that you were gazing upon a *gentleman* . . . one that is gentle, generous, accomplished, brave."

Horace Smith was a practical but not punctilious business man; for instance, he did not on Shelley's death claim the sum of £150 owing to him for postage and small commissions. It was he who tried to buy in Paris the harp that Shelley wished to present to Jane Williams: the guitar and the verses beginning "Ariel to Miranda" took its place. It was to him that Shelley now turned in a last attempt to raise money for William Godwin—which might put an end to the bitter, demanding letters from her father that Mary had asked Shelley to intercept.

During the last months of his life Shelley intended to amend his will. He had revised it in 1817; though he did not assess his friendships in terms of money, it would have been interesting to see what changes he would have made in the second revision. The original will contained bequests of £6,000 to Harriet, £5,000 to each of her children, £2,000 to Peacock and similar amounts to Byron and Hogg. Peacock's legacy was to be invested in an annuity (because he, too, was a bad manager of money) and he was to receive in addition the sum of £150. Mary was to receive the rest, after Claire's bequest had been paid. Shelley meant this to be £6,000, but the omission of a single word, in a second reference to the amount, caused the sum to be doubled. The revision made in February, 1817, omitted the legacy to Harriet and increased by £1,000 each the legacies to Ianthe and Charles; Shelley also included a bequest of £2,000 to William Shelley. It is supposed that in 1822 Shelley intended to amend Claire's legacy to £6,000 and leave £2,000 to Leigh Hunt.

The will could not come into effect till Sir Timothy Shelley died. Mary's first act on probate was to set aside a sum that would insure Hunt a life annuity of £150.

Though there were heavy burdens upon the poet while he lived at Casa Magni, Mary Shelley declared that these two months were the happiest in his life. His last letter from the bay spoke of his contentment. In such a mood, his sense of humour would not desert him. Something must be said about his humour, for it is an essential part of the portrait. The idea of a humourless Shelley is a distortion; but the nature of his humour is so subtle that it is not easily captured in words.

Hogg, whose words were coloured by a desire to become a

facetious novelist, wrote as if Shelley's humour were entirely of the fantastic kind. Other sources show that it was a compound of many elements: verbal wit, the private joke, complex personal irony. His was the humour of the man who in his subtlest jokes is laughing at himself. Liking for the wit of words came early: at Eton a master was disturbed by the noise in Shelley's room, found him experimenting with a galvanic battery, and seemingly enveloped in blue flame, and asked him what he thought he was doing, whereupon Shelley replied pertly, "Please, sir, I'm raising the devil." He liked the humour of situation, too: when oppressed by the severe face of an old woman in the Hampstead coach, he unexpectedly announced to his companion:

> For God's sake! let us sit upon the ground,
> And tell sad stories of the death of kings.

A similar kind of humour broke out when, Hogg records, Shelley as an undergraduate had been arguing that all knowledge was inherent, not acquired. The argument was continued in the street, where Shelley (no doubt tired of the argument and particularly of his own side of it) approached a woman who was carrying a baby and asked politely, "Will your baby tell us anything about pre-existence, madam?" The woman regretted that the child could not, because it had not yet learnt to talk. "How provokingly close are those new-born babes!" Shelley remarked.

One kind of humour that he did not enjoy was the "dirty joke", as Mary termed it when an Italian offended Shelley by telling one in company. This distaste had developed early: it made Shelley unpopular with his first schoolmaster, at whose innuendoes he refused to smile.

When he seemed to be laughing at his friends, he was often laughing at himself. When, in 1816, there was a possibility of Byron's returning to England, Shelley made William behave himself not by threatening to give him to the Corsican Ogre, but by saying, "The great poet is coming!" In his letters there are similar touches of irony at his own expense; in 1821 he was writing to the new Corsican Ogre:

"You felt the strength to soar beyond the arrows; the eagle was soon lost in the light in which it was nourished, and the eyes of the aimers were blinded. As to me, I am, perhaps, morbidly indifferent to this sort of praise or blame; and this, perhaps, deprives me of an incitement to do what now I never shall do, i.e., write anything worth calling a poem. Thanks to that happy indifference, I can yet delight in the productions of those who can; nor has ill-success yet turned me into an unfailing, and malignant critic; that second degree in the descending scale of the Academy of Disappointed Authors."

He was at his wittiest and most ironical when writing about the vanity of the literary mind and the spleen of self-styled critics. Yet malice was lacking in such writings; even *Peter Bell the Third* is an appeal to a poet to be true to his gift, not merely a request to him to refrain from writing drivel.

He did not mind being caricatured, as Peacock caricatured him in *Nightmare Abbey*, as Scythrop. In one scene Scythrop's father reads him a text to console him for a disappointment in love: "One man among a thousand have I found, but a woman amongst all those have I not found." Scythrop replies warmly with a genuine twist of Shelley's humour, reminiscent of a note in *Queen Mab*: "How could he expect it, when the whole thousand were locked up in his seraglio? His experience is no precedent for a free state of society like that in which we live."

One way of understanding the nature of Shelley's humour is to compare his letters with Byron's, and to note especially the letters the two poets exchanged. Byron's correspondence is dashing, witty, malicious, frequently indecent and almost always entertaining; but it is never private; it is always written with an eye to circulation, or to posterity. Byron's conversation was cynical and sharp, coloured by a desire to frighten people into thinking of him as Cain or Mephistopheles, with the worn-out spirit of Don Juan constantly intruding. Shelley's letters, by contrast, seem serious to the degree of heaviness, but there are concealed currents of irony. His reported conversations are mainly serious, but Trelawny captures some of their lighter tones. In Trelawny's reminiscences we see Shelley hurrying out of the house, and stepping over Percy Florence, who is sitting on the doorstep. "Whose child is it?" asks Trelawny. "Don't know," replies Shelley, taking a look. Mary opens the casement and reminds her husband that the child is his own. "You are not the wise man who knows his own child," says Trelawny. "The wise men," Shelley replies, "have none."

Tom Medwin attempted to convey the quality of this humour—humour so deep-rooted in the personality that it is hard to record—by writing:

"At times he was as sportive as his child, (with whom he would play by the hour upon the floor,) and his wit flowed in a continuous stream,—not that broad humour which is so much in vogue at the present day, but a genuine wit, classical I might say, and refined, that caused a smile rather than a laugh."

Since a review dismissed *Prometheus Unbound* as "*nonsense, pure, unmixed nonsense*", and the *Quarterly* referred to "*drivelling prose run mad*", plenty of acid and asterisks have been expended on Shelley's work and his aims as a poet. In the last seven days of tranquillity at San Terenzo, Shelley may have been stocktaking, a process that he had begun the year before when he wrote his *Defence of Poetry*.

Many of his contemporaries found his verse over-intense and obscure; if they were able to stomach his political and religious opinions, they found his mysterious scientific allusions impossible to grasp, and his deliberate mixing of metaphors of body and spirit a literary blemish. The scientific allusions (*Prometheus* is packed with them) now make sense, and the compound metaphor is no longer considered "metaphysical", but natural to the language of poetry.

The cruder blemishes of his verse—repeated imagery involving clouds, caves, serpents, eagles, boat, veils and the sea —had been pointed out by his friend Hunt. In the review of *The Revolt of Islam* in which Hunt drew attention to the monotonous sea-metaphors, he also condemned an "inartificial and yet not natural economy".

The repetitions and the monotony of imagery will not withstand modern criticism, which on the other hand values rather than condemns the remarkable compression of ideas to be found side by side with expanded, tumultuous language. Whence did Shelley derive this talent for condensation; with whom did he share it? Not from John Donne, with whose compressed versions of the ceremonies of love Shelley would have had an affinity, had he read Donne; not wholly from Milton—but perhaps through Milton. For the influences are largely Italian. It was not Italian literature in itself—embellished, rhetorical, often absurdly inflated—that taught Shelley to charge words with ideas, but it may well have been his preoccupation with Petrarch. During his last week at Casa Magni Shelley may have added a hundred or so lines to *The Triumph of Life*. His last poem is not only a kind of imitation of Petrarch, but a form of homage to him.

Though the work of Sophocles and Keats went with him when he was drowned, a volume of Petrarch may have been in his hands during his last week of leisure. Petrarch's influence was the culmination of the influence of Italy itself which had begun to work in Shelley's poetry since 1818; the four great creative years of his life were, after all, Italian years. *Rosalind and Helen*, a poem begun in England and finished in Italy, is in some ways a notebook of impressions, a record of an altered view of nature. It reveals Shelley seeing in a new way, and incidentally removing the sentimentalities of his early poetry. Henceforward there would be little room for such language—commonplace even at that period—as this, from *Alastor*:

> Undulating woods, and silent well,
> And leaping rivulet, and evening gloom
> Now deepening the dark shades.

Compared with the words he used to record his first Italian impressions, such imagery seems a steel engraving side by side with fresh oil or water colours. In *Rosalind and Helen*

> through the intricate wild wood,
> A maze of life and light and motion
> Is woven.

It would not be difficult for the reader who knows Italy well to piece together this poem as Shelley actually composed it, for the contrast between the English and the Italian influence of scenery is so marked. There is the grasshopper's incessant chirping; the "emotion In all that dwells at noontide here"; "the windless sky"; the blue lake; the cypresses that "cleave with their dark green cones the silent skies". Imagination alone would never lead a poet to choose these images for his first jottings, yet to become coherent sentences, on the landscapes of Italy: it was experience that came into Shelley's poetry in 1818—experience swiftly absorbed and soon stamped (in October of that year) on one of his most polished and most Italianate poems, *Lines Written Among the Euganean Hills*.

The "quenchless lamp" had begun to shed its light on Shelley's mind as early as 1813, when the young poet began to study literary Italian in company with Hogg. Not surprisingly, Hogg found nothing to rhapsodize about in Petrarch's devotion to Laura; but Shelley found in Petrarch an affinity with his own unformed ideas about "intellectual beauty" and the painful spiritualizing or etherealizing of human love.

He would find humour as well as platonics in Petrarch's sonnets. A fourteenth-century man, Petrarch was not a poet to sink in abstractions. Whether Laura actually lived, or existed in his imagination only, he gave her a life history, and a lapidary inscription as magnificent as any given by a man to a woman. Real or imaginary, she was a Tuscan woman, a woman who could be angry and ill; who grew old and died.

Neither Shelley nor Hogg could have deeply understood Petrarch's language, much less his thought, in 1813. His syntax is as complicated as Shelley's and designed like Shelley's for the encompassing of an idea; and one finds when reading both poets that unless one tries hard to understand the syntax the words wrap up, rather than encompass, the thought. On arriving in Italy, Shelley naturally had some difficulty in understanding spoken Italian; but it did not take him long to master the language. He was a good linguist (he translated from Italian, Spanish and German and even began to learn Arabic). During his first summer in Italy he wrote:

"We have almost finished Ariosto—who is entertaining and graceful, and *sometimes* a Poet. Forgive me, worshippers of a more equal and tolerant divinity in poetry, if Ariosto pleases me less than you. Where is the gentle seriousness, the delicate sensibility, the calm and sustained energy without which true greatness·cannot be? He is so cruel too, in his descriptions; his most prized virtues are vices almost without disguise. He constantly vindicates and embellishes revenge in its grossest form; the most deadly superstition that ever infested the world. How different from the tender and solemn enthusiasm of Petrarch—or even the delicate moral sensibility of Tasso, though somewhat obscured by an assumed and artificial style."

The predilection became firmer and in September, 1819, he read aloud, to Mary, Petrarch's *Trionfo della morte*. In 1820 he included Petrarch in his list of books for Medwin's library. He lost all interest in Tasso and frequently quoted Petrarch's ode *All'Italia*. A month after the reading aloud of the *Triumph of Death* he wrote *Ode to the West Wind*. He was at this time still working on *Prometheus Unbound*.

Shelley's last poem seems to have been designed as part imitation of, part comment on, Petrarch's *Trionfi*. *The Triumph of Life* was laboriously constructed by Mary from the rough drafts that Shelley prepared while writing at night, with the *sandalino* drawn up on the shore, in the Maralunga and other coves surrounding the bay. Enough remains for the parallel to be quite clear. Shelley adopted Petrarch's rhyming scheme and adapted his metre. The rhyme scheme—*a, b, a; b, c, b; c, d, c,* etc.—is facile in Italian but perilous in English, which demands more varied rhymes in place of the simple vowel-endings of Italian. The result is that in rough draft *The Triumph of Life* appears verbose and occasionally leaden-footed, whereas the *Trionfi* have the compression that Shelley had achieved in *Ode to the West Wind*.

The resemblance between the two poems is more than mechanical. Petrarch's poem, in six parts, describes the triumph of love over man; of chastity over love; of death over both; of fame over death; of time over fame; and of eternity over time. It opens:

> *Nel tempo che rinnova i miei sospiri*
> *Per la dolce memoria di quel giorno*
> *Che fu principio a si lunghi martiri,*
>
> *Scaldava il Sol già l'uno e l'altro corno*
> *Del Tauro, e la fanciulla di Titone*
> *Correa gelata al suo antico soggiorno.*
>
> *Amor gli sdegni e 'l pianto e la stagione*
> *Ricondotto m'aveano al chiuso loco*
> *Ov'ogni fascio il cor lasso ripone.*
>
> *Ivi fra l'erbe, già del pianger fioco,*
> *Vinto dal sonno, vidi una gran luce,*
> *E dentro assai dolor con breve gioco,*
>
> *Vidi un vittorioso e sommo duce,*
> *Pur com'un di color che 'n Campidoglio*
> *Trionfal carro a gran gloria conduce.*

(In the season when I sigh anew at the sweet memory of that day that was the beginning of so long a martyrdom, the sun was warming both horns of Taurus, and Titan's daughter, the dawn, was running cold across the sky. Love, scorn, tears and the season had drawn me back to Valchiusa, where my weary heart re-makes each bond. There on the grass, faint with tears and overcome by sleep, I saw a great light, and surrounded by much sorrow and brief joy I saw a victorious and supreme leader, like one of those who in Campidoglio gloriously lead a triumphal car.)

In other words, Petrarch goes to the place where in the spring he first saw Laura, now dead, and in the cold air of dawn he falls asleep and dreams.

Shelley's opening lines, with a few descriptive embellishments omitted, run thus:

> Swift as a spirit hastening to his task
> Of glory and of good, the Sun sprang forth
> Rejoicing in his splendour, and the mask
> Of darkness fell from the awakened Earth . . .
>   .   .   .   .   .
>
> But I, whom thoughts which must remain untold
>
> Had kept as wakeful as the stars that gem
> The cone of night,—now they were laid asleep,
> Stretched my faint limbs beneath the hoary stem
>
> Which an old chestnut flung athwart the steep
> Of a green Apennine: before me fled
> The night; behind me rose the day; the deep
>
> Was at my feet, and Heaven above my head;—
> When a strange trance over my fancy grew,
> Which was not slumber, for the shade it spread
>
> Was so transparent, that the scene came through
> As clear as, when a veil of light is drawn
> O'er evening hills, they glimmer; and I knew
>
> That I had felt the freshness of that dawn,
> Bathed in the same cold dew my brow and hair,
> And sate as thus upon that slope of lawn
>
> Under the selfsame bough, and heard as there
> The birds, the fountains and the ocean hold
> Sweet talk in music through the enamoured air;
> And then a vision on my brain was rolled.

There follows a description of the coming of Life's triumphal car, in blazing light; but Shelley's great guide is not like Petrarch's:

>   a Shape
> So sate within, as one whom years deform,
>
> Beneath a dusky hood and double cape,
> Crouching within the shadow of a tomb;
> And o'er what seemed the head a cloud-like crape

> Was bent, a dun and faint ethereal gloom
> Tempering the light. Upon the chariot beam
> A Janus-visaged Shadow did assume
>
> The guidance of that wonder-wingèd team.

Petrarch reviews (sometimes tediously, it must be admitted) the lovers of antiquity. Shelley chooses as his representatives of Life first Rousseau and Napoleon, then Voltaire, Frederic, Paul, Catherine and Leopold; later he mentions Plato, Bacon and the Fathers of the Church. His guide is Rousseau:

> What I thought was an old root which grew
> To strange distortion out of the hill-side,
> Was indeed one of those deluded crew.

The first of Petrarch's "crew" is Caesar; Shelley sees "the heirs of Caesar's crime". In the *Trionfo d'amore* the dominating idea is soon stated:

> *Quest' è colui che 'l mondo chiama Amore;*
> *Amaro, come vedi.*

(This is he whom the world calls Love; bitter, as you see.)

Equally promptly, Shelley produces his central idea:

> And much I grieved to think how power and will
> In opposition rule our mortal day,
>
> And why God made irreconcilable
> Good and the means of good.

And in the words of the leader, Rousseau:

> "Their power was given
> But to destroy," replied the leader: "I
> Am one of those who have created, even
>
> If it be a world of agony."

How closely Shelley was imitating Petrarch's method may be judged by the use of the word "leader", a literal translation of the word *duce* used by Petrarch. It is the only instance of the word "leader" used in Shelley's poetry.

Petrarch's theme was the bitterness (but supremacy) of love in the eyes of youth. Shelley's similarly paradoxical statement is that life makes the "heart sick of one sad thought", that it is a battlefield of the will of man, which while appearing to be the means of good, too often turns to power, the instrument of destruction. This much we can interpret from what remains of *The Triumph of Life*, and it suggests that Shelley's intention probably was to rest content with writing his complement to the *Trionfo d'amore*, not to write six Triumphs. The leader describes his youthful vision of love:

> the wondrous story
> How all things are transfigured except Love;

but unfortunately the world is not a world of lovers, and the light is obscured by vampire-bats among men:

> Some made a cradle of the ermined capes
>
> Of kingly mantles; some across the tire
> Of pontiffs sate like vultures; others played
> Under the crown which girt with empire
>
> A baby's or an idiot's brow, and made
> Their nests in it. The old anatomies
> Sate hatching their bare broods under the shade
>
> Of demon wings, and laughed from their dead eyes
> To reassume the delegated power,
> Arrayed in which those worms did monarchise,
>
> Who make this earth their charnel. Others more
> Humble, like falcons, sate upon the fist
> Of common men, and round their heads did soar.

The entire argument is not concerned with the corruption

spread by power over monarchs, prelates and demagogues, however. The vampire-bats settle also on women, "On fairest bosoms and the sunniest hair", to corrupt them:

> And in those eyes where once hope shone,
> Desire, like a lioness bereft
>
> Of her last cub, glared ere it died.

Finally Rousseau (if the punctuation is correct) or Shelley (if as is possible a set of inverted commas has been misplaced) cries "Then, what is life?" and the poem is broken off. We are left to guess in what stage of the history of man, his emotions and aspirations, Shelley was to find the triumph.

Shelley did not borrow from Petrarch, and in many respects the poets are as unlike as might be expected from the space of five centuries lying between them; but they shared several fundamental ideas and there are echoes in Shelley's work of certain terms used by Petrarch.

Petrarch never gave up his verse to extensive descriptions of natural scenery, as Shelley did in his attempts to bring about some magical alchemy, some ecstatic fusion, between the spirit of man and the works of Nature. Petrarch's intensity was expended on the idea of eternity—in relation to his spiritual faith and his early love—just as Shelley in his most difficult work attempted the eternalizing of man's love and human personality: which is no more and no less than a religious idea.

Petrarch believed that all things converged upon eternity, but his view of the corroding power of time is similar to Shelley's:

> Se la mia vita da l'aspro tormento
> Si può tanto schermire e degli affani,
> Ch' i' veggia, per virtù degli ultimi anni,
> Donna, de' be' vostri occhi il lume spento,
> E i cape' d'oro fin farsi d'argento,
> E lassar le ghirlande e i verdi panni,
> E 'l viso scolorir che ne' miei danni

> *A lamentar mi fa pauroso e lento;*
> *Pur me darà tanta baldanza Amore,*
> *Ch' i' vi discovrirò, dei miei martiri*
> *Qua' sono stati gli anni e i giorni e l'ore...*

(If my life can parry harsh torment, and anguish, may I see in its last years, lady, the spent light of your eyes, and your golden hair silvered, and the garlands and youth's green dress worn out; and the fading of that countenance which, to my hurt, makes me foolish and afraid when it shows displeasure. Then at least love will give me enough boldness to reveal to you how many were the years, days and hours of my martyrdom...)

(Sonnet IX)

This sonnet, which ends with the reflection that at least when she has lost her beauty Laura may pity the poet more, has the compression, the grimness and the mixture of cruelty and tenderness that characterize several of Shelley's lyrics.

Shelley's fear of the night is not usually associated with Petrarch, but it is to be found in the poems Shelley read with so much sympathy:

> *Poi quand' io veggio fiammeggiar le stelle,*
> *Vo lagrimando e desiando il giorno.*

(Then, when I see the stars glistening, I go crying and longing for the day.)

(Sestina I)

In Sonnet CXCVII Petrarch writes that though happy lovers love the night and hate the dawn, he is of the opposite persuasion, since for him the dawn mitigates the anguish of the night. The whole spirit of Shelley's love poetry receives, in Petrarch, its finest expression in the first Sestina:

> *Con lei foss'io da che si parte il Sole,*
> *E non ci vedess' altri che le stelle;*
> *Sol una notte; e mai non fosse l'alba:*
> *E non si trasformasse in verde selva*
> *Per uscirmi di braccia, come il giorno*

Che Apollo le seguia qua giù per terra.
Ma io sarò sotterra in secca selva,
E 'l giorno andrà pien di minute stelle
Prima ch'a si dolce alba arrivi il Sole.

(That I might be with her from sunset, and that I should see nothing but the stars; only one night; and never a dawn; and that she might not change into a laurel, to escape from my arms, as Daphne did from Apollo's the day he followed her down to earth. But I shall be below ground, in my coffin, and the day will go by full of small stars, before the sun will shine on so sweet a dawn.)

It is not surprising to find an echo of this thought in *Epipsychidion*:

I stood, and felt the dawn of my long night
Was penetrating me with living light.

It was in 1820, the year when he became absorbed in Petrarch, that Shelley wrote in *Orpheus*, "Where she is, it is dark!"

Petrarch excelled when writing on death; his sonnets written after the death of Laura are superior, for sustained emotion, to those written before. Yet even in the first set he had often taken up the theme: *"Quante volte m'udiste chiamar Morte!"* ("How often you heard me call on death!"). The feeling of *A Lament*, which begins:

O world! O life! O time!
On whose last steps I climb,

is given similar though calmer expression in *Trionfo della morte*, which Shelley read aloud not long before he wrote the above lines:

La morte è fin d'una prigione oscura
Agli animi gentili.

(Death is the end of a shadowy prison, to gentle spirits.)

This thought occurs in *The Cenci* (I, i, 115):

> I rarely kill the body, which preserves
> Like a strong prison, the soul within my power.

Shelley was obsessed by time, the mysterious trinity of past, present and future:

> And the future is dark, and the present is spread
> Like a pillow of thorns for thy slumberless head.
> *(Prometheus Unbound)*

> in form,
> Sound, colour—in whatever checks that Storm
> Which with the shattered present chokes the past.
> *(Epipsychidion)*

> I mix the present with the past,
> And each seems uglier than the last.
> *(Song* for *Tasso)*

> He, by the past pursued,
> Rests with those dead, but unforgotten hours
> Whose ghosts scare victor kings in their ancestral towers.
> *(Ode to Liberty)*

> There is regret, almost remorse,
> For Time long past.
> 'Tis like a child's beloved corse
> A father watches, till at last
> Beauty is like remembrance, cast
> From Time long past.
> *(Time Long Past)*

In the final *Trionfo* Petrarch writes on this theme:

> *Quel che l'anima nostra preme e 'ngombra*
> *Dianzi, adesso, ier, diman, mattino e sera,*
> *Tutti in un punto passeran com'ombra.*

(What now presses upon and burdens our spirit—before, now, yesterday, tomorrow, morning and evening—all in an instant will pass like a shadow.)

Perhaps the simplest expression of Petrarch's sense of past, future and mutability, and that most near to Shelley's several poems on the theme, is to be found in Sonnet IV written after Laura's death:

> *La vita fugge e non s'arresta un'ora;*
> *E la morte vien dietro a gran giornate:*
> *E le cose presenti e le passate*
> *Mi danno guerra, e le future ancora.*

(Life slips away and does not pause for an hour; and death comes behind in great day-long strides; and things present and past wage war against me, and things future even more.)

Shelley frequently wrote about hope and fear—a combination of ideas too persistent to be set aside as a figure of speech amounting to little more than "indecision". In *Epipsychidion* he writes:

> As the state of Death
> And Birth is worshipped by those sisters wild
> Called Hope and Fear.

Behind the painted veil of life, in the sonnet on that theme,

> lurk Fear
> And Hope, twin Destinies.

In the *Revolt of Islam* the twin sources of energy appear in this form:

Necessity, and love, and life, the grave,
And sympathy, fountains of hope and fear:
Justice, and truth, and time, and the world's natural sphere.

Petrarch's use of the image appears in the *Trionfo d'amore*:

> *Da indi in qua so che si fa nel chiostro*
> *D'Amor; e che si teme, e che si spera,*
> *A chi sa legger, ne la fronte il mostro.*

> (From that time till now I know what one does in love's cloister; that one fears, and that one hopes; who knows how to read it sees on one's brow the monster.)

The lines recall Shelley's expression of desolation, in *Prometheus Unbound*, in which gentle spirits

> Dream visions of aëreal joy, and call the monster, Love,
> And wake, and find the shadow Pain.

In Sonnet XC the words are used as a figure of paradox:

> *Pace non trovo, e non ò da far guerra;*
> *E temo e spero, ed ardo, e son un ghiaccio;*
> *E volo sopra 'l cielo, e giaccio in terra;*
> *E nulla stringo, e tutto 'l mondo abbraccio.*

(I find no peace, have no means to wage war; I fear and hope, and burn, and become ice; I fly above the sky and lie on earth; I grasp nothing, and embrace the whole world.)

Like Shelley, Petrarch found paradox effective: *"Perfida lealtate, e fido inganno"* ("Treacherous loyalty, and faithful cunning"). Humour is not absent from his poetry. Tension is dominant in his work, however; his frequent desire is for *"Qualche breve riposo, e qualche tregua"* ("Some brief rest, some truce"). For him, as for Shelley, love is gallwood as well as honey; a prison and a labyrinth:

> *Mille tre cento ventisette appunto,*
> *Su l'ora prima, il di sesto d'aprile*
> *Nel laberinto intrai: nè veggio ond'esca.*

(In thirteen hundred and twenty-seven exactly, at the first hour, on the sixth of April, I entered the labyrinth; nor do I see the way out.)

(Sonnet CLVII)

> *Un lungo error in cieco laberinto.*

(A long wandering in a blind labyrinth.)

(Sonnet CLXIX)

In *Prometheus Unbound*, Shelley uses the metaphor for both body and mind:

> We will be dread thought beneath thy brain,
> And foul desire round thine astonished heart,
> And blood within thy labyrinthine veins
> Crawling like agony.
>
> . . . . .
>
> Like the omnipotence
> Of music, when the inspired voice and lute
> Languish, ere yet the responses are mute,
> Which through the deep and labyrinthine soul,
> Like echoes through long caverns, wind and roll.

He uses the word in the fragment:

> And who feels discord now or sorrow?
> Love is the universe today—
> These are the slaves of dim tomorrow,
> Darkening Life's labyrinthine way.

In *The Revolt of Islam* he combines with the "labyrinth" metaphor his recurrent image of "hope and fear":

> Who shall dare to say
> The deeds which night and fear brought forth, or weigh
> In balance just the good and evil there?
> He might man's deep and searchless heart display,
> And cast a light on those dim labyrinths, where
> Hope, near imagined chasms, is struggling with despair.

There is nothing particularly profound about either Petrarch's or Shelley's use of the words hope and fear, but the phrase is of some interest because it explains why the poetry of both may be called, roughly, "dream-like". If we care to agree, with Sigmund Freud, that a dream is either a hope (desire) or a fear (anxiety), and often a mixture of the two, we can understand the tension in Shelley's poetry very well, and furthermore understand his physical constitution, which exposed him to waking nightmares, and a condition in which the mind, with its command of words, appeared to be translating into poetry the sensations of the body. This condition, which is possibly no more than the ordinary state of a supreme creative artist working at the pitch of his powers, becomes even easier to grasp if one also remembers Freud's warning:

> "It is only too easy to forget that a dream is as a rule merely a thought like any other, made possible by an easing-up of the censorship and by unconscious intensification, and distorted by the operation of the censorship and by unconscious elaboration."

The Eros of Shelley is not very different from the Eros of Freud—and it is equally subject to misinterpretation.

Ode to the West Wind is a dream owing its birth to that personal Eros, or energy, and its chemistry in the imagination may owe a little to three images in Petrarch, the last of which Shelley read aloud to his wife a month before writing the ode. First there are the two practically adjacent sonnets (XXXII and XXXIV) on the death of Laura:

> *Quanta (invidia) porto al ciel, che chiude e serra*
> *E si cupidamente ha in sè raccolto*
> *Lo spirto de le belle membra sciolto.*

(What envy I have for the sky, which shuts and locks in, and has so greedily garnered to itself the spirit dissolved from her beautiful limbs!)

> *Levommi il mio pensier in parte ov'era*
> *Quella ch'io cerco e non ritrovo in terra:*
> *Ivi fra lor che 'l terzo cerchio serra,*
> *La rividi più bella e meno altera.*

(Having raised my thoughts to the place where she was, she whom I seek and do not find on earth, there among those who are enclosed in Heaven's third circle I see her—more beautiful and less severe.)

This reference to the third circle (that of Venus) is used again in the *Trionfo della morte*:

> *la rota*
> *Terza del ciel m'alzava a tanto amore,*
> *Ovunque fosse, stabile ed immota.*

(The third circle of Heaven raised me to such love, where she should be, secure and unmoving.)

In 1820 Shelley wrote in Italian a prose fable, *Una Favola*. It deals with the poet's love for two mistresses, Life and Death, of which Death is the more favoured. It contains a direct reference to Petrarch's "third circle" of Heaven:

> "*La Vita, vergognandosi forse della sua fraude, si celò allora dentro alla spelonca d'una sua sorella abitando colà: ed Amore se ne tornò sospirando, alla sua terza sfera.*"

("Life, feeling perhaps ashamed of her deception, therefore hid herself in the cavern of one of her sisters living there: and Love returned, sighing, to her third sphere.")

Such consonance of thought and occasionally of language between Petrarch and Shelley is not accidental. Mary Shelley knew her husband's absorption with the Italian poet, and resorted to Petrarch when writing about the mysterious poems of 1818, thereby, as we have seen, planting a possible clue to the crisis between them. Furthermore, she used quotations from the same poet to preface the two editions of Shelley's poetry that she herself prepared. One is drawn from Sonnet CLX:

> *In nobil sangue vita umile e queta,*
> *Ed in alto intelletto un puro core;*
> *Frutto senile in sul giovenil fiore,*
> *E in aspetto pensoso anima lieta.*

This is a eulogy transferred from Laura to Shelley: "In noble blood, a life humble and peaceable; and in a high intellect a pure heart; old fruit in a youthful flower, and in a thoughtful aspect, a gay spirit." The end of the sonnet, which is not quoted, runs:

> *E non so che negli occhi che 'n un punto*
> *Può far chiara la notte, oscuro il giorno,*
> *E 'l mel amaro, ed addolcir l'assenzio.*

(And something beyond words which, in those eyes, can suddenly illumine the night, and darken the day, make honey bitter, and sweeten wormwood.)

The second quotation used by Mary Shelley ends Sonnet XXVIII of the second series, and with the gender changed reads:

> *Lui non trov'io, ma suoi santi vestigi,*
> *Tutti rivolti a la superna strada,*
> *Veggio, lunge da' laghi averni e stigi.*

(Him I do not find; only his sacred footprints, turned towards the higher road, do I see, far from the lakes of Avernus and the Styx.)

On Saturday, 29 June, Shelley's books arrived from Genoa, "a good fortune," wrote Williams, "of which I had little hope". On that day Shelley, after trying the boat under sail, wrote his last letter from Casa Magni, and it was to Horace Smith. His old friend had been unable to raise the £400 for Godwin that Shelley had inquired about, and Shelley declared that he was not sorry for the refusal, for he had written with regret, having long been "firmly persuaded that all the money advanced to Godwin so long as he stands engaged in business is absolutely thrown away".

He turned to general matters:

"It seems to me that things have now arrived at such a crisis as requires every man plainly to utter his sentiments on the inefficacy of the existing religions, no less than the political systems, for restraining and guiding mankind. Let us see the truth, whatever that may be. The destiny of man can scarcely be so degraded that he was born only to die—and if such be the case, delusions, especially the gross and preposterous one of the existing religion, can scarcely be supposed to exalt it. If every man said what he thought, it could not subsist for a day. But all, more or less, subdue themselves to the element that surrounds them, and contribute to the evils they lament by the hypocrisy that springs from them. . . .

England appears to be in a desperate condition, Ireland still worse; and no class of those who subsist on the public labour will be persuaded that *their* claims on it must be diminished. But the government must content itself with less in taxes, the landholder must submit to receive less rent, and the fundholder a diminished interest, or they will all get nothing. I once thought to study these affairs and write or act in them—I am glad that my good genius said *refrain*—I see little public virtue, and I foresee that the contest will be one of blood and gold, two elements which however much to my taste in my pocket and my veins, I have an objection to out of them."

He gave news of Byron, of Hunt, of the *Don Juan* and of the projected review:

"Between ourselves, I greatly fear that this alliance will not succeed; for I, who could never have been regarded as more than the link of the two thunderbolts, cannot now consent to be even that; and how long the alliance may continue, I will not prophesy. Pray do not hint my doubts on the subject to any one, or they may do harm to Hunt; and they *may* be groundless."

He concluded:

"I still inhabit this divine bay, reading Spanish dramas, and sailing, and listening to the most enchanting music. We have some friends on a visit to us, and my only regret is that the summer must ever pass, or that Mary has not the same predilection for this place that I have, which would induce me never to shift my quarters. Farewell."

On Sunday the books were being unpacked, and Williams was enthusiastically reading *Queen Mab*—

"an astonishing work. The enthusiasm of his spirit breaks out in some admirable passages in the poetry and the notes are subtle and elegant as he could now write."

Nine

THE SILENT ISLE

> Noon descends, and after noon
> Autumn's evening meets me soon.
>   .   .   .   .   .
>
> And the soft dreams of the morn
> (Which like wingèd winds had borne
> To that silent isle, which lies
> 'Mid remembered agonies,
> The frail bark of this lone being),
> Pass, to other sufferers fleeing,
> And its ancient pilot, Pain,
> Sits beside the helm again.
>   *Lines Written Among the Euganean Hills*

MONDAY, 1 July, dawned a calm and clear day, and at four o'clock Williams was preparing to alter the topsails of the *Don Juan* in the hope that a strong breeze would spring up, sufficient for the run of forty-five or fifty miles along the coast. This time Williams's judgment of the weather was correct, for by midday "a fine breeze from the westward tempted us to weigh for Leghorn". Mary was too weak to accompany the men, as she had wished. When the time of parting came, she called Shelley back two or three times, and when he finally stepped on board and hauled up the *sandalino* she was crying bitterly. She had given the voyagers a letter written to Leigh Hunt, in which she implored him not to accept any invitation that Shelley might extend to him to visit "this dungeon" during the summer.

It was two o'clock when the *Don Juan* moved across the bay to Lerici. By half past two Captain Roberts was aboard with Shelley, Williams and Charles Vivian, and with a sidewind to propel them, they set course. Seven hours later, having made six or seven knots without any delays, they sailed into Leghorn harbour. It was half past nine, and the health office had shut at nine o'clock. They could not land without clearance papers (they were a "foreign" ship coming from another state), so they anchored astern the *Bolivar*, borrowed some cushions from aboard Byron's ship, and spent the night on board their own boat.

Next morning brought complications. They learned from the crew of the *Bolivar* that that ship was due to sail for Genoa. The story was that Lord Byron would leave Tuscany and establish his household on Genoese soil, for Count Gamba's family were in a scrape, and had been given but a few days to leave Tuscany. Very soon they received confirmation of at least the second part of this story, for on landing they met the Gambas, who had just left the police office, where they had been summoned to receive the official order of expulsion. There had been a brawl between Byron's and Gamba's servants, in which Gamba had been slightly wounded. It was a bad moment to discuss with Byron the scheme for the *Liberal* which had brought Leigh Hunt and his family out to Italy. Hunt had arrived at Byron's country house outside Pisa, indeed, immediately after the brawl. Byron had lost his enthusiasm for the project and the thought of living in proximity with Hunt and his numerous family now horrified him. He was very soon (as Trelawny noticed) to exhort his bull-dog, "Don't let any Cockneys pass this way."

The *Liberal* project had not escaped the notice of the Tuscan Government, who watched Byron and the Gambas closely. The Tuscan authorities learned that Byron and another English poet intended to start a newspaper against the Italian Government and its Austrian masters. This information has the air of having been culled not among Byron's associates but from gossip circulating among the members of the English Factory at Leghorn, a group of merchants who had reason to dislike the proximity of such politically dangerous compatriots as Byron and Shelley. Two years earlier, a panic had arisen among these merchants. It began when the British Minister at Florence, Lord Burghersh, whose mind was haunted by fears of secret societies, frightened his consul at Leghorn, John Falconar, by demanding:

"I beg you to give me an answer to this question, have you ever been present at any meeting of persons designating themselves as a political society, under the name of *European* or any other? Have you ever received them at your house particularly once when a *German* was admitted a member of the organization?"

Falconar hastily denied the charge, protested his loyalty to the British diplomatic service, and unwisely mentioned with contempt one Grant, a local merchant, "foremost in all the Jacobin Clubs of the day". In reply, Lord Burghersh ordered Falconar to do what he had ordered him as early as July, 1818—namely to report not only ships' movements but to "give yourself pains to find out what is taking place at Leghorn with regard to the Societies I mentioned to you".

Falconar's counter-accusation, and his stupidity in having a libellous notice about Grant placed in the consular office at Genoa, designed to dissuade English sea-captains from having anything to do with the man, came to Grant's knowledge, and the matter nearly ended with Falconar's dismissal for the indiscretion in the very month of July, 1822. Lord Castlereagh had looked into the matter himself. Falconar had no reason to be happy on account of the presence of the English poets at Leghorn; nor would the members of the English Factory hesitate to pass on any damaging information they might have, for their livelihood was endangered by the taint of Jacobinism that had touched one of their members.

"Jacobinism" was only a bogey, which Burghersh fostered in the mind of Castlereagh. Like all spies and not a few ministers, ambassadors and consuls, Burghersh reported chiefly what he thought would please his master. In fact, hatred of the Austrians was alive among the Italians as

among the English poets. In the very year when Lord
Burghersh had frightened his Leghorn consul with scare-
stories about Jacobins, he filed a document in French containing an Italian opinion, which stated among other things:

> "Austria, by reason of the clumsiness of some of her
> agents, seems to wish to govern the Italians by means of
> her great weight, as if the spirit could be replaced by the
> mass."

The writer added that the Italians did not wish to be looked
upon as "good-for-nothings".

It was in an atmosphere of general as well as personal
suspicion, therefore, that Shelley and Williams met Byron in
the Via Ferdinando at the shop of Henry Dunn, an Englishman
who kept a general store. Apparently there was little time to
discuss the troublesome situation that had developed; in any
case, Shelley was anxious to meet Leigh Hunt after their four
years' parting. He therefore took Williams to the hotel where
the family were staying.

Later, Leigh Hunt described the meeting in fictional form:

> "What a moment it was! I had often wondered to see
> men embrace, and disliked the custom; but I found, on
> this occasion, how quickly great emotions dash aside
> preconceived judgments. My friend's manners had as little
> of the foreigner in them as mine; and yet the moment he
> entered the room, the mutual impulse was so strong upon
> us, that we rushed as heartily together as a Pylades and
> Orestes; and both, in separating, were in tears."

And then he looked at Shelley and saw that time had marked
his face. It had not lost its youthfulness, which all the features
except the eyes contained; but the forehead was wrinkled, the
temples seemed beaten in, and grey had crept among his glossy
brown hair. He stooped as he sat; but his eyes were finer than
Hunt had ever seen them. To Thornton Hunt, a boy of twelve,
Shelley seemed stronger than he had been at Marlow in 1817;

his chest was better developed, his voice stronger, and his manner more confident.

Williams was introduced to Marianne Hunt, who was ill in her room, and he was hurt by the way Byron had received her. Shelley and Hunt had much to talk about, but they also had much to see and experience together. They went to the docks and boarded the ship that had brought Hunt to Italy, and in the cabin Shelley made a dot in the centre of a sheet of paper and said, "*That* is the experience of mankind." "The white then," Hunt said, "is our inexperience—is time past or future, or what we don't know?" "No," Shelley explained; "if all the paper in the world were put together, the white would not be enough for the inexperience, and yet the dot would be the true representation of the other. *All space is the white; and the dot is all history.*"

But the poet did not spend the whole day talking metaphysics, for it must have been on this day, and not as Trelawny said on Shelley's return to Leghorn the following week, that the *Bolivar* and the *Don Juan* put out of port for a sail in the open sea. Williams, meanwhile, shopped and strolled about, and met an old schoolfellow and shipmate, a lieutenant on board the *Rochefort*, which was anchored at Leghorn at the time.

Williams stayed at Leghorn next day (3 July), while Shelley accompanied the Hunts to Pisa, and installed them in the ground floor of Byron's Palazzo Lanfranchi, overlooking the Arno. Byron had moved in from his country house near Monte Nero, in spite of the heat, not so much to discuss Hunt's position as to consider his own. He said at first that he would not publish anything in the *Liberal* under his own name. In the ensuing days Shelley exerted all his powers of tactful persuasion on both Byron and Hunt. He finally extracted from Byron a promise that he would offer, for the first issue, the copyright of his *Vision of Judgment*. He probably had a shorter, though not less delicate, job in bringing to Hunt's notice the fact that he must always give Lord Byron his title, in both conversation and writing. Shelley always did so; but Hunt had once dedicated a poem to his collaborator, innocently and warmly beginning "Dear Byron . . ."

Shelley was particularly fond of Marianne, of whose farewell kiss he had been deprived, as he himself complained, when on the evening before he sailed for the Continent the Hunts allowed him to finish his sleep of exhaustion rather than wake him to say good-bye. He now called in his friend Vaccà, a celebrated and witty doctor who shared at least two of Shelley's interests—atheism and agriculture. His diagnosis on this occasion added nothing to his reputation as a doctor: he examined Marianne Hunt, declared that she was in a decline, and stated that she probably would not outlive the year. She survived the judgment, and died thirty-five years later. Between Byron and Vaccà, Italy gave a dismal welcome to Leigh and Marianne Hunt; but there could be no thought of return to England now, so Shelley persisted in his efforts to win Byron's support for the unhappy and worried family. He could not know that his triumph, in acquiring Byron's *Vision of Judgment* for the review, was to turn out badly; it landed Leigh Hunt's brother John into gaol in England, as the publisher of a blasphemous composition.

On Thursday, 4 July, Edward Williams sat down in Leghorn and wrote in his diary:

"Fine. Processions of Priests and religiosi have for several days past been active in their prayers for rain—but the Gods are either angry or Nature is too powerful."

They were the last words he wrote in that little book.

Shelley wrote to both Mary and Jane that day—to his wife to report Vaccà's sentence upon Marianne, and to explain that Byron, after talking of emigrating to America, then of moving to Genoa, then of settling in Switzerland, seemed finally to have settled for the Duchy of Lucca, ten miles away from Pisa; to Jane to assure her that he would return to Leghorn that night and urge Williams to sail home with the first fair wind.

"I have thus the pleasure of contributing to your happiness when deprived of every other, and of leaving you no other subject of regret, but the absence of one scarcely worth regretting. I fear you are solitary and melancholy at Villa Magni, and, in the intervals of the greater and more serious distress in which I am compelled to sympathize here, I figure to myself the countenance which has been the source of such consolation to me, shadowed by a veil of sorrow.

How soon those hours passed, and how slowly they return to pass so soon again, perhaps for ever, in which we have lived together so intimately, so happily! Adieu, my dearest friend! I only write these lines for the pleasure of tracing what will meet your eyes."

Next morning Shelley received a cheerless letter from Mary. She was obsessed by a feeling of impending doom. The letter has been lost—no doubt it floated away in the Tyrrhenian Sea when the *Don Juan* sank—but Mary explained to a friend later that her fears were not on account of Shelley. She was worried about the child Percy Florence. Williams heard about this letter the next day, and Leigh Hunt saw Shelley open and read it.

The letter referred to another source of discontent: Mary wanted Shelley to look for a house at Pugnano, near Florence. She was not for long to endure Casa Magni; it was Trelawny who eventually removed her from that detested spot. Depressed by her fears, anxious on account of Hunt and his family, and no doubt feeling guilty because Williams, in Leghorn, was aching to join his wife after this, the longest parting they had experienced, Shelley nevertheless brought his famous obstinacy into play and spent the day persuading Byron to make firm his promise to support Hunt in the *Liberal* project. He kept in touch with Williams, no doubt by messenger, for Leghorn was little more than an hour's ride from Pisa.

On the evening of 5 July he was able to feel, with as great a certainty as he had ever enjoyed during his uncertain life, that Hunt would not be utterly abandoned, and that the powerful if unwilling support of Byron had been won over.

On Saturday, 6 July, his diary forgotten, Williams was writing to Jane:

"I have just left the quay, my dearest girl, and the wind blows right across to Spezzia, which adds to the vexation I feel at being unable to leave this place. For my own part, I should have been with you in all probability on Wednesday evening, but I have been kept day after day waiting for Shelley's definite arrangements with Lord B. relative to poor Hunt, whom, in my opinion, he has treated vilely. A letter from Mary, of the most gloomy kind, reached S. yesterday, and this mood of hers aggravated my uneasiness to see you; for I am proud, dear girl, beyond words to express, in the conviction, that *wherever* we may be together you could be cheerful and contented.

Would I could take the present gale by the wings and reach you tonight; hard as it blows, I would venture across for *such* a reward. However, tomorrow something decisive shall take place; and if I am detained, I shall depart in a felucca, and leave the boat to be brought round in company with Trelawny in the *Bolivar*. He talks of visiting Spezzia again in a few days. I am tired to death of waiting—this is our longest separation, and seems a year to me. Absence alone is enough to make me anxious, and indeed unhappy; but I think if I had left you in our own house in solitude, I should feel it less than I do now.—What can I do? Poor S. desires that I should return to you, but I know secretly wishes me not to leave him in the lurch. He too, by his manner, is as anxious to see you almost as I could be, but the interests of poor H. keep him here—in fact, with Lord B. it appears they cannot do anything—who actually said as much as that he did not wish his name to be attached to the work, and of course to theirs."

Williams then speaks of Byron's plans for the future, reporting that Trelawny has been dispatched to feel the way with the Governor of Lucca, carrying letters on the subject:

"All this time Hunt is shuffled off from day to day, and now heaven knows when or how it will end.

Lord B.'s reception of Mrs. Hunt was—as S. tells me—most shameful. She came into his house sick and exhausted, and he scarcely deigned to notice her; was silent, and scarcely bowed. This conduct cut H. to the soul; but the way in which he received our friend Roberts, at Dunn's door, must be described when we meet: it must be acted. How I long to see you; I had written *when*, but I will make no promises, for I too well know how distressing it is to both of us to break them. Tuesday evening at the furthest, unless kept by the weather, I *will* say 'Oh, Jane! how fervently I press you and our little ones to my heart.'

Adieu! Take body and soul; for you are at once my heaven and earth—that is all I ask of both."

On this very day, Jane was writing to Shelley and reporting to him, in a note which he probably never received, a curious hallucination reminiscent of the evening when she had seen his image on the terrace at Casa Magni:

"Your few melancholy lines have indeed cast your own visionary veil over a countenance that was animated with the hope of seeing you return with far different tidings. We heard yesterday that you had left Leghorn in company with the *Bolivar*, and would assuredly be here in the morning at five o'clock; therefore I got up, and from the terrace saw (or I dreamt it) the *Bolivar* opposite in the offing. She hoisted more sail, and went through the Straits. What can this mean? Hope and uncertainty have made such a chaos in my mind that I know not what to think. My own Neddino does not deign to lighten my darkness by a single word. Surely I shall see him tonight. Perhaps, too, you are with him. Well, *pazienza*!

Mary, I am happy to tell you, goes on well; she talks of going to Pisa, and indeed your poor friends seem to require all her assistance. For me, alas! I can only offer sympathy, and my fervent wishes that a brighter cloud may soon dispel the present gloom. I hope much from the air of Pisa for Mrs. Hunt.

Lord B.'s departure gives me pleasure, for whatever may be the present difficulties and disappointments, they are small to what you would have suffered had he remained with you. This I say in the spirit of prophecy, so gather consolation from it.

I have only time left to scrawl you a hasty adieu, and am,

Affectionately yours,

J. W."

Jane added a postscript, referring to what Shelley had written in his melancholy note to her:

"Why do you talk of never enjoying moments like the past? Are you going to join your friend Plato, or do you expect I shall do so soon? *Buona notte.*"

On Sunday, 7 July, all appeared to be settled. Hunt's affairs were at least stable enough in appearance for Shelley to spend the last day with him sight-seeing in Pisa. In his *Autobiography* Leigh Hunt described Shelley as he remembered him:

"His eyes were large and animated, with a dash of wildness in them; his face small but well shaped, particularly the mouth and chin, the turn of which was very sensitive and graceful. His complexion was naturally fair and delicate, with a colour in the cheeks. He had brown hair, which, though tinged with grey, surmounted his face well, being in considerable quantity, and tending to a curl. His side face upon the whole, was deficient in strength, and his features would not have told well in a bust."

Hunt had been too worried, humiliated and despairing, and Shelley too active in the Byron affair, for either of them to think of touring Pisa before this day; so naturally they walked along the narrow streets to see that curious, chequered arrangement so reminiscent of a giant cruet-set, the Cathedral and the Leaning Tower. On the way, Shelley laughed at some jokes made by Hogg, which Hunt reported, and spoke with affection of Horace Smith. In the Cathedral the organ was playing, and Shelley agreed with Hunt's opinion, "that a truly divine religion might yet be established, if charity were really made the principle of it, instead of faith".

They went to visit Shelley's friend Lady Mountcashell, who had now been settled in Pisa for three years. She was a cheerful woman of about forty-seven, for whom Shelley had much affection. (She had "a disposition rather to like me", he had written to Leigh Hunt shortly after making her acquaintance.) She and her lover, George William Tighe, had long lived together in contentment under the title of "Mr. and Mrs. Mason". She had been Mary Wollstonecraft's pupil before her unsatisfactory marriage to Lord Mountcashell. She was highly democratic—and a wit. After the cobbler Thomas Hardy had been acquitted of High Treason, with Thelwall, Horne Tooke and their friends, in 1794, she called at his shop to buy shoes; they were uncomfortable, and she remarked that his lasts were too aristocratic for her democratic feet.

During this last visit, Shelley said, in a vein both philosophical and prophetic:

"If I die tomorrow, I shall have lived to be older than my grandfather; I am ninety years old."

He had said something similar to Trelawny when talking to him about the nonagenarians of Florence, and in yet another conversation which Trelawny noted down in the appendix to his *Records*:

"TRE.: Byron said to me the other morning: 'I was reminded by a letter from my sister that I was thirty-four; but I felt at that time that I was twice that age. I must have lived fast.'

SHELLEY: The mind of man, his brain, and nerves are a truer index of his age than the calendar, and that may make him seventy.

When Shelley at a later date said he was ninety, he was no doubt thinking of the wear and tear of his own mind."

When Shelley left Lady Mountcashell, she recalled his

saying, and his parting look—the happiest she remembered—and the following night she dreamt of him.

He went home with Hunt and they talked about Plato as they watched the fireflies dancing over the black waters of the Arno. Shelley had to return to Leghorn that night. He borrowed Keats's last volume of poems from Leigh Hunt, promised that he would not sail if the weather was treacherous, said good-bye, and drove once more towards the sea.

Next morning, in Leghorn, he and Williams had shopping to do. Shelley had run short of money—he had had to borrow £50 from Byron—so he called at his bankers, Guebhard & Co. Trelawny, back from his mission to Lucca, accompanied him. They went to a store—doubtless Dunn's, in the Via Ferdinando—to buy household provisions, including some bottled beer and a hamper of wine for Maglian, the harbour-master at Lerici. As midday approached they went down to the harbour in the sultry heat. A banker from another banking house, named De Young, is believed to have accompanied the party to the pier, trying to persuade Shelley not to sail. But as Trelawny noted, "Williams was fretting and fuming to be off." Trelawny went aboard the *Bolivar* after one o'clock and Shelley and Williams joined Charles Vivian in the *Don Juan*. Captain Roberts did not like the look of the weather, but his professional opinion bore no more weight than the landsmen's. At two o'clock both ships were under weigh.

Trelawny's intention was to accompany the *Don Juan* outside the port, but the guard-boat crew boarded him and, though he had gone out before without clearance, this time permission was refused. The *Bolivar* returned to the quayside as the *Don Juan* passed the end of the mole. As Trelawny watched his friends the Genoese mate of the *Bolivar* gave it as his opinion that they should have sailed twelve hours earlier, and that they were standing too much in shore—"the current will set them there". Trelawny thought that they would soon have a land-breeze, but the Genoese thought that they would soon have too much: "That gaff topsail is foolish in a boat with no deck and no sailor on board." He pointed to the south-east in the direction of Corsica. "Look at those black lines and the dirty rags hanging on them out of the sky—they are a warning;

look at the smoke on the water; the devil is brewing mischief."

The sea fog had come up by three o'clock, when Roberts, feeling anxious, went to the watch-tower. He thought that he saw the *Don Juan* about ten miles out at sea, off Viareggio; but this is unlikely, for it is scarcely possible to see an eighteen-foot vessel, twenty miles away, in the malignant sea-smoke that rises before a storm in that part of the world. Overcome by the oppressive heat, Trelawny had gone to his cabin to sleep. When he woke, at half past six, it was to hear his crew letting go another anchor, and to find the sky almost dark, and the sea "as solid and smooth as a sheet of lead".

A storm on the *ponente* coast is a frightening sight. The serene sky turns rapidly sullen and the sea, having lost its green limpidity inshore and its rich blue farther out, turns purple, then black, as a kind of smoke rises from the ominously flat surface. The horizon approaches you, then disappears as sea and sky are joined by the black ribbon of fog. The rain falls not with the coolness of a sub-tropical deluge, but with a viciousness, a chill that depresses both mind and body. The lightning makes savage stabs into the valleys among the mountains, the thunder wandering now near, now far, among the peaks. Life is suspended by these storms: they depress rather than exhilarate. Everything and everyone, except for rain, the thunder, and the occasional whiplash of lightning, becomes silent. The Italians have a superstition that to sing or play music during such a storm will attract the lightning.

At Leghorn the fishing craft ran for the shelter of the harbour. The storm, according to Trelawny's account, lasted no longer than twenty minutes. If the conversation of Taaffe, reported four years later, is to be trusted, two Livornese boats sighted the *Don Juan* shortly after Roberts, in the watch-tower, had lost sight of her. The captain of the first offered to take the crew aboard, but was refused. A large wave broke over the boat, and he shouted, "For God's sake reef your sails or you are lost." One of the crew, supposed to be Williams, began to lower the sails but was restrained, supposedly by Shelley. The crew of the second vessel threw no light on the matter. Whether the fact has significance or not, Shelley's watch, preserved in the Bodleian Library, is stopped at 5.16.

P

That night there were gusts and showers and, says Trelawny, "the lightning flashed along the coast". Lady Mountcashell, in Pisa, had a dream. Shelley approached her, pale and dejected, and she invited him, "You look ill, you are tired, sit down and eat." "No, I shall never eat more," he replied; "I have not a *soldo* left in the world." "Nonsense, this is no inn—you need not pay." "Perhaps it is the worse for that," he remarked. The dream merged into one in which she thought that Percy Florence was dead, and she woke crying bitterly.

Petrarch had written, in Sestina IV:

> *Chi è fermato di menar sua vita*
> *Su per l'onde fallaci e per gli scogli,*
> *Scevro da morte con un picciol legno,*
> *Non può molto lontano esser dal fine:*
> *Però sarebbe da ritrarsi in porto*
> *Mentre al governo ancor crede la vela.*
>
> *L'aura soave a cui governo e vela*
> *Commisi entrando a l'amorosa vita,*
> *E sperando venire a miglior porto,*
> *Poi mi condusse in più di mille scogli;*
> *E la cagion del mio doglioso fine*
> *Non pur d'intorno avea, ma dentro al legno.*

. . . .

He who is firmly pledged to lead his life
On the misguiding waves, among the rocks,
Chosen by death, housed in some fragile craft,
Cannot be distant from his journey's end:
Yet he could turn, back to the friendly port,
While to the helm the mainsail still responds.

The smooth-tongued breeze to which both helm and sail
I gave in trust at the start of a life of love,
Hoping to anchor in a better harbour—
That was my guide to more than a thousand rocks;
And the occasion of my sorry end
Was in my craft; not in the winds of love.

Ten

THE GOAL OF TIME

It is deserted now, but once it bore
Thy name, Prometheus; there the emulous youths
Bore to thy triumph through the divine gloom
The lamp which was thine emblem; even as those
Who bear the untransmitted torch of hope
Into the grave, across the night of life,
As thou hast borne it most triumphantly
To this far goal of Time.
Prometheus Unbound

THE briefest account of happenings at Casa Magni during the fortnight that followed the storm is carved in stone, above the central supporting arch of the terrace, in the words of Roccatagliata Ceccardo Ceccardi:

"*Da questo portico in cui si abbateva l'antica ombra di un leccio, il luglio del MDCCCXXII, Mary Godwin e Jane Williams attesero con lagrimante ansia Percy Bysshe Shelley, che da Livorno su fragil legno veleggiando era approdato per improvisa fortuna ai silenzii de le isole elisee. O benedette spiagge, ove l'amore, la libertà, i sogni non hanno catene.*" ("From this porch, in which beat down the ancient shadow of a holm-oak, in July, 1822, Mary Godwin and Jane Williams in weeping anxiety awaited Percy Bysshe Shelley, who, sailing from Leghorn in a fragile craft, had come to shore by sudden chance among the silences of the Elysian Isles.—O blessed shores, where love, liberty and dreams have no chains.")

The three bodies, scattered by the currents, were washed up on the ninth and tenth day after the wreck. The corpse of Edward Williams was cast up on 17 July near the mouth of the River Serchio, where he, Shelley and Trelawny had often sailed in their flat-bottomed boat. Next day Shelley's body was cast on shore six miles farther up the coast, very near to the port of Viareggio; on the same day Charles Vivian's body was washed on to the beach at Massa, nine or ten miles beyond Viareggio in the direction of Lerici.

After the storm which swallowed the *Don Juan*, Trelawny sent the mate of the *Bolivar* to find out whether any of the craft that had scurried into Leghorn had seen Shelley's boat. No one appeared to have sighted it. Next day the mate pointed out on board a fishing-boat an English-made oar which he thought he had seen on the *Don Juan*, but the crew maintained that it was their own oar. On the third day, Trelawny went to Pisa to see whether any letters had arrived from San Terenzo, but there was nothing. He spoke to Hunt and to Byron. Then, having sent to Leghorn instructions for the *Bolivar* to cruise along the coast, he rode in the same direction himself, and dispatched a courier to cover the coast as far as Nice. Having ridden eighteen miles, he learned at Viareggio that a small boat, a water-keg and some bottles had been found there on the beach. He recognized the *sandalino*. Though he feared the worst, he had the coastguards keep a good look-out, and patrolled the coast himself during ensuing days.

At Casa Magni the women were not at first unduly alarmed. On the day of the disaster, Williams's letter of the 6th was received, so the *Don Juan* was expected by Tuesday, the 9th. When she did not appear, Mary and Jane assumed that the vessel was storm-bound at Leghorn. But Wednesday and Thursday were fine, and on Friday Jane Williams would have sailed to Leghorn for news had the weather not taken a turn for the worse. A letter arrived from Leigh Hunt. It fell from Mary's hands, and Jane picked it up and read, "Pray write to tell us how you got home, for they say that you had bad weather after you sailed on Monday, and we are anxious."

Jane at once assumed that it was all over, but Mary, who had been despondent and unsmiling for so long, would not give up hope, and in spite of the fact that she was ill she took a coach from Lerici to Leghorn at once. She showed outstanding physical and moral courage throughout her ordeal. At Lerici no news of a wreck was reported. It was nearly midnight when the women reached Pisa. They went to the Palazzo Lanfranchi to seek Hunt, assuming that Byron was still at Leghorn. Hunt was already in bed, and it was Teresa Guiccioli who came out to find Mary, white-faced, asking the maid for news. Neither Teresa nor Byron had any news to give, so the two women continued their way to Leghorn, to arrive between two and three o'clock in the morning. They chose the wrong inn and waited, sleepless, till six o'clock, when they went to the inn where Roberts was staying and learned what he knew.

Three hours later they started back for San Terenzo, and when passing through Viareggio, they saw and identified the objects Trelawny had seen two days earlier. He joined them, and the three continued the journey home.

It was 10.30 at night when, having passed through Sarzana, they forded the wide, stony bed of the Magra, between the forbidding trees. When the carriage wheels touched the water, and she looked to her left and saw the beacon light at the river's mouth, seven miles away, Mary knew that the sea was Shelley's grave. An hour later they were rowed across the bay from Lerici to San Terenzo, to find the village illuminated for a *festa*, and the villagers dancing and singing on the seashore—a wild celebration which continued for some days afterwards.

It was Saturday night, 13 July. They waited till the following Thursday, the 18th, then Trelawny went back to Leghorn. The slender hope intended to sustain them during those days was that the *sandalino* and the other objects might have been lost or discarded, and that the *Don Juan* might have been driven across to Corsica. The sea between the mainland and that island had varied perils. The previous August, for example, Consul Falconar had reported to his Minister the news that a Neapolitan vessel had been boarded between Corsica and Capraia by four armed Algerians, supposed to be cruising in search of Spanish merchant vessels.

The bodies had already been washed on shore, as Trelawny discovered on reaching Leghorn. Williams's body, which lay near the Tower of Migliarino, at the mouth of the Serchio, suggested that he had been the last survivor, and that he had attempted to strip and swim. Shelley's body, at Viareggio, was fully clothed; in the left-hand jacket pocket was a volume of Sophocles, now preserved in the Bodleian, and in the right-hand pocket the volume of Keats's poems lent by Leigh Hunt, doubled back as if Shelley had thrust it away, while reading, to respond to some emergency. Charles Vivian's body, like the other two, was unidentifiable except by the clothes; it was later burnt on the beach at Massa and the ashes were buried in the sand.

Trelawny had not returned to Casa Magni by the evening of Friday, 19 July, but Claire Clairmont had known the truth since that morning. Roberts had sent a letter addressed to Trelawny, reporting the finding of the bodies. She opened it and, though a later official letter from Viareggio had stated that nothing had been found, she said nothing to Mary or Jane. She wrote instead to Leigh Hunt, asking him to come and break the news. Possibly she misunderstood Roberts's letter, for she wrote:

"I doubt the report, because we had a letter from the captain of the port of Via Reggio, July 15th, later than when Mr. Roberts writes, to say nothing had been found.... I pray you answer this by return of my messenger. I assure you I cannot break it to them, nor is my spirit, weakened as it is from constant suffering, capable of giving them consolation, or protecting them from the first burst of their despair."

Roberts's letter could not have been written before 18 July.

Claire did not have to keep her knowledge secret for many hours. Late that evening Trelawny, who walked to San Terenzo after putting up his horse at Lerici, entered Casa Magni and startled Caterina, the nurse. He went upstairs unannounced and the women read the end of their hope in his expression. Next day he persuaded them to return with him to Pisa.

· · · · ·

The bodies had been buried above the reach of the sea, according to custom, but they were not to lie in unmarked graves on that desolate coast. Trelawny went to work, with the help of British diplomatic representatives at Leghorn and Florence, to make arrangements for exhumation and cremation. Williams's body lay on Tuscan soil; Shelley's was within the confines of the Duchy of Lucca. The British Minister at Florence, Lord Burghersh, was on leave, and it was his chargé d'affaires, Edward James Dawkins, who helped Trelawny in his negotiations with the authorities of both states.[1]

The first account of the accident received by Dawkins was a much-garbled one, for he reported to the Tuscan authorities, in August, that Shelley and Williams had embarked on 12 July, and, surprised by the tempest, had lost their lives the following day; he added that Shelley's remains had been thrown up near the mouth of the Serchio. Williams's relatives had asked permission to cremate the body and remove the ashes to the Protestant cemetery at Leghorn, and Dawkins had addressed "a similar request on behalf of the family of Mr. Shelley" to the Duchess of Lucca.

Matters were in fact placed in the hands of Dr. Trevor, British Chaplain at the Ximenes Palace, Florence, and on 3 August Consul Falconar was directed to apply to the Governor of Leghorn. He replied two days later with the Governor's permission for the body of Williams to be disinterred and reburied near the spot where it lay; or for a monument to be erected nearby. On the 8th permission came from the Tuscan Government for the cremation of Williams's body, under the supervision of the sanitary guards of Leghorn, and for the transfer of the ashes to the cemetery there.

Finally Dawkins was able to communicate to Trelawny the permission of the Lucchese authorities for the cremation of Shelley's body: "I said that they were to be removed to Leghorn for interment, but that need not bind you." It had been decided in the interim to inter the ashes near William Shelley's grave in Rome; those of Williams were to be sent to England.

[1] Trelawny prints a letter from "W. Dawkins"—an understandable misreading of E. J. Dawkins's signature which has been repeated in subsequent accounts. No letters from Trelawny or anyone else connected with Shelley or Williams remain in Dawkins's official files.

What Dawkins meant by the following words is open to conjecture: "I am very sensible of Lord Byron's kindness, and should have called upon him when I passed through Pisa, had he been anybody but Lord Byron." Possibly he was thinking of the Masi affair at Pisa the previous March, an account of which, signed by Byron and Shelley, he had sent to the Foreign Office; it still ranked as unfinished business.

On 13 August, provided with a furnace, fuel, wine and spices, Trelawny sailed up the coast in the *Bolivar* towards the Bocca del Serchio. With fitful breezes, it took thirteen hours to travel as many miles. All was made ready, and Byron and Hunt were asked to be present next day at noon.

There were many spectators, including, as Trelawny reports, "many ladies richly dressed", near the Tower of Migliarino, when at noon next day, on the desolate shore near the pinewoods, Williams's shapeless body was exhumed. Byron, watching the grisly operation, commented:

"Is that a human body? Why, it's more like the carcass of a sheep, or any other animal, than a man: this is a satire on our pride and folly. The entrails of a worm hold together longer than the potter's clay of which man is made . . . Don't repeat this with me; let my carcass rot where it falls."

The heat of the sun and of the fire drove the attendant soldiers to the shade of the pines, but Byron had the melodramatic idea of testing "the strength of these waters that drowned our friends". Trelawny warned him that he was not in condition, but he persisted, so when frankincense and salt had been thrown on the fire, and a flask of wine and oil had been poured on the remains, Byron, Trelawny and Captain Shenley, a friend of Trelawny, swam out to sea in the ferocious heat. A mile out, Byron was sick, and Shenley got cramp; Trelawny, a very strong swimmer who had no mock-modesty and who was not afraid to excel Byron, helped them both back to the shore. The furnace was cooled at four o'clock, the ashes put into a small oak box and placed in Byron's carriage, and

Byron went back to Pisa with Hunt. Trelawny and his party slept at an inn nearby and next morning took the implements to Viareggio for the second ceremony.

Shelley's body had been buried in quicklime between the sea and the ragged pines which have long since disappeared. Mary had seen the spot, and doubted whether the authorities would allow a cremation so near to the town; the grave was, indeed, only three or four hundred yards from the Burlamacca canal leading to the sea and forming in itself a tiny harbour for Viareggio. The scene was not the romantic one, featuring battlemented towers, marble-crested Apennines and clear views of Corsica, Elba and Capraia that Trelawny wrote into his various accounts of the cremation. Far from there being "not a human dwelling in sight", the central square of Viareggio, Piazza Paolina, was two hundred yards away; beyond the writhing pines which then wrestled with the *ponente* wind the length of that wild coast, the Apennines would rise in a heat haze, grey and ominous, the peaks flecked with dull marble.

It took the party an hour's digging to locate the body, buried two feet under the sand. The remains, horribly decomposed, were placed in the furnace and the fire lit. Trelawny recorded that Byron wished to preserve the small, delicate skull, which fell to pieces; but Leigh Hunt wrote in his *Autobiography* that Byron got out of the carriage and wandered away, not wishing to see the spectacle. Hunt himself remained in the carriage and watched Trelawny perform the rites, pouring "more wine . . . over Shelley's dead body than he had consumed during his life". The volume of Keats that Shelley had borrowed was burnt with the body and, in Hunt's words,

> "the Mediterranean, now soft and lucid, kissed the shore as if to make peace with it. The yellow sand and the blue sky were intensely contrasted with one another: marble mountains touched the air with coolness; and the flame of the fire bore away towards heaven in vigorous amplitude, waving and quivering with a brightness of inconceivable beauty. It seemed as though it contained the glassy essence of vitality."

The white heat of the furnace must have driven away even the sanitary guards appointed to see that no one touched the remains save with irons; for Trelawny stayed near the furnace and was able to snatch from it the blood-gorged heart and a fragment of the jaw-bone. Byron swam to the *Bolivar*, which was standing off-shore, and this time, apparently, his friends let him try the Tyrrhenian waters alone. He lived for two years afterwards, but it is said that he never fully recovered from the effects of sun and salt water suffered after his reckless action in swimming for three hours in the glare of the August sun. As he drove back through the pinewoods to Pisa, Byron began to sing and shout, and Leigh Hunt, infected by his hysteria, joined him, to the astonishment of the coachman.

Williams's ashes were sent to England and ultimately, after Jane had lived for many years with Hogg, the oak box accompanied her to her grave in Kensal Green. Shelley's ashes were sent to Rome; William's grave could not be found, so the ashes were buried alone on 21 January, 1823, but afterwards removed to a site which Trelawny considered more worthy. To Leigh Hunt's inscription *"Cor cordium"* were added, on the tombstone, the lines from *The Tempest* suggested by Trelawny:

> Nothing of him that doth fade,
> But doth suffer a sea change
> Into something rich and strange.

Trelawny is one of the very few writers whose inaccuracies are almost endearing, rather than irritating. His are the fullest accounts of the cremation of Shelley, yet they are riddled with errors relating to dates, places and incidents. He contradicted himself in successive accounts, and printed with the date "15 August, 1822" an account that was obviously written long afterwards; his imperfect knowledge of Italian made him invent a hitherto unknown topography for Viareggio and the adjacent land and sea. He even misquoted the lines from *The Tempest*. But he was the only man who remained with Shelley to the end, till the last flame died away against the ochre sand.

Tempted perhaps to put right some of Trelawny's errors, Guido Biagi went to Viareggio in 1890 and held a kind of court of inquiry, at which witnesses of the cremation gave their evidence. Raffaello Simonetti, scarcely aged five, was there; Giacomo Bandoni, aged ten, took his father's dinner to the spot; his friend Giovan-Francesco Simonetti, a year younger, was also there. Among others who told Biagi what little they knew was Maria Pietrini, who was twenty-five at the time, and ninety-three when the inquiry was held. Carlo Simonetti, born in the year of Shelley's death, went to sea at the age of four and heard the fishermen's oath: "May I be burned like the Englishmen at the Due Fosse!" Francesco Petrucci, who was thirteen at the time, remembered the superstition which declared that when the ashes were taken to England, the dead men would come to life.

It is to Biagi, also, that we have to go for a true account of the discovery of the *Don Juan*. According to Trelawny's account, he sent two feluccas to dredge for the vessel with ground-tackling the day before Williams's body was reduced to ashes. Within five or six days the *Don Juan* was found about two miles off the coast. The feluccas could not raise her so Trelawny, on his way to Rome, asked Roberts to return from Genoa and finish the business, which he did in September, reporting:

"I consulted Lord Byron on the subject of paying the crews of the felucca employed in getting up the boat. He advised me to sell her by auction, and to give them half the proceeds of the sale. I rode your horse to Viareggio. On Monday we had the sale, and only realized a trifle more than two hundred dollars.

The two masts were carried away just above board, the bowsprit broken off close to the bows, the gunwale stove in, and the hull half full of blue clay, out of which we fished clothes, books, spy-glass, and other articles. . . .

We found in the boat two memorandum books of Shelley's, quite perfect, and another damaged; a journal of Williams's, quite perfect, written up to the 4th of July. I washed the printed books: some of them were so glued together by the slimy mud that the leaves could not be separated: most of these things are now in Lord Byron's custody. The letters, private papers, and Williams's journal, I left in charge of Hunt. . . .

P.S. On a close examination of Shelley's boat, we may find many of the timbers on the starboard quarter broken, which makes me think for certain that she must have been run down by some of the feluccas in the squall."

The official account of the matter, to be found in the archives of the Duchy of Lucca, shows that on 12 September the Governor of Viareggio reported that two fishing smacks belonging to Stefano Baroni "have, while fishing, discovered, at the bottom of the sea, at a distance of about 15 miles from the shore, a small vessel, schooner rigged". The *Don Juan* was taken back to Viareggio and placed in quarantine with Baroni's vessels and their crews. "A trunk, locked with a key, containing clothing, and 245 francesconi, some bottles, books and other small objects used on board have been found." Six days later the sanitary guards of Leghorn had officially identified the vessel.

The Italian sailors' memory of the salvage operations was that the two fishing-boats of Stefano Baroni, captained by Giuseppe Giampieri, caught the hull of the schooner in their nets and brought it in to Viareggio. One of the crew, Antonio Canova, aged nineteen, said that the *Don Juan* lay five miles out (not two, as Trelawny recorded, or ten, as is stated in an official report), in the direction of the Tower of Migliarino, and that she was caught in the nets. He and another man towed the damaged vessel into Leghorn, and when she was sold, each man received twenty-five scudi and twenty-five bolognini. At the *festa* of the Santa Croce on 14 September, Giampieri wore one of the suits found in the boat.

The fact that the trunks, books and hamper of wine were in the vessel when she was salvaged suggested to Roberts that the *Don Juan* had not capsized, but had been swamped, and the damage to the starboard quarter suggested a collision, though how the damage to the masts could do so is difficult to tell. The damage was quite possibly done during the salvage operations. Taaffe's conversation about the Livornese felucca whose crew was said to have seen the *Don Juan* shortly before she sank added to the suspicious circumstances, though no one troubled to find out whether any vessel showed signs of having been involved in a collision. The *Bolivar's* mate's talk about an oar from the *Don Juan* also helped to lay the foundation of the story which was given to the world fifty-three years later in the correspondence columns of *The Times*.

Trelawny's daughter wrote to him from Rome that she had heard of an old sailor who had died at La Spezia after confessing to a priest that he had been one of a crew that ran down Shelley's boat under the impression that Byron, in possession of a large sum of money, was on board; the intention was to board the boat and murder Byron, but she sank as soon as she was struck. "This account was sent to my friends the K——s by a person they are intimate with, and who lives at Spezzia, and, I believe, knows the priest."

This was not a very reliable piece of information and, though the damage to the *Don Juan* could as logically be explained by its having been dashed about for over two months on the sea-bed, and by the salvage operations, the story proved irresistible to Trelawny. It also prompted a certain "V.E.", living in Rome, to write that he or she had visited San Terenzo and heard from "my hostess, who is an old friend of the Shelley family" the story "of which a somewhat garbled version has now appeared in print". According to this correspondent, who considered his name "quite immaterial to the object in view", the old sailor had died in 1863, and the priest had told the story to a noble, who passed it on to the writer's informant, who forthwith communicated it to "the person most interested", which unknown recipient of the information said nothing. V.E. pointed out that the noble had died, so there would be no point in naming him. The boatman died near Sarzana, according to this involved, fanciful and mysterious account, and no explanation is given of the quite remarkable fact that a Viareggian sailor should ever stray so far from home, much less go inland.

The conception and birth of the story are shown clearly

enough, and its dubious value is indicated, by the conclusion of the letter:

> "My informant has resided during the last twenty years in the neighbourhood of Spezzia, and has always placed entire faith in the truth of the above. But it has crept into the papers without my agency, although I am responsible for having mentioned it as an interesting anecdote to some friend of the Trelawny family in Rome, and I have obtained the permission of my original informant to offer this explanation."[1]

Thanks to Trelawny's acceptance of the story, it persisted in spite of the slender evidence on which it was based. But the mystery of Shelley's death, unlike the mysteries of marriage and birth in his life, is not impenetrable. If the felucca had miraculously escaped showing signs of a collision, its crew would scarcely have picked up an oar and some spars and brought them back to Leghorn, as Trelawny said his Genoese mate suggested. Nor is the idea of a collision, manœuvred during a squall, an easily credible one; the *Don Juan* was a faster craft than the feluccas of Leghorn. The truth seems to have been that Shelley and Williams raised too much sail, and perhaps their uncertain seamanship caused the *Don Juan* to get athwart the heavy seas when the squall began. Their sailing time suggests strongly that they were caught in the squall, which would quite conceivably break off Viareggio, some time after five o'clock, before sweeping along the coat to Leghorn, where Trelawny witnessed it at about half past six. The *Don Juan* was riding a little high in the water after her recent overhaul, and was not easily manageable at the best of times, as the men who brought it from Genoa, and Shelley's friends, had said themselves. In 1827, after the vessel had been bought by a group of military officers at Zante, she broke her moorings and was smashed in a gale.

The heart of Shelley, which Leigh Hunt gave up unwillingly to Mary, appears to have been preserved by her in a silk pouch

---

[1] An Italian writer, Enrico Montecorboli, says the whole story was invented for money by one Moscovia.

attached to her copy of *Adonais*, where it was found, a handful of dust, on her death, and in 1889 buried with the body of Sir Percy Florence Shelley.

In 1894 Viareggio honoured the poet whose corpse its sands had received, by changing the name of the Piazza Paolina to "Piazza Shelley", and erecting there a monument. Today, the old people of Viareggio still call the square "Paolina", and they remember where the Englishman's body was cremated—in the nearby Piazza Mazzini, in front of the Public Library, where an expanse of shadeless palms surround a simple fountain and a broad pool. The Piazza Mazzini contains the Albergo della Pace, but it is also a noisy bus terminus; one side of it presents to the view some of Italy's screaming advertising hoardings; and in summer, as you look towards the sea, you perceive mile after mile of bathing umbrellas, punctuated by petrol stations and the remnants of the contorted pinewoods which in 1822 extended along the greater part of the coast between here and Massa.

There are no pines near that scene now, but a mile or so farther up the coast stands an oddity in the Italian scenery: a garden consisting of perfectly trimmed lawns in the centre of which rises, despite the vulgarity of the surrounding bathing establishments, a nymph fashioned in Carrara marble, her limbs dissolving into a tree-trunk and her hair into the wind.

On the Shelley monument in the town is engraved the tribute of a Catholic country, curiously more generous than any that his own country ever officially extended to "the Atheist":

"*A P. B. Shelley, Cuor de Cuori, nel MDCCCXXII annegato in questo mare, arso in questo lido, lungo il quale meditava al Prometeo Liberato, una pagina postreme in cui ogni generazione avrebbe segnato la lotta, le lacrime, la redenzione sua.*" ("To P. B. Shelley, *cor cordium*, in 1822 drowned in this sea, cremated on this shore, along which he meditated *Prometheus Unbound*, a last page in which each generation has discovered its conflict, its tears, and its redemption.")

· · · · · ·

In September the surviving members of the Pisa circle left Tuscany. They travelled variously by sea and land, but met at Lerici. The *Bolivar* lay three miles offshore, and Byron challenged Trelawny to swim to the ship, dine in the water alongside her while treading water, and return to the shore. They did so, and in addition to eating a meal and drinking ale, Trelawny smoked a cigar. Byron became ill, and Trelawny persuaded him to return to the *Bolivar* and rest on the accommodation-ladder; but he insisted on swimming ashore. The result was that Byron spent two days in bed, at a poor hotel. "Luckily," writes Trelawny, "the medico of Lerici was absent," so within two or three days the party went on their way to Genoa, where, "left to our own devices, we degenerated apace".

During this stay at Lerici, Trelawny took Leigh Hunt across the bay to see Shelley's house, and Hunt recorded the visit in the words:

"All my melancholy was put to its height by seeing the spot which my departed friend had lived in, and his solitary mansion on the seashore. Lerici is wild and retired, with a bay and rocky eminences; the people suited to it, something between inhabitants of sea and land. In the summer time they will be up all night dabbling in the water and making wild noises. Here Trelawny joined us. He took me to the Villa Magni (the house just alluded to); and we paced over its empty rooms and neglected garden. The sea fawned upon the shore, as though it could do no harm."

Mary Shelley lived unhappily at Genoa, saw Jane Williams off to England and eventually followed her, thanks to Trelawny's generosity in raising her fare; but not before she had endured humiliation at Byron's hands, and had had to come to the rescue of Leigh Hunt, about whom Byron had written contemptuous comments to Murray, who had relished showing them to John Hunt. Trelawny had also to intervene in a quarrel between Byron and Daniel Roberts. Nevertheless, Trelawny stood by Byron till the end, running about to perform his commissions by land and sea.

On one of his last journeys along the coast alone, Trelawny took an evening walk to Casa Magni.

"I walked in. Shelley's shattered skiff, in which he used to go about adventuring, as he termed it, in rivers and canals, was still there: in that little flat-bottomed boat he had written many beautiful things:

> Our boat is asleep on Serchio's stream,
> Its sails are folded like thoughts in a dream,
> The helm sways idly, hither and thither;
> Dominic, the boatman, has brought the mast,
> And the oars and the sails: but 'tis sleeping fast.

And here it was, sleeping still on the mud floor, with its mast and oars broken. I mounted the stairs or rather ladder into the dining-room they had lived in. . . . As I surveyed its splotchy walls, broken floor, cracked ceiling, and poverty-struck appearance, while I noted the loneliness of the situation, and remembered the fury of the waves that in blowing weather lashed its walls, I did not marvel at Mrs. Shelley's and Mrs. Williams's groans on first entering it; nor that it had required all Ned Williams's persuasive powers to induce them to stop there."

A SHELLEY CHRONOLOGY

1792   4 *August:* Percy Bysshe Shelley born at Field Place, Warnham, Sussex, son of Timothy Shelley.
1793   *February:* France declares war on England. Publication of William Godwin's *Political Justice.* Edward Ellerker Williams born.
1794   The "English Terror". Horne Tooke treason trial.
1795   1 *August:* Harriet Westbrook born. *October:* John Keats born.
1797   30 *August:* Mary Wollstonecraft Godwin born.
1798   27 *April:* Clara Mary Jane Clairmont (Claire Clairmont) born; later step-daughter of William Godwin.
1802   *March:* Peace of Amiens.
1803   *May:* Resumption of war against France.
1804   Shelley goes to Eton.
1810   1 *April: Zastrozzi* published. *Michaelmas:* Shelley goes to University College, Oxford; meets Thomas Jefferson Hogg.
1811   *January: St. Irvyne* published. *March: The Necessity of Atheism* published; several copies burned twenty minutes later, and printers ordered to destroy MS. and type. 25 *March:* Shelley and Hogg expelled. 25 *August:* Elopes with Harriet Westbrook. 28 *August:* Marries Harriet. *October:* Hogg attempts to seduce Harriet. *November:* Shelley meets Southey.
1812   Cantos I and II of Byron's *Childe Harold* published. *January:* Shelley writes to William Godwin. *February:* Shelley's first visit to Ireland. *April–October:* Wanderings in Wales and Devon. *June:* England at war with America. *October:* Shelley meets Godwin; French retreat from Moscow. *November:* Shelley and Harriet return to Wales.
1813   *January:* Completion of *Queen Mab. February:* Leigh Hunt sentenced to two years' imprisonment for libel against Prince Regent; Shelley offers help. *March:* Second journey to Ireland. *April:* Return to London. 28 *June:* Ianthe Shelley born. *July–December:* Wanderings in Berkshire, Lake District, Edinburgh and return to London.

1814   *A Refutation of Deism* published. 22 *March:* Shelley remarries Harriet. *May:* They are estranged. *June:* Shelley meets Mary Wollstonecraft Godwin. 28 *July:* Shelley and Mary elope to Continent, accompanied by Claire Clairmont. 13 *September:* Return to England after tour of France, Switzerland, Germany and Holland. 14 *November:* Reconciliation with Hogg. 30 *November:* Charles Bysshe Shelley born to Harriet.

1815   5 *January:* Timothy Shelley succeeds to baronetcy. *January–April:* Mary's "affair" with Hogg; Shelley pursued by creditors. 22 *February(?):* Seven-months child (girl) born to Mary. 6 *March:* The child dies. *March:* Defeat of Napoleon. *June–July:* Shelley house-hunting in Devon. 18 *June:* Napoleon finally defeated at Waterloo. *August:* Shelley writes *Alastor* at Windsor.

1816   24 *January:* William Shelley born to Mary. *Spring:* Claire Clairmont's affair with Byron. 25 *April:* Byron leaves England. *May–September:* Second Continental journey of Shelley, Mary and Claire; Shelley meets Byron. *September–December:* Shelleys at Bath. 9 *November:* Supposed suicide of Harriet Shelley. 30 *December:* Shelley marries Mary.

1817   Publication of Keats's *Poems*; Godwin's *Mandeville*. 8 *January:* Westbrooks begin Chancery proceedings for custody of Charles and Ianthe Shelley. 12 *January:* Birth of Alba (later Clara Allegra) Byron to Claire Clairmont. *February:* Shelley meets Hazlitt, Keats, Horace Smith. *March:* Moves to Marlow. *A Proposal for putting Reform to the Vote throughout the Kingdom*. *Summer:* Writing *The Revolt of Islam*. 2 *September:* Clara Everina Shelley born. *December: History of a Six Weeks' Tour* (by Mary and Shelley).

1818   Keats's *Endymion* published; and Mary Shelley's *Frankenstein*. 11 *March:* Shelleys leave for Italy. *April:* Chancery decision announced. *May:* Shelleys settle in Pisa. *August:* Completion of *Rosalind and Helen*. 24 *September:* Death of Clara Everina Shelley. *October: Lines Written Among the Euganean Hills* and (probably) *Julian and Maddalo*; Shelley begins *Prometheus Unbound*. *November:* Arrival in Rome. 27 *November:* Shelleys go to Naples. 27 *December:* Supposed birth of Elena Adelaide Shelley.

1819   27 *February:* Baptism of Elena Adelaide; departure of Shelleys and Claire for Rome. *April:* Completion of

Prometheus Unbound; Shelley working on *The Cenci*. 7 *June:* Death of William Shelley. 10 *June:* Departure for Leghorn. *August:* "Peterloo" riot at Manchester; Shelley completes *The Cenci, Ode to the West Wind, The Masque of Anarchy*. *November: Peter Bell the Third; A Philosophical View of Reform.* 12 *November:* Birth of Percy Florence Shelley.

1820 Publication of Keats's *Lamia and Other Poems*. *January:* Shelleys move to Pisa. 29 *January:* Death of George III. *Summer:* Paolo Foggi attempts blackmail. 9 *June:* Death of Elena Adelaide Shelley. Shelleys move to Leghorn. 2 *July:* Revolution in Naples. 10 *August:* Shelleys move to Lucca. *The Witch of Atlas; Ode to Naples; Ode to Liberty; Swellfoot the Tyrant. September:* R. B. Hoppner reports to Byron Elise's accusation against Shelley. *October:* Shelleys return to Pisa. *December:* They meet Emilia Viviani in Florence.

1821 *January:* Shelley writes *Epipsychidion*, to Emilia. *February–March: A Defence of Poetry.* 23 *February:* Death of Keats. *June:* Shelley completing *Adonais*. *August:* Shelley visits Byron at Ravenna, is shown Hoppner's letter. 10 *August:* Mary Shelley writes refutation of slander to Mrs. Hoppner. *November:* Completion of *Hellas.*

1822 *January:* Shelley working on *Charles the First. February:* Trip to La Spezia. 24 *March:* The Masi affair (a street brawl) involving Byron, Shelley and others. 27 *April:* Shelley moves to Lerici. *May–June:* Working on *The Triumph of Life.* 1 *July:* Shelley and Williams go to Leghorn and Pisa. 8 *July:* They are drowned when the *Don Juan* sinks off Viareggio. 18 *July:* Shelley's corpse washed up near Viareggio. 18 *August:* Trelawny superintends cremation of Shelley's remains.

1823 Mary Shelley returns to England.
1824 Death of Byron.
1836 Death of William Godwin.
1851 Death of Mary Shelley.
1879 Death of Claire Clairmont.
1881 Death of Edward Trelawny.
1884 Death of Jane Williams.

BIBLIOGRAPHY AND SOURCES

Following is a selection of works consulted during the writing of this book:

SHELLEY TEXTS.—*The Complete Works of Percy Bysshe Shelley* (Julian edition, ed. Ingpen and Peck, 1926-29). *The Complete Poetical Works of Shelley* (Oxford edition, ed. Hutchinson, 1904 and later). *The Poems of Percy Bysshe Shelley* (ed. Locock, 1911). *Posthumous Poems of Percy Bysshe Shelley* (ed. Mary Shelley, 1824). *The Poetical Works of Percy Bysshe Shelley* (ed. Mary Shelley, 1839). *The Letters of Percy Bysshe Shelley* (ed. Ingpen, 1915). *New Shelley Letters* (ed. W. S. Scott, 1948). *Bibliography of Shelley's Letters* (S. de Ricci, 1927). *The Choice* (Mary Shelley, 1876).

BIOGRAPHIES.—*The Life of Percy Bysshe Shelley* (Edward Dowden, 1886; I vol. edition reissued 1951). *The Life of Shelley* (Hogg, ed. Humbert Wolfe, 1933). *Revised Life of Shelley* (Medwin, ed. H. B. Forman, 1913). *Memoirs of Shelley* (Thomas Love Peacock, 1860). *Shelley: His Life and Work* (Walter E. Peck, 1927). *Shelley. A Life Story* (Edmund Blunden, 1946). *Shelley* (Newman Ivey White, 1947). *The Young Shelley. Genesis of a Radical* (Kenneth Neill Cameron, 1951).

MISCELLANEOUS.—*Shelley and his Friends in Italy* (Helen Rossetti Angeli, 1911). *Recollections of the Last Days of Shelley and Byron* (Edward J. Trelawny, 1858). *Records of Shelley, Byron and the Author* (Trelawny, 1878). *Mary Shelley* (R. Glynn Grylls, 1938). *Claire Clairmont* (R. Glynn Grylls, 1939). *The Friend of Shelley, a Memoir of Edward John Trelawny* (H. J. Massingham, 1930). *Trelawny* (R. Glynn Grylls, 1950). *The Shelley Legend* (Robert M. Smith and others, 1945). *Shelley, Godwin and their Circle* (H. N. Brailsford, 1913, reissued 1951). *Autobiography* (Leigh Hunt, 1850). *Lord Byron and Some of his Contemporaries* (Leigh Hunt, 1828). *Child of Light. A Reassessment of Mary Wollstonecraft Shelley* (Muriel Spark, 1952). *Lord Byron's Correspondence* (ed. Murray, 1922). *Byron, Shelley and their Pisan Circle* (L. C. Cline, 1952).

ITALIAN WORKS.—*Le Rime di Francesco Petrarca* (ed. Leopardi, Ambrosoli, Camerini, Carducci and others). *Gli ultimi giorni di P. B. Shelley* (Guido Biagi, 1892). *P. B. Shelley e l'Italia* (M. L. Giartosio de Courten, 1923). *Saggio di Studi Shelleyani: Shelley in Italia* (Bernheimer, 1923). *La Spezia a P. B. Shelley* (1907). *Per l'erezione in Viareggio di un busto a Shelley* (Pellegrini, 1894). Italian texts of Shelley by: Faccioli, Rapisarti, de Bosis, Sanfelice, Renzolli, Parato and others. *Lerici e il suo castello* (Francesco Poggi).

MS. SOURCES.—Quotations from Edward Ellerker Williams's journal are drawn from the MS. in the British Museum (Add. 36622), which was salvaged from the *Don Juan*; Richard Garnett's published version of the journal (1902) is inaccurate in various minor respects. I have consulted various MS. material by the Shelleys, Trelawny, the Gisbornes and others where this is available at the British Museum. MS. material relating to conditions in Italy are drawn from various diplomatic and consular documents (1814-1830) in the archives of the Public Record Office.

For valuable help and suggestions I wish to thank Lady Mander (Miss R. Glynn Grylls), Miss Ray Allister, Miss Dorothy Hewlett, Dr. Marion Kingston (Colorado), Mr. Raymond Anderson, Mr. Edmund Blunden, Professore Giacopello (Lerici) and Signor Renato Di Maio (Naples). I am also grateful to Mrs. Rosalie Sabine and the young ladies who so patiently worked on the typescript of the book.

INDEX

A

A'Court, Sir William, 172
Alexander, William, 93
Ariel, the (*see Don Juan*, the)
Ariosto, Ludovico, 196
Arno, River, 58, 217, 224
Arnold, Matthew, 71
Atheism (*see* Religion; and Shelley, P. B.)
Austria, occupation of Italy by, 107, 215–16 (*see also* Metternich)

B

Bacon, Sir Francis, 199
Bagnacavallo, convent at, 30
Bagni di Lucca, 170
Bandoni, Giacomo, 235
Baroni, Stefano, 236
Bath, Mary Shelley at, 124
Berlinghieri, Dr. Vaccà (*see* Vaccà)
Betta (or Beta), the Shelleys' cook, 62, 69, 85
Biagi, Guido, 71, 235
Birmingham, riot at, 98
Blake, William, 91
Blessington, Lady, 129
Boating (*see* Shelley, P. B.)
Bodleian Library, 225, 230
Bolivar, the, Byron's ship, 60, 115, 120, 121, 156, 160, 183, 214, 217, 220, 221, 224, 228, 232, 234, 240
Buffon, Count, 105
Burghersh, Lord, British Minister to Tuscany, 108, 215, 231
Burke, Edmund, 101, 102
Burlamacca, canal at Viareggio, 233
Byron, Alba (*see* Byron, Clara Allegra)
Byron, Clara Allegra, daughter of Claire Clairmont, 20, 28, 30, 31, 33-4, 72, 132, 134, 140, 162, 163, 172, 173–4, 178

Byron, Lady Noel, 76
Byron, Lord: 18, 58, 97, 154, 157, 192, 228, 229; writing habits, 64; friendship with Shelley, 74–9; religious opinions, 89; hatred of Southey, 129; opinion of Austrians, 177; dislike of Leigh Hunt, 214; use of his title, 217; Edward Williams's opinion of, 220; treatment of Hunts, 221; Jane Williams's opinion of, 221–2; on cremation, 232; swimming exploits, 232, 234, 240; at cremation of Shelley, 233–4; advises on salvage of *Don Juan*, 235; illness at Lerici, 240; relations with Claire Clairmont, 20–1, 72, 74, 163, 164–6, 173; relations with Mary Shelley, 32, 129, 164; attitude to Shelley, 21, 30, 61, 73, 78, 79, 116, 117, 128, 162–3, 167; *Cain*, 161, 182; *Vision of Judgment*, 217, 218

C

Cain, 161, 182
Calderon, Don Pedro, 161
Campbell, Adelaide Constance, 171
Campbell, Lady Charlotte, 171
Canova, Antonio, sailor, 236
Carbonari (*see* Secret societies)
Carducci, Giosuè, 71
Carlyle, Thomas, 80–1
Carrara, visit of Shelley and Jane Williams to, 62
Cartwright, Major John, 98, 103
Casa Magni, 22–3, 26, 63–4, 240, 241
Castlereagh, Lord, 106–7, 108, 172, 215
Caterina, servant of the Shelleys, 230
Ceccardi, R. C., 227

Index

Censorship, Italian, 69
Chancery, Court of, 91, 92–3, 124, 127, 152
Chesterfield, Lord, 101
Christianity (*see* Religion and Shelley, P. B.)
Clairmont, Allegra (*see* Byron, Clara Allegra)
Clairmont, Claire (Clara Mary Jane Clairmont): 20, 86, 109, 132, 144, 156, 160, 166, 180, 230; and Trelawny, 118; and Elise, 167–8, 178; and Naples mystery, 169–70; relations with Byron, 20–1, 33–4, 77–8, 146, 183; relations with Mary Shelley, 28, 31–2, 122, 127–8, 129, 146, 148–9, 164, 165, 166; relations with Shelley, 22, 28, 30, 77, 84–5, 111, 145, 162, 163, 164, 165, 166, 172–4, 190
Clairmont, Mrs. (*see* Godwin, Mrs.)
Clifton, Mary Shelley at, 151
Coachmaker's Hall, debates at, 98
Cobbett, William, 105
Consular records (*see* Foreign Office archives)
Cremation: of Shelley, 233–4; of Edward Williams, 232–3

D

Dante Alighieri, 24–5, 49, 185–6
Darwin, Erasmus, 66
Dawkins, E. J., 108, 231
Day, Thomas, 98
Del Rosso, Federico, 163, 177, 179
De Quincey, Thomas, 102
De Young, Mr., 224
Dissenters, 100–1
Di Lorenzo, Antonio, 169
Domenico, servant of the Shelleys, 62, 69, 241
Don Juan, the: 33, 115, 117, 118, 156, 157, 158, 160, 181, 182, 184, 213, 214, 217; arrival at Lerici, 58–63; loss of, 224–5; search for, 228; salvage of, 235–8; theories on wreck of, 237–8; destruction at Zante, 238
Donne, John, 54, 194
Dowden, Edward, 103, 109–10
Drummond, Sir William, 40
Dublin, Shelley in, 90
Dundas, Henry, 99
Dunn, Henry, 216, 224

E

Eldon, Lord, 92–3, 111
Eliot, T. S., 82
Elise (*see* Foggi, Elise)
Este, Shelley at, 132
Eton, 94, 191
Examiner, the, 73

F

Falconar, John, consul at Leghorn, 215, 229, 231
Fiorenzano, Pasquale, 176
Florence, 47, 231
Florimonte, Francesco, 169
Foggi, Elise, 76, 161–4, 167–8, 169, 171–2, 174, 178, 179
Foggi, Paolo, 162, 163, 164, 168, 171–2, 177, 178, 179–80
Foreign Office archives, 171
Fox, Charles James, 98, 102
France, the Shelley's journey across (1818), 173
Francis I supposedly at Lerici, 25
French Revolution, 97, 98
Freud, Sigmund, 207–8

G

Gamba, Pietro, 34, 214
Genoa (*see* Piedmont)
Ghibellines, 25
Giacopello, D., 26
Giampieri, Giuseppe, 236
Ginocchio, Domenico, 25
Gisborne, John, 159, 160, 161, 162, 163, 166, 168, 177, 179, 180

Index

Gisborne, Maria, 58, 85, 161, 162, 163, 166, 168, 177, 179, 180
Godwin, Fanny, 148
Godwin, Mrs. Mary Jane, 28, 83
Godwin, William: 18, 39, 72, 82–4, 85, 98, 99, 107, 122, 124, 127, 190, 210; *Mandeville*, 82; *Political Justice*, 18, 82
Goethe, Johann, 34, 97, 160
Greece, movement for independence of, 108
Grove, Harriet, 50, 121
Guebhard & Co., 157, 224
Guelphs, 25
Guiccioli, Teresa, 229

H

Habeas Corpus, suspension of, 99
Hardy, Thomas, the shoemaker, 98, 223
Haydon, Benjamin, 29
Hazlitt, William, 29, 79–80, 102
Hesperides (see *Liberal*, the)
Hitchener, Elizabeth, 143, 144
Hobhouse, John Cam, 78
Hogg, Thomas Jefferson: 16, 29, 64, 121, 122, 188, 190, 191, 195, 222; and Harriet Shelley, 143–4; "affair" with Mary Shelley, 144–53; relations with Shelley, 142; after Shelley's death, 153–5; relations with Jane Williams, 155, 234; *Memoirs of Alexey Haimatoff*, 149–50
Hookham, Thomas, 124
"Hope and Fear", theme in Shelley's works, 52–3, 104, 205, 207–8
Hoppner, Maria Isabella May Frances Louisa, 162–5, 166, 167, 168, 169, 170, 178, 179
Hoppner, Richard Belgrave, 31, 76, 78, 162–5, 166, 167, 168, 169, 171, 172, 175, 179
Hunt, John, 218, 240

Hunt, Leigh: 16, 29, 67, 87–8, 102, 151, 157, 159, 160, 165, 185, 211, 213, 228, 230, 234; imprisoned for libel, 72–3; on Shelley and orthodoxy, 94–5; arrival in Italy, 181; on Horace Smith, 189; Shelley's bequest to, 190; on Shelley's work, 193; meeting with Byron, 214; reunion with Shelley, 216; with Shelley at Pisa, 216–23; last meeting with Shelley, 224; at cremation of Williams, 232–3; at cremation of Shelley, 233–4; gives up Shelley's heart, 238; visits Casa Magni, 240; *Autobiography*, 222, 233
Hunt, Marianne, 217, 218, 220–1
Hunt, Thornton, 130, 216

I

Ireland, visit to, 90
Italy: situation in, 106–9; Shelley on, 25–6

J

Jacobin movement, 97–104, 215
Johnson, Samuel, 101

K

Keats, John, 97, 102, 112, 194, 224, 230, 233

L

Lamb, Charles, 81
Lanfranchi, Palazzo, 217, 229
Lawrence, Dr., 146
Leghorn: English Factory at, 214–15; Shelley's last voyage to, 182, 184, 213–14; Shelley's last days in, 216, 224; visited by Mary Shelley and Jane Williams, 229

Lerici, 21-2, 24-7, 115, 187-8, 240
Liberal, the, 73-4, 181, 214, 217, 219
Liguori, Antonio, 176
Locock, C. D., 47
Lofft, Capel, 98
London Registry Office, 172
Longdill, P. W., 124
Lucca, Duchy of, 218, 231, 236

M

Maglian, harbour-master at Lerici, 22, 59, 61, 70-1, 224
Magra, River, 229
Manners (of Byron and Shelley), 116
Mantegazza, Paolo, 23
Maria, servant of the Shelleys, 85
Marlow, 28, 130, 172
Marriage, Shelley's views on, 89, 142
Masi affair at Pisa, 74, 171, 182, 183, 232
Mason, Mr. (*see* Tighe)
Mason, Mrs. (*see* Mountcashell, Lady)
Massa, 70-1, 85, 86, 228, 230, 239
Mavrocordato, Prince, 108
Maxwell, Colonel, 122
Mazzini, Giuseppe, 25, 26
Medwin, Thomas, 29, 32, 39, 112, 162, 168, 171, 193, 196
Memoirs of the Life and Writings of Lord Byron, by John Watkins, 158, 160
Memoirs of Prince Alexey Haimatoff, by T. J. Hogg, 149-50
Metternich, Count, 177
Migliarino, Tower of, 230, 232, 236
Milan, Shelleys at, 173
Milman, Henry, 78
Milton, John, 194
Monarchy, Shelley's views on, 88
Montecorboli, Enrico, 238 n.
Montenero, 217
Moore, Thomas, 78, 184

Moscovia, 238 n.
Mountcashell, Lady, 84, 223-4, 226
Murray, John, 65, 78, 79, 80, 240
Musto, Gaetana, 178

N

Naples: 106, 108, 109, 161-2, 164-6, 168-72, 174-7; State archives, 168-9, 170; British Residency, 171, 172; revolution at, 177
Napoleon, 191, 199
Napoleonic war, 95, 105
Nightmare Abbey, by T. L. Peacock, 192
Nightmares, Shelley's, 120, 183-5, 207-8
Nugent, General, 108

O

Ollier, Charles, 80, 165
Oxford, Shelley's expulsion from, 88, 121, 144, 171

P

Paine, Tom, 98, 104, 105
Palmaria island, 62, 115
Peacock, Thomas Love: 16, 29, 40, 122, 130, 144, 188, 190, 192; *Nightmare Abbey*, 192
Peck, W. E., 33, 49
"Peterloo" riot, 107
Petrarch, Francesco: 24, 68, 112, 131-2, 135, 141, 194-210; *All' Italia*, 196; Sestinas, 202, 202-3, 226; Sonnets, 24, 201-2, 205, 206, 208, 209, 210; *Trionfo d'amore*, 196-200, 205; *Trionfo della divinità*, 204; *Trionfo della morte*, 196, 203, 209; works quoted, 24, 131, 132, 197, 199, 201, 202, 203, 204, 205, 206, 208, 209, 210, 226
Petrucci, Francesco, 235

Piedmont, 21, 69, 210
Pietrini, Maria, 235
Pisa: Shelley's last visit to, 217–24; Mary Shelley's return to, 230
Pitt, William (the Younger), 98, 99, 102
Plato, 56, 60, 118, 199, 222
Political background in England, 95–102, 211
Portovenere, 25, 62, 115
Price, Dr., 98
Priestley, Joseph, 66
Primogeniture, Shelley's views on, 88
Prince Regent, 73
Public Record Office, 172

Q

Quarterly Review, the, 78, 80, 193

R

Religion: in England, 87–95, 100–1; Shelley's views on, 111, 210–11, 222–3
Reveley, Henry, 65, 66, 179
Roberts, Captain Daniel, 59, 60, 115, 157, 181, 214, 221, 224, 225, 229, 230, 235–7, 240
Robinson, Henry Crabb, 129, 166
Romantic movement, 97
Rome, Shelley's burial at, 231, 234
Rossetti, William, 155
Rousseau, Jean-Jacques, 105, 199, 201
Ryan, Major, 122, 123

S

San Terenzo, 19, 21–2, 26, 229, 237
Sarzana, 25, 34, 62, 229, 237
Secret societies, 106, 108, 175
Sedition, Proclamation against, 98
Serchio, River, 33, 228, 231, 232, 241
Shakespeare, William, 191, 234
Shaw, G. B., 91, 96

Shelley, Sir Bysshe, 65, 147
Shelley, Charles Bysshe, 190
Shelley, Clara Everina, 30, 37, 50, 76, 131, 133, 134, 141, 152–3, 172, 178
Shelley, Elena Adelaide, 30, 37, 52, 76, 128, 131, 134, 161–81
Shelley, Elizabeth, 121–2
Shelley, Harriet, 50, 53, 92, 121–7, 128–9, 135, 141, 143–4, 148, 155, 190
Shelley, Ianthe, 37, 190
Shelley, Lady Jane, 123, 128, 144, 154
Shelley, Mary: 18, 32, 46, 76, 114, 115, 121, 128, 156, 163–5, 166–7, 171–2, 178, 180–1, 190, 213, 228–30, 240, 241; relations with Claire Clairmont, 31–2, 127–8, 164–6; relations with Byron, 32, 153, 240; knowledge of Elena Adelaide Shelley, 162–7; relations with T. J. Hogg, 141–56, 209–10; relations with Shelley, 35, 41, 43, 45–6, 47, 50, 51–2, 121, 122, 123–5, 127–41; relations with Trelawny, 115, 118; opinion of San Terenzo, 26
SHELLEY, PERCY BYSSHE: appearance, 29; as described by others, 17, 28, 29, 189, 216, 222; boats and boating, 33, 39, 58, 60, 70–1, 114, 115, 118–19, 120, 196, 228, 241; relations with Byron, 21, 30–1, 34, 61, 72, 74–9, 85, 135, 159, 160, 163, 167, 177, 182–3, 190, 191–2, 211, 217–18, 219; conversations, 16, 41, 65, 87, 110, 184, 189, 192–3, 223; chronology of life, 243–5; cremation, 233–5; habits of life, 64, 66, 67; hallucinations, 36–7; hates, 110–11; health, 39, 71, 146; heart, 234, 238–9; humour, 190–3; imagery, 193–209; on Italy, 25–6; "labyrinth" idea, 181, 206–7; as linguist, 195; on

254 Index

Shelley, Percy Bysshe—*cont.*
love, 54–7; marriage to Harriet, 121–7; marriage to Mary, 127–41; mechanical interests, 65–6; memory, 67; money matters, 18, 34, 65, 83, 127, 147, 148, 157, 176, 189, 210, 224; monument to, in Viareggio, 239; nightmares, 120, 183–5, 207–8; Petrarch, influence of, 194–209; on poetry, 16, 111; on primogeniture, 88; reading and study, 54, 55, 60, 64, 65; religious views, 111, 210–11, 222–3; republicanism, 95; and the sea, 63; on suicide, 157; wager with Byron, 76; will, 76, 190; writing habits, 63, 64, 115, 160

    Letters quoted—34, 41, 72, 85, 88, 95, 107, 110, 122, 143, 143–4, 170, 176, 182; on Bay of Lerici, 211–12; on Byron, 74, 77, 159, 160, 167; to Byron, 182–3, 192; to Byron, on calumny, 174; to Byron, on Claire Clairmont, 173; on Chancery case, 152; on damnation, 89; on *Don Juan*, 60, 61, 160; to Godwin, 83; on Hoppner scandal, 163–4, 165, 167, 180; on Italian poets, 196; on Italy, 25–6; on Charles Lamb, 81; on the *Liberal*, 73; on reviewers, 78; on Elena Adelaide Shelley, 52, 179, 180; on Harriet Shelley's death, 124; to Southey, on calumny, 80; on the state of England in 1822, 210–11; on suicide, 157; on Emilia Viviani, 47, 48; to Jane Williams, 218–19; on writing, 160–1

    Works referred to and quoted (q):

Address to the Irish People, 90, 92; 94 (q)
Adonais, 159, 239
A Lament, 203 (q)
Alastor, 194 (q)
An Exhortation, 10 (q)
Boat on the Serchio, The, 241 (q)
Cenci, The, 80, 81; 204 (q)
Charles the First, 160
Death, 37 (q)
Defence of Poetry, 193
Epipsychidion, 15, 47, 48–56, 159; 49–56, 188, 203, 204, 205 (q)
Fragments: "And where is truth?", 68, 159 (q); "And who feels discord", 181, 207 (q); "Lines", 70 (q); "On Keats", 112 (q); "On Love", 56 (q); "Song of a Spirit", 36 (q); "When a lover clasps his fairest", 46 (q)
Hellas, 32
Invitation, The, 40
Julian and Maddalo, 51, 79, 144; 9, 74–5, 135–40, 186 (q)
Letter to Maria Gisborne, 58, 66, 188 (q)
Lines: The Serpent is Shut Out, 42 (q)
Lines to a Reviewer, 79 (q)
Lines Written Among the Euganean Hills, 195; 107, 133, 187, 213 (q)
Lines Written during the Castlereagh Administration, 110 (q)
Lines Written in the Bay of Lerici, 38, 44–5, 46; 44 (q)
Lines (1815), 126 (q)
Magnetic Lady to her Patient, The, 40 (q)
Masque of Anarchy, The, 103, 107 (q)
Mutability (I), 67, 126 (q)
Mutability (II), 67–8 (q)
Necessity of Atheism, The, 88, 142, 171
Ode to Liberty, 87, 88, 109, 204 (q)
Ode to the West Wind, 196, 208
On a Faded Violet, 133 (q)

Index

Shelley's Works—*cont.*
Orpheus, 133, 203 (q)
Past, The, 112, 133 (q)
Peter Bell the Third, 111, 192; 54, 55, 81 (q)
Philosophical View of Reform, 103
Posthumous Poems, 152
Prometheus Unbound, 96, 103, 193, 196, 239; 63, 93, 96, 184–5, 204, 206, 207, 227 (q)
Proposal for Putting Reform to the Vote, 103–4 (q)
Queen Mab, 81, 91, 96, 107, 142, 192, 212; 40, 90, 142 (q)
Recollection, The, 40–1, 70 (q)
Review of Alexey Haimatoff, 150 (q)
Review of Mandeville, 82 (q)
Revolt of Islam, The, 80, 193; 126, 151, 205, 207 (q)
Rosalind and Helen, 171; 55, 194–5 (q)
St. Irvyne, 171
Sensitive Plant, The, 40, 150; 111 (q)
Song for Tasso, 133, 204 (q)
Sonnet: England in 1819, 103 (q)
Sonnet: Lift not the painted veil, 133; 53, 205 (q)
Sonnet: Political Greatness, 104 (q)
Stanzas (1814), 125 (q)
Time Long Past, 204 (q)
To Mary, 131 (q)
To Mary Shelley, 133 (q)
To Sophia Stacey, 47 (q)
To William Shelley (I), 93, 151–2 (q)
To William Shelley (II), 152 (q)
Triumph of Life, The, 63, 112, 115; 27, 100–201 (q)
Two Political Characters of 1819, 110 (q)
Una Favola, 209 (q)
We Meet Not As We Parted, 38, 45, 46; 45, 47 (q)

When passion's trance is overpast, 134 (q)
When the Lamp is Shattered, 43, 114 (q)
With a Guitar: To Jane, 190; 41, 63 (q)
Woodman and the Nightingale, The, 133; 112 (q)
Zastrozzi, 18, 185
Zucca, The, 43, 45; 41–2 (q)
Shelley, Percy Florence, 18, 52, 123, 142, 154, 169, 193, 219, 226, 239
Shelley, Sir Timothy, 65, 77, 88, 153–4, 190
Shelley, William, 30, 50, 51, 82, 93, 130–1, 151–3, 172, 190, 191, 231
Shenley, Captain, 232
Shields, Amelia (Milly), servant of the Shelleys, 172
Simonetti, Carlo, 235
Simonetti, Giovan-Francesco, 235
Simonetti, Raffaello, 235
Smith, Horace, 29, 73, 83, 188–90, 210, 222
Society for Constitutional Information, 98
Society for the Suppression of Vice, 95
Sophocles, 194, 230
Southcott, Joanna, 75
Southey, Robert, 80, 94, 99, 129, 174
Spezia, 22, 60, 69
Stacey, Sophia, 47, 64, 171
Stanhope, Earl of, 98
Stewart, Lord Vane, 108
Suicide, Shelley's view of, 157
Swift, Jonathan, 91
Switzerland, Shelley's visit to, 74, 151, 168
Symposium, the, of Plato, 56

T

Taaffe, Count or Mr., 89, 225, 237
Tasso, Torquato, 196
Thelwall, John, 98–102, 223

Tighe, George William ("Mr. Mason"), 223
Times, The, 237
Tinetto, island, 62
Tino, island, 62, 114
Tita, servant of Byron, 34
Tooke, Horne, 98, 102, 223
Tortiglione, Alberto, 168–9
Trelawny, Edward John: 29, 41, 58–9, 60–1, 71, 112, 129, 144, 154, 160, 192–3, 214, 219, 220; on the Bay of Lerici, 21–2; on plans for the *Don Juan*, 58; on Shelley's writing habits, 63; conversation with Wordsworth, 81; on Shelley's religious opinions, 87; visit to Casa Magni, 115–21; described by Mary Shelley, 115; on Shelley's and Byron's manners, 116–17; on Shelley and Williams as sailors, 118–19; fanciful stories, 119–21; on Shelley's separation from Harriet, 123; on Shelley's maturity, 223; account of storm off Leghorn, 224–6; search for *Don Juan*, 228–9; conduct of cremation, 230–4; salvage of *Don Juan*, 235; accepts fictitious account of wreck, 237–8; with Byron at Lerici, 240; last visit to Casa Magni, 240–1
Trevor, Dr. S. H., 231
Tuscany, government of, 214, 231

V

Vaccà, Dr., 218
Venice, 135, 174, 186
Vesuvius, visit to, 169–70
Viareggio, 71, 72, 85, 225, 228, 229, 230, 233, 235–6, 239
Vienna, postal censorship in, 177
Villa Magni (*see* Casa Magni)
Vision of Judgment, 217, 218
Vivian, Charles, 59, 86, 214, 224, 228, 230

Viviani, Teresa Emilia, 42, 47–8, 50, 51, 53

W

Wager, Shelley's and Byron's, 76
Watkins, John, 160
Wesley, John, 101
Westbrook, Eliza, 110, 122, 124, 125
Westbrook, Harriet (*see* Shelley, Harriet)
White, Newman Ivey, 29, 46, 120, 123, 152, 169, 171
Williams, Edward Ellerker: 35, 39, 58, 59, 60, 61, 84, 114–15, 155, 157, 158, 160, 181, 184, 213, 216, 217, 219, 224, 225, 228, 230, 231, 234, 235–6, 238, 241; career, 19–20; as poet, 32; cremation of, 232–3; last letter to Jane Williams, 219–21; journal quoted—30, 34, 36, 39, 42, 59, 60, 62, 69, 71, 85, 114, 115, 119, 121, 182, 183, 188, 210, 218, 220
Williams, Edward Medwin, 20
Williams, Jane: 19–20, 31, 35, 47, 61–2, 114, 118, 120, 184, 190, 228, 234, 240, 241; alleged affair with Shelley, 32–3; Shelley's friendship with, 37–46; association with T. J. Hogg, 153–5; sees vision of Shelley, 156; Shelley's comments on, 160; Shelley's last letter to, 218–19
Williams, Rosalind, 20
Wollstonecraft, Mary, 18, 54, 82, 127, 223
Wordsworth, William, 81, 97, 111

Y

York, Shelley and Harriet at, 143

Z

Zante, and loss of *Don Juan*, 238

Magra
SPEZIA
SAN TERENZA
SARZANA
LERICI
PORTOVENERE
Palmaria
Tino
CARRARA
MASSA
GAR
PIETRASANTA
Lucc
VIAREGGIO
Serchio
PISA
CASCIN
T
Metoria
LEGHORN
MONTENERO
Pi
Gorgona